To Rhonda and Sara

Christianity and Moral Identity in Higher Education

Christianity and Moral Identity in Higher Education

Perry L. Glanzer

and

Todd C. Ream

First published in 2009 by
PALGRAVE MACMILLAN®
in the United States—a division of St. Martin's Press LLC,
175 Fifth Avenue, New York, NY 10010.

Where this book is distributed in the UK, Europe and the rest of the world,
this is by Palgrave Macmillan, a division of Macmillan Publishers Limited,
registered in England, company number 785998, of Houndmills,
Basingstoke, Hampshire RG21 6XS.

Palgrave Macmillan is the global academic imprint of the above companies
and has companies and representatives throughout the world.

Palgrave® and Macmillan® are registered trademarks in the United States,
the United Kingdom, Europe and other countries.

ISBN: 978–0–230–61240–2

Library of Congress Cataloging-in-Publication Data

Glanzer, Perry L. (Perry Lynn)
    Christianity and moral identity in higher education / Perry L.
Glanzer and Todd C. Ream.
        p. cm.
    Includes bibliographical references and index.
    ISBN 0–230–61240–7
        1. Education, Higher—Moral and ethical aspects. 2. Moral education
(Higher) 3. Education, Higher—Religious aspects—Christianity.
    I. Ream, Todd C. II. Title.

LB2324.G53 2009
378'.014—dc22   2009023757

A catalogue record of the book is available from the British Library.

Design by Newgen Imaging Systems (P) Ltd., Chennai, India.

First edition: December 2009

10 9 8 7 6 5 4 3 2 1

Printed in the United States of America.

Contents

**Part III   Strengthening the Moral Tradition of
Christian Humanism**

Acknowledgments

The older we have become, the more we realize that any labor, particularly labors of love, are far more communal endeavors than individual. Ideas do not merely come to us in isolation but through the relationships we are fortunate enough to share with others. As a result, any list of acknowledgements will prove to be insufficient. Persons in our past and present have helped shape our passion for seeing how colleges and universities can fulfill their rightful duties as instruments of character formation. We have encountered some of these persons through more theoretical work. They made their presence known to us through their words both spoken and in print. To this end, we are deeply indebted to figures past and present such as Aristotle, Thomas Aquinas, Alasdair MacIntyre, Stanley Hauerwas, and Charles Taylor. We have encountered some of these persons through more practical work. They made their presence know to us through administrative decisions that needed to be made. Although confidentiality demands that we must protect their anonymity, we think of students we have driven to rehabilitation centers, sat with in court and even suspended hoping and praying that they would decide to return to campus with the virtues more firmly pressed upon their hearts and minds.

The communities of Baylor University and Indiana Wesleyan University provided us with places to live out our commitments to the academic vocation. This project started several years ago with a Horizons Grant offered by the Baylor's Institute for Faith and Learning. Both Baylor University and Indiana Wesleyan University were also generous in their subsequent provision of additional travel funds and summer sabbaticals. For the gracious support we received from both universities, we thank Jade Avelis, Michael D. Beaty, Ronnie L. Fritz, Douglas V. Henry, David Lyle Jeffrey, Jerry Pattengale, and Alleta Tippey. We would also thank The Louisville Institute and its Executive Director, James W. Lewis, for providing us with the funding needed to expand the breadth and depth of this effort. Finally, we would like to thank the research assistants we have had the pleasure to work with over the course of the last couple of years, Brian C. Clark, Edith Davis, Konstantin Petrenko, and Pedro Villarreal. This project is much improved as a result of their keen eyes, critical minds and gracious spirits.

Throughout the course of this project, we visited campuses across the country. The hospitality alone that we received was impressive. In addition, we were overwhelmed by their willingness to take time out of their very busy schedules to talk with us about their institutions. We believe that their voices make a unique contribution to this work. We only hope that we represent their voices with charity and integrity. We thus would like to thank representatives from the following schools for their time and for their hospitality: Bethel University (MN), Calvin College, Colorado State University, Eastern Mennonite University, George Fox University, Hampden-Sydney College, Hillsdale College, Mary Baldwin College, St. Olaf College, Seattle Pacific University, the United States Air Force Academy, University of Dallas, the University of St. Thomas (MN), Xavier University (OH), and Yale University.

Julia Cohen, her colleagues at Palgrave Macmillan, and a number of anonymous reviewers encouraged us to think beyond our initial inclination to hide behind data. They saw something in our proposal that we, at first, did not see. They encouraged us to go beyond the data and offer not only an overview of what we taking place on particular campuses but also offer a vision for what many of these campuses could become if they only embedded themselves more deeply in their respective traditions. Without their encouragement, this book would be much smaller in terms of not only its aspirations but what it can offer those who take the time to read it.

Original portions of this book were previously published in academic journals and magazines. Parts of chapter four first appeared as Perry L. Glanzer and Todd C. Ream, "Addressing the Moral Quandary of Contemporary Universities: Rejecting a Less than Human Moral Education," *Journal of Beliefs and Values* 29.2 (2008): 113–23. Portions of chapter seven appeared in Todd C. Ream and Perry L. Glanzer, "The Moral Idea of a University: A Case Study," *Growth: The Journal of the Association for Christians in Student Development* (Winter 2009): 2–14. Parts of chapter nine were taken from Perry L. Glanzer and Todd Ream, "Whose Story? Which Identity? Fostering Christian Identity at Christian Colleges and Universities," *Christian Scholars Review* 35 (2005): 13–27 and Perry L. Glanzer, "Course Correction," *Touchstone*, September 2007, 18–19. Finally, parts of chapter ten were taken from Perry L. Glanzer, "Why We Should Discard the Integration of Faith and Learning: Rearticulating the Mission of the Christian Scholar," *Journal of Education and Christian*

Belief 12.1 (Spring 2008): 41–51 (Copyright © 2005 by *Christian Scholar's Review*; reprinted by permission). We thank the respective editors, William S. Campbell, Skip Trudeau and Tim Herrmann, Don King, James Kushiner, and David Smith for allowing us to edit and reprint some of that material in this book.

Our deepest gratitude goes to our respective families and to our churches, First Baptist Church in Woodway Texas and Jerome Christian Church in Jerome/Greentown, Indiana. In these two contexts, we have learned not only about the virtues in theory but also have been fortunate enough to also see them in practice in ways our imaginations may otherwise envision. Our children, Bennett and Cody Glanzer and Addison and Ashley Ream, help us each day to see how their embodiment of the virtues can transform each and every person around them. Finally, we thank our wives for their love, their support, and for their embodiment of the virtues. Our work and more importantly our lives have been transformed through their willingness to walk alongside us. To them, Rhonda Glanzer, and Sara Ream, we dedicate our efforts in these pages. We hope, in some way, that this book returns to them a small measure of what they have so graciously given to us.

Hewitt, Texas & Greentown, Indiana
Lent 2009

Introduction

The Turn to Less than Human Moral Education: The Moral Reservations of Contemporary Universities

> If trees or wild beasts grow, men, believe me, are fashioned...If this fashioning be neglected you have but an animal still.
>
> —Desiderius Erasmus, 1529[1]

> We bring all of you here, brim full of needs and desires and hormones, let you loose on each other like so many animals in a wildlife sanctuary and hope for the best.
>
> —Professor Andrew Abbott to the University of Chicago's Class of 2006[2]

National Lampoon's *Animal House*, a well-known 1978 movie about college life, now appears quite outdated. The reason why has nothing to do with the wild members of the Delta Tau Chi fraternity depicted in the film. For 800 years students have always posed moral challenges to university leaders and these leaders have always grumbled about the moral lives of students. Even from the thirteenth to the fifteenth centuries, Rainer Schwinges tells us university leaders complained:

> Students are bawling and brawling, carousing and whoring, singing and dancing, playing cards and chess, are addicted to dice and other games of chance, are up and about town day and night, are swanking around in inappropriate, fashionable clothing, are behaving provocatively to burghers, guild members, and town law-and-order forces, are carrying arms, and are even making use of them.[3]

Life at American universities proved no different. In 1849, soon after the creation of fraternities, University of Michigan professors complained about this "monster power" that threatened to bring "debauchery, drunkenness, pugilism, dueling...disorder and ravigism."[4]

Complaints about the moral conduct of students and the negative influence of their organizations have always existed. Of course, a few things have changed regarding what constitutes a moral problem. Colleges now sponsor clubs related to singing, dancing, and chess and some now have majors related to the design of fashionable clothing. The most significant change in university life, however, is a university's sense of responsibility for the overall moral lives of students. Even in *Animal House*, one finds the dean (however incompetent) making various unsuccessful attempts to control the hedonism of the "animals" in the fraternity house.

Throughout history, university leaders usually made efforts to take the young "animals" brim full of needs, desires, and hormones and make them more fully human. The university leadership sought to humanize students, because they shared the perspective of Erasmus quoted above. They believed that men (and later women) needed to be formed or fashioned according to some particular moral ideal. The natural growth or even the choices of young people did not produce this ideal. Humans were created and not born. In fact, many of the disciplines now comprising the humanities were even justified at one point for this very reason.[5]

Today, college administrators and faculty may take a different approach. Professor Abbott's quote in the opening may be seen as an extreme, but one can find a similar attitude among other university leaders. For example, in an *Atlantic Monthly* article about Princeton University, David Brooks found that Princeton does not "go to great lengths to build character" and one of its administrators claimed, "We've taken the decision that these are adults and this is not our job. . . . There's a pretty self-conscious attempt not to instill character."[6] Princeton administrators appear to believe that the students admitted should already be considered humans and will likely not revert to being animals. Thus, the university does not need to shape character. Such comments would appear to reinforce Harry Lewis' claim in *Excellence without a Soul* that "the university has lost, indeed, has willingly surrendered, its moral authority to shape the soul of its students."[7]

It would be more accurate to say that most universities have surrendered the moral authority to shape the whole soul of students. Our central argument in this book is that most universities have shifted from what we call fully human approaches to moral education to less than human approaches. When universities lack agreement about the overall human purpose and function, they must find partial agreements about the purpose and function of particular aspects of human identity. They search for agreement about what it means to be a good professional or good citizen instead of what it means to be a good human being. Outside of these areas, the vast majority of universities largely leave students to their own autonomy and freedom until they pose a legal liability to the university or to its students.

What accounts for this transformation? The change, we argue, cannot be chalked up merely to "guns, germs and steel."[8] The historical reason, we will argue, stems from the failed quest to find a nonsectarian or universal form of humanism as a basis for moral education. When universities were birthed in medieval Europe, agreement existed regarding a common moral tradition, particularly what it would mean to be fully human. Although it would be foolish to say that disagreements did not exist, there was greater consensus regarding the basic metaphysical narrative that shaped an understanding of human nature and purpose. Christian humanism served as the foundation for moral formation in early European and American universities and colleges.

As religious pluralism increased and consensus broke down regarding our views about what it means to be a good human being or what a good society would look like, Enlightenment thinkers believed that reason alone could solve our moral disagreements. Thus, a quest began that still continues to this day. Scholars embarked on a search to find and implement a common approach to moral education. They hoped for a tradition-free humanism. Usually, they based their approach on a broad and inclusive vision of individual and social good by relying upon methods or foundations that they deemed to be universal and free from sectarian moral traditions. Nonetheless, particular thinkers and communities have always risen up to point out the particular problems with these universal visions. In a world that rests on the precipice between modernity and postmodernity, scholars now recognize that reason has also failed to provide significant agreement about what it means to be fully human. As a result, debate now reigns over the nature of moral education that should be offered in universities or whether moral education should even be included as a purpose of higher education.

Some contemporaries argue that in light of the failed search for a universal humanism, universities should merely stick to professional forms of moral education. Others, however, want to continue the search. We argue that neither option should be promoted. Instead, academe needs to recognize and accept a whole range of less than human and fully human approaches to moral education. It should also understand how moral identity proves to be a crucial category by which to understand these various approaches. In his forthcoming book, *What Is a Person?*, Christian Smith sets forth the importance in this way:

> Are we simply self-conscious animals improbably appearing for a moment in a cosmos without purpose or significance? If so, that has implication for life, which even ordinary people can work out. Or are we rather illusions of individuality destined to dissolve in the ultimately real Absolute? That would make a difference. Are we instead really materially acquisitive hedonists or carnally desiring sensualists who have nothing higher to which to aspire than the gratifications of possessions and physical sensations that we can use our money and relations to consume? Or mainly only bodies with the capacities to define by means of the exercise of will and discourse our identities through self-description and re-description? Or perhaps are we children of a personal God, whose perfect love is determined to rescue us from our own self-destructive brokenness, in order to bring us in to the perfect happiness of divine knowledge of worship? Or maybe something else? The differences matter for how life ought to be lived, how *we* ought to live.[9]

The differences also matter for how universities shape their moral order and education.

Because anyone seeking to understand, critique or defend a particular approach to moral education will need to speak from within a specific tradition, we will address our own moral tradition of Christianity, although we will also examine secular approaches as well. Thus, in the second half of this book we will set forth our research regarding moral education in the Christian tradition, describe some of the weaknesses we found, and defend the model against some common critiques. For example, whether universities that set forth a more comprehensive humanist vision are truly universities is a question some would answer in the negative. We think differently. Thus, we will defend the importance of universities and colleges committed to a moral tradition that can set forth a comprehensive moral ideal for the university and its students about human well-being. This book explains our argument, offers examples from various institutions of higher education, and then responds to possible criticisms about how moral education in a comprehensive humanist moral tradition may short-change diversity, autonomy, and critical thinking. We conclude with ways of strengthening Christian universities and colleges that espouse and implement visions for a more human moral education.

Audience

In terms of audience members for this book, we hope to address three groups. First, since colleges and universities contribute in significant ways to what it means to be human, our book hopes to address students and scholars in a variety of disciplines interested in this debate. Conversations occur around this topic in general in disciplines such as anthropology, philosophy, psychology, sociology, and theology.

Second, our book obviously intersects with work being done by higher education scholars. For too long, discussions concerning the moral identity of students in higher education have revolved around theories generated by scholars in developmental psychology. Many believe these discussions have now run their course and have left us with perhaps fewer answers than we had when we started. Regardless of whether such scholars prove interested in how Christianity can inform the moral identity of students, such interest may come via our argument that particular traditions inform the moral fabric of a campus and thus the moral identity of its students.

Finally, we believe our work will be of interest to faculty members and administrators serving Christian colleges and universities. Too often, these individuals have forsaken their respective strands of the Christian tradition to foster appeal to a larger constituency. Nonetheless, a fine line exists between parochialism and an appreciation for a tradition that can grant both a sense of form and direction to an otherwise amorphous community. Given the research we conducted, campuses which exhibit the deepest respect for practices such as hospitality and academic freedom are also campuses which have been granted the deepest sense of identity by their particular Christian tradition.

Summary of Contents

Part I—The Story of Moral Education in Higher Education

Our book begins in chapter one by providing a framework by which we can understand the conversations about moral education in higher education that are currently taking place. In chapter two, we provide the major historical background to our argument. We contend that while university leaders in early European and American colleges clearly had their differences, they still shared enough common views about the essential human purposes and functions, because they generally agreed upon a common meta-identity and a common metanarrative arising from that identity—the Christian identity and story. However, as disagreements emerged over how to interpret that story, a quest began within the university. University leaders and scholars attempted to search for a nonsectarian approach to moral education. The underlying reason why, by the 1950s, university administrators and faculty made fewer attempts to shape students' character is that after nearly 200 years of the quest, the academy stood further away from agreeing upon what it means to be fully human than ever before. The third chapter then describes how events in the 1960s revealed dissatisfaction with the marginalization of ethics. Efforts began to be made to bring ethics back from the margins. Ironically, the attempts actually fostered what we call less than human approaches to moral education. Finally, this part concludes with a chapter that critically examines the various proposals contemporary scholars have made for addressing the current situation.

Part II—A More Human Education: Moral Identity and Moral Orientation

In part II, we open by distinguishing between what we call less than human and more human approaches to education. In chapter five, we then discuss the various ways that colleges and universities attempt to find moral agreement that stems not from our common humanity but from the functional commonalities associated with being a citizen or person of a particular ethnic or gender group. In chapter six, we then move to a discussion of how various versions of humanism can and do inform the moral vision in place at particular institutions. Chapter seven offers a typology of how different Christian traditions inform the moral ideals and practices at several colleges and universities we deem significant, as well as an in-depth discussion of how two of those traditions inform campuses we deem exemplary in terms of their efforts. In chapter eight we explore the possibility that too many colleges and universities understand what it means to be human as a cognitive endeavor. In the end, we contend that what we call more human institutions of higher learning can aid in the development of critical thinking in ways that institutions which refrain from setting forth specific visions of human flourishing cannot.

Part III—Strengthening the Moral Tradition of Christian Humanism

In the final two chapters we offer a vision for how Christian colleges and universities can go about strengthening their distinctive moral visions and practices. In chapter nine we argue that one of the key components of any approach to moral formation involves the formation of a person's identity. In essence, we propose a Christian understanding of identity and identity formation that can assist Christian colleges and universities in shaping the moral character of their students. In chapter ten we offer a robust vision for how Christian colleges and universities can go about offering a balanced and comprehensive vision of moral education for the curricular and co-curricular arenas. In both chapters we seek to expand the Christian community's theological imagination regarding this topic while grounding our discussion in the concrete realities of current practices of Christian colleges and universities.

Overall, we hope to provide ways that colleges and universities can draw upon the moral resources of particular traditions to help students realize their full humanity. For while the animals may be taking over the moral culture at many universities, there is hope that colleges and universities can still try to form humans. Such efforts can prove immensely more important than an education undertaken for acquiring job skills and information or even moral education that attempts to create good professionals or good citizens. As Erasmus reminds us, if moral education "be contrived earnestly and wisely, you have what may prove a being not far from a God."[10] At least perhaps, one may fashion a moral education that helps humans bear that image.

Part I

The Story of Moral Education in Higher Education

Chapter One

Love in the University: Moral Development and Moral Orientation

> There is a threshold question, then that every college needs to debate. Should moral development be merely an option for students who are interested (and for college authorities when it is not too costly or controversial)? Or should it be an integral part of undergraduate education for all students and a goal demanding attention, effort, and on occasion, even a bit of courage and sacrifice from every level of the college administration. After so many years of neglect, surely it is time to address this question with the care and deliberation it deserves.
>
> —Derek Bok, former Harvard president[1]

Should moral education be an integral part of undergraduate education? Although we agree with Derek Bok that every college needs to debate this question, we do not believe it should be the threshold question. Before we talk about whether moral development should be an option for students or an integral part of the university, we need to answer the prior question. Do we even agree about what "moral development" means or what fostering it entails? Although higher education scholars often assume that we do, we contend that we do not.

In this first chapter we explore some of the reasons higher education scholars assume common agreement about the concept of moral development and suggest more disagreement about the concept exists than these scholars often acknowledge. This disagreement stems from the existence of what John Rawls terms "reasonable comprehensive doctrines"[2] or what we call different moral traditions. Due to this reality, we must abandon the pretence of talking about moral development from some objective, universal standpoint since we can only talk about moral development and other associated concepts (e.g., moral education, moral formation[3]) from within a particular moral tradition. Consequently, we outline the particular conceptual approach we will use when we talk about moral development and moral education.

What Is Moral Development?

Discussions about growth or development are quite different when discussing physical versus moral development. Unlike the physical realm, where a parent can go to the doctor and ask, "How is my child developing?" and receive reports about the child's weight, height, word usage, et cetera in percentage terms that indicate the child's status in relation to others, we have tremendous disagreement about the empirical markers for human flourishing in regard to the good life. We do not use the average moral characteristics of the population to designate whether someone's moral development is at the fiftieth or the seventieth percentile marks.

We tend to use two general types of markers which reflect two different dimensions of the term "moral development." First, there are those in the social sciences, particularly developmental psychology, who point to reasoning changes in individuals as they (hopefully) move through particular stages of a universal developmental process. Scholars such as William Perry, Lawrence Kohlberg, Carol Gilligan, Mary Belenky et al., and James Rest fall into this category.[4] In fact, James Davison Hunter notes that this "psychological regime" has dominated our conceptions and understandings of moral development.[5] The job of the person engaged in moral education, according to those who employ these theories, is to help students move through different stages of cognitive, moral development. According to this view, various forms of socialization linked to various philosophical or theological visions of the good life should not be considered moral education. In fact, Kohlberg went so far as to say that the stimulation of development as understood within cognitive-developmental framework "is the only ethically acceptable form of moral education."[6] Thus, the important end of moral education involves encouraging someone to reason from moral principles as opposed to demonstrating a particular "bag of virtues" or learning various "'irrational' or 'arbitrary' cultural rules and values."[7]

Much of the scholarship and practice of moral education in American higher education subscribes to this outlook. Derek Bok articulates this dominant view, although he demonstrates more openness to virtue theory and encouraging students to acquire certain virtues than Kohlberg did. Bok believes we can discover a tradition-neutral understanding of particular means and ends of moral development with which "no reasonable person can disagree"[8] that can then be employed in colleges and universities to improve students' moral reasoning and perhaps even their character.

We remain less optimistic than Bok. For example, parents who ask a college administrator or faculty member how their child is developing morally could hear from an administrator that the student is now reasoning at a higher level according to some cognitive structural scale. However, such a response would probably mean little to parents who believe their student may be declining in virtues such as self-control, responsibility, and compassion or rebelling against their moral ideals and principles. Both would be talking to each other using different conceptions of moral development. The parents understand moral development as a life increasingly lived more consistently with a particular understanding of the good life or the good society. The two are using different paradigms for understanding moral development which are rooted in different narrative conceptions of the moral life. Of course, one could understand why the parent might use this language, since the marketing material of universities, if it says anything about morality at all, usually discusses moral development in this manner.

Thus, we need to recognize a second conception of moral development with roots in the Aristotelian tradition but one that takes many forms. According to this view, a person develops morally when they demonstrate the thinking, affections, and behavior associated with a particular ideal of the good life grounded in a particular understanding of the moral order. Because a plurality of views about the good life and the moral order exist, a plurality of moral traditions have developed around the diverse ways to conceptualize the process, means and ends of moral development. Although descriptive cognitive structural theories can be helpful in outlining some common ground found among moral traditions of the good, we believe we must turn to the second understanding of moral development to understand institutional missions related to moral ends in higher education. Within this understanding, moral exemplars are not those who reason at a certain level.[9]

To help us understand the difference between these views, we find it helpful to consider the example of a well-known six-year-old girl named Ruby Bridges. In the early 1960s, Ruby Bridges participated in a school desegregation effort in New Orleans. Robert Coles, a Harvard psychiatrist, became fascinated by the moral heroism that Ruby demonstrated during the months she walked to school through heckling mobs. One teacher related to Coles how Ruby smiled at her antagonists and even prayed for them. When Coles asked Ruby why, she said, "I go to church every Sunday, and we're told to pray for everyone, even the bad people, and so I do."[10] Perhaps, according to a

scale of moral reasoning, Kohlberg might find Ruby at a level one obedience orientation. Yet, Coles probed further and found more than simple obedience. Ruby stated reasons for her actions: "The minister says if I forgive the people and smile at them and pray for them, God will keep a good eye on everything and He'll be our protection." When asked if she believed the minister, she replied, "Oh yes...I'm sure God knows what's happening. He's got a lot to worry about; but there is bad trouble here, and He can't help but notice. He may not rush to do anything, not right away. But there will come a day, like you hear in church."[11] For those who hold to the second view of moral development, even a child can reach moral heights not reached by adults who may be level six moral reasoners according to Kohlberg's scale. Christians, for instance, may contend that Ruby imitated Christ-like love by praying for and forgiving her racist antagonists.

Moreover, the reasons behind the actions of a child may be deeply influenced by a moral tradition in ways not captured by broad stage theory generalizations. Why did Ruby Bridges react this way? Coles sought to understand where and how she found the strength to undertake her moral actions:

> Although from a poor family, she had somehow managed to obtain: strength to integrate a southern school; strength to be a young activist in the face of extreme hostility and plenty of danger; strength to believe not only in a social and political effort but also in herself as someone able and worthy to take part in it; and strength to maintain her high hopes, to keep her spirits up, no matter the serious obstacles in her way. Whence such strength—in a child whose parents were illiterate, unemployed, with few prospects?[12]

Coles admits that his psychiatric frameworks did not help him understand the moral courage of Ruby Bridges and others like her. Instead, he turned to a different sort of explanation rooted in a particular social context and moral tradition:

> If I had to offer an explanation, though, I think it would start with the religious tradition of black people, which is of far greater significance than many white observers, and possibly a few black critics have tended to allow. In home after home I have seen Christ's teachings, Christ's life, connected to the lives of black children by their parents.[13]

Coles' questioning reveals that Ruby's courage and mercy stemmed from the Christian teaching that she received at home and church.

The moral reasoning she used (appealing to God's justice and not merely an abstract form of fairness), the moral practices she demonstrated (praying for her antagonists) and her hopeful heart for ultimate justice from God were all reflections of living within a Christian conception of the moral order. In a similar manner, to appreciate and help conceptualize a university's role in contributing to this second view of moral development, we will also need to pay more attention to social context and moral traditions than stages of moral reasoning.

Moral Development and Moral Order

Bok's quote at the beginning of this chapter also contains a second assumption that we find problematic. Bok poses his question as if the university has a choice about whether to engage students in moral development. We contend that universities, by the very way they structure student learning and life, cannot help but be involved in promoting a particular tradition of moral development.

The reason why we talk as if the university has a choice about moral development is that the scholarly community in higher education has been enamored with the cognitive structural approaches to moral development described above. The problem with this approach, as James Davison Hunter notes, is that it tends to "view the sequence of moral development in terms that are highly individualistic and psychological as though the process is simply a dynamic of the isolated personality alone."[14] Again, while we should not abandon the insights provided by this approach, we believe that we must abandon its pretence of objective neutrality, its overly cognitive approach to moral development, as well as its overly individualistic tendencies.

If we want to examine the social dimension of moral education in universities, sociologist Christian Smith's, *Moral, Believing Animals* provides a better starting place. As our introduction revealed, the language of "animal" and "human" often infiltrates works that address moral education.[15] The reason why is that to discuss moral development at all, we need to discuss the question of who we are, or as Smith frames the question at the beginning of his book, "What kind of animals are human beings?" Smith's answer is that we humans are unique because we possess "the ability and disposition to form strong evaluations about our desires, beliefs, and feelings that hold the potential to transform them."[16] In other words, humans have the capacity not only to love and hate but to think about, judge and evaluate those desires in light of some higher moral ideal. We are moral lovers and dreamers and we have the ability to evaluate our loves and dreams that have implications for their possible transformation.

We also create institutions that embody this characteristic. In fact, Smith argues that the best way to theorize about human culture, including universities, is to conceive "of humans as moral, believing animals and human social life as consisting of moral orders that constitute and direct social action."[17] By moral, Smith means "an orientation toward understandings about what is right and wrong, good and bad, worthy and unworthy, just and unjust, that are not established by our own actual desires, decisions or preferences but instead believed to exist apart from them, providing standards by which our desires, decisions, and preferences can themselves be judged."[18] The order to which Smith refers penetrates the social and psychological world of humanity and is "thickly webbed with moral assumptions, beliefs, commitments and obligations."[19] Or as Don Browning observes, "[O]ur practices are always surrounded by—always assume— some story about the meaning of life."[20]

We would go one step farther than Smith and argue that not only are humans moral dreamers and evaluators, we are also worshippers. James K.A. Smith describes us in this way, "We humans are liturgical animals."[21] Our social gatherings also reflect this fact. As Philip Kenneson observes:

> Indeed, all human gatherings are a kind of worship to the extent that they presuppose and reinforce certain ascriptions of worth. For this reason, human gatherings are inevitably formative, not least because such gatherings construct an imaginative landscape (a "world") within which all future action and reflection upon it will take place. People come to have a world as they gather together and share stories about the shape and meaning of that world, as well as their place and role within it. People come to have a world as they gather together and engage in common practices that only "make sense" with a world so understood. People come to have a world as the above activities presuppose, instill, and intensify certain desires and dispositions, and as certain virtues are commended and instilled as being requisite for flourishing in this kind of world. People come to have a world as they construct and maintain institutions that order and support ways of life that are congruent with the ways they understand the world and their place within it.[22]

In brief, we all worship and create social groups and institutions to foster that worship—a particular ordering of our desires and affections toward particular beings and objects.

Cognitive structural theorists, such as Lawrence Kohlberg, have tended to downplay this part of moral formation as merely aspects of external socialization. Yet, it is important to note that the moral order created in such situations is not merely something external to individuals or institutions. As Christian Smith writes,

> These morally constituted and permeated worlds exist outside of people, in structured social practices and relationships within which people's lives are embedded. They also exist "inside" of people in their assumptions, expectations, beliefs, aspirations, thoughts, judgment, and feelings.[23]

Thus, when discussing moral development in higher education, we must recognize that universities already represent a particular moral order or way of shaping our social world. As Smith observes, "All social institutions are embedded within and give expression to moral orders that generate, define and govern them."[24] According to this theory and understanding of culture, universities cannot escape from both representing and transmitting a particular understanding of the moral order. As Smith points out,

> Universities are more fundamentally stable configurations of resources (buildings, personnel, budgets, reputations, and so on) grounded in and reproducing moral order. American universities, for instance, are expressive incarnations of certain moral narratives, traditions and commitments concerning the good, the right, and the true regarding human development, student character, the nature of knowledge, the purposes of education, equality and merit, academic freedom, liberal arts and technical training, racial justice, gender relations, socioeconomic background, collegial decision-making, the place of the arts, the limits of religion, the informed consent of human subjects, the value of sports, and so on. And these, of course, are themselves rooted in even deeper moral traditions and worldviews about the nature of human personhood, epistemologies, historical progress, liberty and equality, legitimate authority and more.[25]

In light of Smith's point, identifying and understanding these deeper moral traditions that shape the moral ideals and identity of the university will prove vital to understanding moral education within the context of higher education. In these respects, Smith's argument here echoes philosopher Charles Taylor's claim that we cannot dismiss the importance of ontological frameworks when discussing how we think and talk about the moral life.[26]

Moral Identities within the Moral Order

Charles Taylor begins his well-known work, *The Sources of the Self: The Making of Modern Identity*, with the simple observation that if one wants to explore the topic of the good, one must begin by examining the topic of identity. This approach is necessary because, "Selfhood and the good, or in another way selfhood and morality, turn out to be inextricably intertwined themes."[27] The reason why he contends these themes are important is due to the fact that, "To know who you are is to be oriented in moral space, a space in which questions arise about what is good or bad, what is worth doing and what is not, what has meaning and importance for you and what is trivial and secondary."[28] There is certainly some truth to this point. Contemporary scholars find that the underlying reason many individuals move from moral understanding to action emanates from a sense of identity.[29] Colby, Ehrlich, Beaumont, and Stephens summarize the findings this way, "Most explanations of the psychological constructs and processes that mediate moral judgment and action have converged on the important role of the individual's sense of moral identity. In this view, moral understanding acquires motivational power through its integration into the structures of the self."[30]

While our identities orient us morally, they also confuse us. After all, our identities are complex. We may be at the same time a Christian, a Democrat, a Coloradan, a woman, an American, a daughter, a mother, and more. These identities may all carry with them certain normative expectations, and we may experience a conflict between what we perceive as the moral obligations with being a good Christian and being a good Democrat or a good woman and a good mother. In truth, what orients us are not only our identities, but our ascription of value to a particular meta-identity or metanarrative that can help us order our other identities, loves, and responsibilities. The same holds true for the social institutions we create, such as universities.

In general, early university leaders believed their institutions should help shape young "animals" into "men" or "humans." This view stemmed from the classical Aristotelian tradition, in both Greek and medieval versions, which understood men or humans as having an essential nature and purpose. Since universities grew and prospered during the time the Thomistic expression of this Aristotelian tradition gained influence, it is no surprise that this tradition dominated the university's approach to moral education. As Alasdair MacIntyre has demonstrated, the strength of this approach is that it helps one overcome what later became labeled the naturalistic fallacy. According to one version of the naturalistic fallacy, we cannot derive moral conclusions from factual premises. In other words, we cannot derive an "ought" from an "is." Identity labels and the functions we associate with them, as MacIntyre and others have shown, provide a way around this problem. MacIntyre writes, "[F]rom the premise 'He is a sea-captain,' the conclusion may be validly inferred that 'He ought to do whatever a sea-captain ought to do'"[31] Identities serve as functional concepts that carry moral content. Of course, there is always some debate about the skills, habits, attitudes, et cetera of a good sea-captain or any other normative identity label, but there are clearly many elements on which those debating can find agreement.

If agreement also exists about the nature and function of humans, we can also derive ought statements based on our agreement about what a good human ought to do. As MacIntyre writes, "Within this tradition moral evaluative statements can be called true or false in precisely the way in which all other statements can be called." However, when disagreement about essential human purposes or functions occurs, a problem emerges, "[I]t begins to appear implausible to treat human judgments as factual statements."[32] With the development of the Enlightenment tradition, as MacIntyre recounts, the functional view of humanity was indeed discarded and agreement about the essential nature and essential purpose of humanity dissipated.

What this development has meant for moral education in universities and colleges will be the subject of this book. Basically, universities shifted from attempting to form humans to what we will call less than fully human forms of moral education. In other words, despite books discussing the moral decline of the university or even the marginalization of morality, universities have never given up moral formation. Universities and colleges continue to encourage students to adopt particular normative identities and seek to enrich students' understanding of those identities and to encourage beliefs, affections, and practices that would involve the perfection of those identities. The key difference involves the type and range of human identities universities attempt to form and the identities used to provide moral orientation to moral education. By placing moral education in more limited identity contexts, the task of moral education shrinks.

The Levels and Elements of Identity Formation

In this book, we will discuss three general levels of identity formation that take place in the university. First, there exists the most basic level of identity formation that is common to every university. Universities attempt to form good students and good professionals. In other words, universities ask students to make a vocational choice and commitment and then engage in an intellectual and morally formative process to help a student become a good historian, biologist, psychologist, et cetera. Second, most *residential* colleges and universities also attempt to form additional aspects of student identity. They may seek to shape good citizens, neighbors, et cetera. Finally, but also increasingly rarely, they may seek to shape good human beings. And since our views of what a good human being is varies greatly, this shaping will always be linked to a particular moral tradition that helps inform and shape all of our different identities. We will expand upon all these types of formation throughout this book and give numerous examples. Nonetheless, before we begin, we will need to provide some explanation of the elements of the moral formation involved in shaping any of these identity types.

First, the perfection of identities, such as professional, civic or human identities, always involves both technical dimensions and moral aspects that cannot be easily separated. In fact, to separate fact from values and talk solely about values transmission obscures what universities actually do when trying to form an aspect of a student's identity. The best way to think about this task is to think about the most basic form of identity formation in which universities engage—that related to professional or vocational identity. If leaders at an institution want to help a student become a good teacher, accountant or nurse, they do not merely transmit facts and discuss values. They motivate, teach, train, and coach them similar to how an athletic coach might coach or train an athlete. As Isaac Kandal noted many years ago, there is:

> One part of our educational system, secondary and higher, in which there is no compromise with standards, in which there is rigid selection

both of instructors and students, in which there is no soft pedagogy, and in which training and sacrifice of the individual for common ends are accepted without question. I refer, of course, to the organization of athletics.[33]

In fact, the athletic example provides a more concrete illustration. For example, basketball coaches may tell their students stories about what it is like to play on a Pan American, an Olympic, an NBA, or a WNBA championship team. Of course, they also teach them the rules. They help them practice the virtues/skills of dribbling, shooting and passing. They encourage them to think critically about their practices, habits, and strategy. They cultivate team work and help them understand the relationship between a good player and a good team. They want the player to understand the "pure" end of basketball is not entertaining the crowd (although like the Harlem Globetrotters, basketball can be used for such ends), but it is scoring the most points to win. They also help them find coaches and role models (e.g., Michael Jordan, Lebron James, Cheryl Miller, Candace Parker) who inspire them and give them wisdom about all the above aspects.

The same is true when universities attempt to form good professionals (e.g., musicians, engineers, historians, accountants, etc.), good citizens or good human beings. Universities are always perpetuators of moral identities and transmit complex forms of moral order that involve:

1. Telling narratives that inspire and shape views about ends;
2. Teaching skills or virtues acquired by habituation and refined through critical thinking and practice;
3. Transmitting rules, general principles and wisdom;
4. Cultivation of the above by studying role models, listening to mentors, continual practice, and communal participation in those things associated with the perfection of the functional identity;
5. Teaching the learner to think critically and independently about his or her performance in light of all of the above.

We can and do speak about this singular form of formation within a particular identity as a type of moral tradition. For instance, we may mention that a particular school has a long tradition of developing good lawyers, historians, teachers, psychologists, et cetera. While professional training influences other spheres of life, it remains focused upon one sphere of a human's life.

Beyond Professional Moral Formation

As mentioned above, one of the major dilemmas facing universities is how comprehensive they should be about the formation of a student's identity. Universities always attempt to form and educate good professionals in a particular professional tradition. Few question this function. Other missions receive more debate. Should they also seek to form additional identities such as what it means to be good American citizens, global citizens, ladies or gentlemen, et cetera? Those in favor of any one of these approaches support multiple identity education.

Even if universities deny that they engage in moral formation or education beyond professional formation, they usually cannot escape other forms of moral formation. For instance, in the introduction, we quoted a Princeton university administrator who claimed that at Princeton, "There's a pretty self-conscious attempt not to instill character."[34] Of course, such a comment ignores the variety of ways Princeton attempts to shape the professional identity of students. We doubt Princeton would deny it is neglecting the moral aspects of what it means to be a good biologist, historian or psychologist. Furthermore, a more honest appraisal of Princeton as a place that builds and transmits a particular order would acknowledge that Princeton engages in additional forms of moral formation outside of professional identity. John Wright observes:

> While Princeton may consciously attempt not to instill character, such a concerted attempt across a community most certainly forms the character of its members. Princeton communally forms the character of its students to believe that they are individuals with the power of their own self-determination—i.e., students have the ability to steer themselves. The community naturalizes a political order of a morally neutral, technical, public realm of knowledge and an individual realm of values. Morality belongs to the private realm of the individual, not subject to the communal oversight of the university. Such an understanding fundamentally embodies liberal political presuppositions. Princeton disciplines its students to a character made to assume and perpetuate the liberal democratic political order of the U.S. In this way Brooks is absolutely correct in stating, "Princeton doesn't hate America. It reflects America."[35]

In other words, far from being morally neutral Princeton seeks to form both good American citizens, as described by Wright, as well as good professionals.

Recently, Anne Colby, Thomas Ehrlich, Elizabeth Beaumont, and Jason Stephens, in their book *Educating Citizens: Preparing America's Undergraduates for Lives of Moral and Civic Responsibility* provide detailed examples of the perspectives and practices various schools use "when educating citizens is a priority."[36] Not surprisingly, they found that colleges and universities that address moral and civic education typically engage in the types of moral formation we have identified above. For example, they note that colleges and universities promoting ideals of good citizenship teach certain skills or virtues acquired by habituation and refined through critical thinking and practice. They also encourage communal participation in these skills or virtues. Such universities typically identify a common range of moral and civic competencies (e.g., moral consciousness raising) although they also set forth "a distinctive quality to their vision of these goals."[37] They summarize these distinctive qualities into three general themes: (1) the community connections approach, which focuses upon "connections with and service to particular communities"; (2) the moral and civic virtue approach, which uses an "emphasis on personal virtues and values" such as integrity, courage and responsibility; and (3) the social justice approach, which they describe as a concern with "systematic social responsibility."[38]

While we believe this categorization is helpful at identifying the types of virtues and skills prized in forming citizens, these authors do not emphasize that these approaches are undertaken with the liberal democratic moral tradition that has a particular liberal democratic narrative, particular procedural rules and principles, views about mentors and moral heroes and a particular community that is politically defined. In other words, Colby et al.'s categorization tells us only about some general virtues and skills and little about the substantive moral identity and tradition guiding different approaches.

The tendency to discuss virtues, skills and other elements of the moral life apart from an orienting identity often characterizes discussions in higher education. Derek Bok provides a good example of a proponent of this sort of method. Bok claims that universities should focus upon ends such as the ability to communicate, critical thinking, moral reasoning, preparing citizens, living with diversity, living in a more global society, providing a breadth of interests, and preparing them for work.[39] Bok's list combines both skills and general ideas related to identities (e.g., good worker, citizen). Yet, skills or virtues only gain meaning when oriented within a particular identity. We think and reason differently based on whether we prioritize our human, professional, democratic, or Christian identity. Therefore, we must take into consideration both individual and institutional identities when examining the moral ends of the university.

How Will Universities Handle Identity Conflicts?

If universities do choose to engage in multiple types of identity formation and enrichment, they must address two questions: (1) How will they deal with conflicts within moral identities? (2) How will they prioritize the identities and the multiple moral traditions associated with those identities when conflicts occur between traditions?

The first question proves important when undertaking single-identity moral formation. For instance, there are different traditions of thought regarding what it means to be a good citizen. These traditions have different moral heroes and different conceptions of the good citizen which will always influence understandings of moral development. Democrats and Republicans may think differently about this type of moral development, but so do those who may think and live outside the democratic political tradition. In the former Soviet Union, for instance, the models of communist virtue were Lenin, Stalin and those who died for their country (heroes of the Great Patriotic War). A teacher from Kiev shared during one of our qualitative studies of communist moral education, "The children were taught about the moral life of Lenin, great historical leaders like Stalin and other people. So they taught us the example of their lives and we were supposed to imitate their lives....In every class we have the portrait of Lenin, in the very front above the blackboard."[40] This example points to the role that our identities, those aspects about ourselves which define who we are and link us to larger moral traditions, play when understanding larger concepts such as moral development or particular virtues such as patriotism. There is no ideal of good citizenship or the virtue of patriotism associated with citizenship on which we all can agree that is divorced from our particular moral traditions.

Second, there may be conflicts between our various identities. We may face conflicts between being a good historian, a good athlete, a good liberal democrat, a citizen of the world, or even a good husband or wife. How do we order our loves? The most obvious identity tension in this area in universities today involves student-athletes. While two types of formation may coexist, there are bound to be tensions and conflicts that will have to be resolved in favor of one identity.

Universities always answer these questions in multiple ways both through their practices and official literature. For instance, when an institution such as Princeton University chooses as its motto, "In the nation's service, in the service of all nations," it perpetuates a particular view of which identity or identities should be prized or promoted. Of course, the prioritization of a particular identity poses problems with other identities. The virtues associated with being a good American or a citizen of the world may conflict. They may also be different than those associated with being a good mother or a good Christian. Few mothers want their sons to go to war, something Benjamin Rush found problematic[41] or as the movie *Chariots of Fire* recounts, a Christian may view the demands of a nation-state to impinge upon his or her moral conscience. Of course, universities can merely leave students to sort out these conflicts themselves, which actually reflects adherence to liberal individualism, or they can introduce another level of moral identity formation. They cannot be morally neutral. "The university is not only, and maybe not even primarily, about knowledge," observes James K. A. Smith, "It is...after our imagination, our heart, our desire. It wants to make us into certain kinds of people who desire a certain telos, who are primed to pursue a particular vision of the good life."[42]

What More Human Universities Add

As mentioned above, there are universities that seek to embody a humanistic approach to moral education. They forthrightly attempt to provide some overall enrichment and ordering of human identities within a particular understanding of the moral order as interpreted by a particular tradition. These types of moral traditions contain the following additional elements that they use to help inform and order various human identities and their concept of the good life and society:

A Meta-identity and Metanarrative

A meta-identity takes first priority over one's other identities. These identities usually link to larger metanarratives. By metanarrative we mean a story which provides individuals with a guiding identity by which to order and understand their other identities, purpose and the overall story of the world.[43] This knowledge then becomes the basis by which they discover what qualities or virtues a person should acquire to be fully human and what characteristics should be associated with an ideal society. These metanarratives can be sacred, secular or both. For instance, in America some of these metanarratives may be associated with colleges identified as Catholic, African-American, tribal, women's, military or Jewish. Political philosophies, such as liberal democracy or communism could supply this metanarrative. Since moral traditions with different metanrratives compete with each other for social and individual supremacy, we should realize as ethicist James McClendon observes: "We exist as in a tournament of narratives" or as we would describe them, metanarratives.[44]

A Moral Orientation by Which to Understand and Prioritize One's Identities

Both individuals and institutions understand their identities in light of these larger stories. Alasdair MacIntyre writes, "[T]he story of my life is always embedded in the story of those communities from which I derive my identity.... What I am, therefore is what I inherit, a specific past that is present to some degree in my present."[45] The same is true for institutions. The communities associated with an institution's identity tell, write, and live stories that shape an institution's identity and become bearers of living traditions.

The understanding of identity these stories provide proves crucial for how one understands moral issues. As Charles Taylor observes, "Our identity is what allows us to define what is important to us and what is not."[46] Although Taylor is speaking about individuals, the same can be said for institutions such as colleges and universities. Colleges and universities, by their identity as colleges and universities, as well as their other identities (e.g., liberal arts, service academy, state—liberal-democratic, Catholic, Jesuit, etc.) locate themselves within an intellectual and moral order tied to various moral traditions and their associated narratives. Moreover, since the narratives associated with various identities supply social and individual ends, they help order an individual's or institution's identities. This identity ordering proves vitally important since identity conflicts are usually at the root of various disagreements. Does one serve one's self, one's family, one's country, one's religion, one's ethnic group, one's profession, or humanity first? What should be the most important constituency for a university or college? What are the limits of academic freedom or religious freedom at a college or university? The answer, of course, will depend on the situation but also upon the moral tradition that informs and guides an individual's or institution's understanding of his, her, or its identity and the priority of various identities. For example, one finds this type of moral orienting occurs in the 1940 *Statement on Academic Freedom and Tenure*. The Statement highlights the following identities as the basis for understanding moral obligation in this area, "College and university teachers are citizens, members of a learned profession, and officers of an educational institution."[47] It then seeks to outline the moral obligations of professors, citizens, and university employees in light of these three identities. The orientation stems from the originators of the statement, such as John Dewey, who largely understood moral knowledge and obligations in light of professional and political (democratic) practices and identity. Nonetheless, such an approach clearly downplays other identity commitments that could stem from the prioritizing of one's faith, family, ethnicity, or humanity. To only single out these three identities shapes the humanity and moral orientation of those involved. This ordering of identities also proves crucial for how one understands and orders the virtues in one's life.

A Means of Prioritizing and Defining Individual and Social Virtues and Vices

A group's or individual's primary narrative or narratives will have a tremendous influence on the priority and understanding of various virtues and vices, because it explicitly or implicitly contains a conception of the individual and the communal *telos*. This understanding of the human telos will then influence which virtues are prized and which vices are shunned.[48] A university concerned with creating good professionals may focus on developing virtues necessary for achieving high standards within a particular profession. Similarly, universities concerned with creating good citizens may prize different virtues. For example, Soviet educators wanted to develop in students certain qualities (patriotism, discipline, a strong work ethic, etc.) that would help them reach "the new socialist future." Since the specific virtues imparted advanced society toward a communist ideal, one did not find forgiveness, love for one's enemy or mercy among The Moral Code of the Builders of Communism that Soviet teachers were expected to present each year.[49] A survey of virtues that U.S. state laws require or suggest that public schools teach American school

children demonstrates a similar bias toward virtues that sustain liberal democracy instead of virtues central to other moral traditions.
While only one state requires the teaching of forgiveness, almost all of
the twenty-four states with virtue lists require the teaching of respect
and responsibility.[50]

Furthermore, even if a school attempts to teach students virtues
such as responsibility and respect, obscurities will remain regarding
the definitions or understandings of these virtues based on one's tradition. Tim Stafford tells of one such difference in understanding:

> At the annual back-to-school night, our principal took a few minutes
> to explain the theme ("Respect and Responsibility–We Can Do It
> Together") to us parents, then turned the program over to the cheer-
> leaders. They illustrated *respect* by lip-synching a bump-and-grind
> rendition of Aretha Franklin's song of the same name. At the final
> beat, they turned around, bent over, flipped up their cheerleader's
> skirts, and displayed the word RESPECT, spelled out on pieces of
> paper pinned to their bottoms. I nudged my wife: "I don't think they've
> completely grasped the concept."[51]

Some of these different understandings about virtues will not always
be so comical to those in different traditions.

Kohlberg observed this sort of difference and derided what he
called the "bag of virtues" approach because it appeared quite arbitrary.[52] What Kohlberg failed to acknowledge was the important role
of metanarratives and moral traditions in setting forth different justifications for and understandings of virtue at different levels of identity. Aristotle or Aquinas may believe the virtues perfect one's soul
while other virtue advocates, such as the author the 1923 "Children's
Morality Code," may see them as having a particular social utility for
the nation (e.g., "Good Americans Control Themselves").[53] If the virtues are considered apart from a particular understanding of what it
means to be fully human the virtues appear to be quite arbitrary. One
can only understand the different "bags of virtues" by tracing them to
the larger metanarrative used to prioritize and define them.

Unique Practices and Unique Moral Principles for Common Practices

Every moral tradition develops particular rituals and practices[54] that
seek to reinforce the ends, virtues, and identity prized by the tradition.

Numerous colleges and universities may use an opening orientation to instill an understanding and reverence for the honor code. There may even be an explanation of the practices associated with the honor code and a ritual signing of the code by all freshmen. Similarly, both lower and higher educational institutions employ certain rituals to encourage the development of good citizenship. In the United States, children in most educational settings open the day by placing their hands over their hearts and reciting the pledge of allegiance. Attendees at college sporting events begin such events with playing of the "Star Spangled Banner." Such practices reinforce the understanding that the loyalty of all participants is intended to serve the larger collective needs of the nation-state in which they exist. Universities with attachments to particular metanarratives will also have unique practices and rituals. For examples, religious traditions may have distinct practices that cultivate the tradition such as prayer, confession, partaking in particular sacraments, singing worship songs, et cetera.[55]

In addition to creating unique rituals and practices, a moral tradition with a meta-identity and metanarrative usually provides various rules and moral principles that guide common social practices. Courtship, marriage, and sex are perhaps three of the practices about which traditions disagree upon both the ends and the principles or rules that should govern it. Thus, we should not be surprised to find tremendous disagreement among diverse moral traditions about such practices. Similarly, professional ethics classes are also filled with textbooks and discussions about the goods internal to the practice of law, business, medicine, journalism, et cetera, and the rules and principles that should govern the practice. Some educators attempt to separate these discussions from the tournament of moral traditions but such a separation always proves impossible.

The History of American Higher Education: Seeking Escape from Sectarian Humanism

As we have laid out the options for moral education in higher education, we have not included what might be called a form of nonsectarian humanism—an approach to moral education to which all universities could possibly subscribe. The reason is that we believe no such approach is possible. In fact, moral education in American higher education today can be described as a tournament of moral identities, narratives, and traditions in which the universities and colleges become instruments through which individuals and communities seek to reproduce an understanding of and commitment to a particular understanding of the moral order (or even the nonexistence of such an order). This reality means that humanist approaches to moral education will always take place within a particular conception of the moral order that others deem "sectarian." As our next chapter will show, various individuals and groups within colleges and later universities have struggled against this reality and sought to overcome it. Thus, college, and later university, leaders began the quest or search for an elusive ideal. They dreamed of an inclusive vision of moral education that overcomes the particularity and diversity of American thought and practice regarding the good life and what it means to be a good human and good society.

Chapter Two

Searching for a Common, Tradition-Free Approach to Moral Education: The Failed Quest

There is no "public" that is not just another particular province.
—John Howard Yoder, *The Priestly Kingdom*[1]

"Is, then, anything settled in respect to university education?" Daniel Coit Gilman asked at his 1876 inaugural address as the first president of the Johns Hopkins University.[2] In the midst of the dramatic changes taking place in American higher education in the late-nineteenth century, including the development of the research university, Gilman reassured his audience that they could find general agreement on some issues. One of twelve settled points Gilman outlined related to the moral task of the university. He confidently proclaimed that "the object of the university is to develop character—to make men. It misses its aim if it produced learned pedants, or simple artisans, or cunning sophists, or pretentious practitioners."[3]

At another opening ceremony over 131 years later, at a different research university, another academic leader made a very different point with equal assurance. John Mearsheimer told entering freshmen that the University of Chicago "makes little effort to provide you with moral guidance. Indeed it is a remarkably amoral institution. I would say the same thing, by the way, about all other major colleges and universities in the country."[4] One critic later tried to refute Mearsheimer by pointing to the various elective courses at the University of Chicago addressing ethics.[5] Mearsheimer countered that this claim missed his central point. The basic feature of the university is that "faculty invariably leave it to students to figure out their own answers to moral questions."[6] As Mearsheimer pointed out, "We all might wish that this were not the case, but universities would have to undergo far-reaching structural changes for moral education to become central to their mission."[7]

The contrast between Gilman's confident assertion of the university's moral purpose and Mearsheimer's observation about the lack of moral guidance provided by the postmodern university illuminates one dimension of the historical changes that have taken place in American higher education. However, Mearsheimer's observations about the contemporary situation are not entirely accurate. As this book makes clear, Mearsheimer clearly overlooks numerous colleges and universities that do make moral education central to their mission. Moreover, Mearsheimer fails to acknowledge the way in which all universities, even his University of Chicago, perpetuate a particular moral order. Within this moral order, faculty may leave "students to figure out their own answers to moral questions" in certain areas, but there are also clearly areas where faculty do not. After all, universities require that students not cheat, falsify scientific results, or sexually harass other students. Clearly, we need to think about both contemporary moral education and the history of moral education in more sophisticated ways than the simplistic narrative Mearsheimer proposes.

The story of moral education in American higher education would be better understood, we argue, as a tournament of moral traditions in which the universities and colleges become instruments through which individuals and communities seek to reproduce an understanding of and adherence to a particular moral order. Various individuals and groups within colleges and later universities, however, have struggled against this reality. They have continually fought against attempts to provide moral education linked to a particular conception of the moral order that seemed "sectarian." Thus, college, and later university, leaders began the quest or search for an elusive ideal. To appeal to a wider audience they needed an inclusive vision of moral education that could overcome the particularity and diversity of American thought and practice regarding the good life. Throughout the history of higher education, various thinkers have proposed and various institutional leaders attempted to teach and implement these inclusive visions. Usually, they relied upon methods or foundations that they deemed to be universal and free from a particular moral tradition. Nonetheless, particular thinkers and communities have always risen up to challenge these universal visions.

This chapter will briefly outline this failed quest from early American history to the mid-1900s and it will identify some of the historical factors that played a role in this story. Obviously, the chapter will not be an exhaustive history. Instead, it will merely try to illuminate the failed quest for a common, nonsectarian moral tradition. It also pays particular attention to how changes in the moral identities and traditions guiding colleges and later universities altered the focus of moral education throughout this period.

The Christian Traditions of Moral Education in Colonial American Colleges

In 1716, Cotton Mather wrote in his diary a note to himself that he needed to give public testimony to a subject that agitated him. The son of former Harvard president Increase Mather ruminated that the colonial colleges, by which he probably meant Harvard and Yale, were spending too much time on a particular subject. He fumed about "the employing of so much Time upon *Ethicks* in *Colledges*. A vile Peece of Paganism."[8] One might expect this conservative Puritan to affirm the colleges for teaching ethics. After all, the Puritan founders of Harvard understood college, first and foremost, as a place to shape students' souls and character in order to form their vision of the good life—"a life of discernment and piety, shaped by the example of the great men of the past and enlivened by a deep and unassailable love of God."[9] In other words, the founders of Harvard, and later Yale and Princeton, undertook moral education primarily in the Christian tradition. Such an education started from the premise that "every one shall consider the mayne End of his life and studies, to know God and Jesus Christian which is Eternall life."[10] To help students fulfill this purpose, the colleges required courses in theological ethics, chapel services, attendance at prayer times, and various other rules related to Christian practices. Of course, Puritan views of human nature would not have led them to be optimistic about the results of these efforts.

What Mather ruminated about though did not pertain to the success of their endeavors. It had to do with the challenge of how to handle competing moral traditions. Underneath his distress lay the question of how the Christian tradition should respond to the Greek and Roman, or what Mather termed the "pagan," moral traditions. Puritan intellectual leaders did not agree about how to approach the issue.

Actually, the Puritans were not alone in their disagreement. From the early beginnings of universities, the relationship between Christian and classical moral traditions often created controversy. When the universities originated in the late-twelfth and early-thirteenth centuries, ethics, or what later became known as moral philosophy, did not exist as a separate discipline. Professors taught the subject as part of theology (moral theology) or within grammar or rhetoric classes using classical works.[11] After the rise in popularity of Aristotle's ethics during the medieval period, however, moral philosophy began to receive additional attention in the curriculum. This change precipitated an important curricular controversy because it remained unclear what relationship Aristotelian moral philosophy should have to moral theology. In essence, how should the moral traditions of Athens relate to those of Jerusalem?

Two basic types of responses to classical moral philosophy can be found in the writings of Thomas Aquinas and Martin Luther. Aquinas' famous *Summa Theologica* incorporated Aristotle's thought into his work as incomplete truth.[12] He still believed that one needed to add the theological virtues (faith, hope, and love) and theological perspectives to complete Aristotle's work. Nonetheless, he contended and demonstrated how Aristotle's views could be successfully integrated into a Christian worldview. Martin Luther took the opposite view. In his address *To the Christian Nobility* he wrote:

> What are [the universities] but places where loose living is practiced, where little is taught of the Holy Scriptures and Christian faith and where only the blind, heathen teacher Aristotle rules far more than Christ? . . . his book on ethics is the worst of all books. It flatly opposes divine grace and all Christian virtues, and yet is considered one of his best works. Away with such books! Keep them from Christians.[13]

Luther's views, it should be noted, did not characterize Protestants as a whole. In fact, Luther's suspicions about pagan authors and the possibility of natural revelation were not held by his successor Philip Melanchthon, but they would find expression in the Anabaptist tradition and in other Protestant and even Catholic thinkers.

John Calvin, the father of the Reformed movement that influenced many Puritans, tended to follow Aquinas' approach. He believed that Christians could glean truth from pagan philosophers such as Aristotle. Calvin essentially agreed with Aquinas that in creation God bestowed humans with reason and moral capacities that allow humans to advance in moral discoveries and knowledge without special or supernatural grace from God. Nonetheless, both thinkers still saw certain limits to human reason. As Fiering notes of this approach, " . . . explicitly incorporated in this theory was the reservation that *recta ratio*, or that 'right reason' by which Natural Law is known, is inadequate, without the aid of scriptural revelation, to attain *complete* moral truth"[14] The exact nature of the limitations of Natural Law or Common Grace also diverged among scholars within the Puritan tradition.

At Harvard College, the most influential Puritan thinkers tended toward Luther's position of completely rejecting ethical teaching from pagan traditions outside Christianity. Peter Ramus, a professor at the Collège de France and one of the most respected thinkers in Puritan New England, spoke harshly against teaching Aristotle's ethics to students, since he believed it contained falsehoods "such as that the sources of happiness are found within oneself and that all the virtues are in our power and may be acquired by natural means."[15] William Ames, the most quoted Puritan thinker read at Harvard shared Ramus' view about Aristotle as well as a distrust of natural reason apart from divine revelation. He argued:

> The sole rule in all matters which have to do with the direction of life is the revealed will of God.... When the imperfect notions about honesty and dishonesty found in man's mind after the fall are truly understood, they will be seen to be incapable of shaping virtue.... Therefore, there can be no other teaching of the virtues than theology which brings the whole revealed will of God to the directing of our reason, will and life.[16]

Ames instead proposed that ethics should be studied under the discipline of theology.

Despite Ramus' and Ames' intellectual influence in New England, Harvard's first designers apparently rejected their ethical views for something closer to Calvin's outlook. Students not only studied theology (which included theological ethics) and practical ethics ("a practical exposition of what the Word of God did and did not permit, illustrated by concrete cases")[17], but early documents indicate that faculty taught Aristotle's ethics and that they devoted one-third of the second year to "Ethicks and Politicks."[18] From 1687 to 1751, ethics or moral philosophy disappeared as a separate subject in Harvard commencement theses, but moral philosophy texts, including Aristotle's ethics, still served as part of the curriculum.[19] Thus, twelve years after Cotton Mather's diary entry one still finds him ruminating about Aristotle's ethics and the teaching of moral philosophy as a separate subject in a way reminiscent of Luther. He complained:

> It presents you with a *Mock-Happiness*; It prescribes to you *Mock Vertues* for the coming at it: And it pretends to give you a Religion

without a CHRIST, and a *Life* of PIETY without a *Living Principle*: a
Good Life with no other than *Dead Works* filling of it.... Study not
other *Ethics*, but what is in the *Bible*."[20]

Mather would likely have been even more disturbed by later developments in Harvard and the other new American colleges. Moral philosophy as a separate area of study eventually began to make a
comeback at Yale (1733) and later at Harvard (1751).[21]

The Rise of Two Additional Moral Traditions in Early American Colleges

1. *The Enlightenment Moral Tradition*[22]

The revival of interest in moral philosophy that began to infiltrate
the colleges did not grow out of fondness for the Aristotelian ethics
criticized by Luther, Ames, and Mather. Throughout educational
institutions in the West, Aristotle's dominance in various fields,
including natural philosophy, began to be replaced by a new "scientific" moral philosophy. The new ethics, derived in part from the
new science, suggested that physical phenomena could be explained
by universal laws accessible and understood by human reason. This
new scientific view resulted in the growth of natural theology. Those
who subscribed to natural theology believed, as did almost all
Christians, that God had designed and ordered the world. What
made proponents of natural theology different was their belief that
humans who studied the laws of nature without the aid of Scripture
could still gain insight into God's nature and will. As Julie Reuben
notes, "According to natural theology, studying 'the tiniest of
insects' or 'the most significant atom of dust could ultimately lead to
greater spiritual and moral truths."[23] Therefore, the study of nature
now had supreme moral significance and could help people lead
moral lives.
    The teaching of natural theology spread to moral philosophy
through thinkers such as Samuel Clarke, Francis Hutcheson, and the
third Earl of Shaftsbury. They propounded the belief that moral truth
existed as a part of a larger moral order that could be discovered by
reason. In other words, with regard to moral epistemology reason
could prove nearly sufficient to Biblical revelation. The development
of both natural theology and an independent branch of moral

philosophy would prove to be two of the most significant changes in eighteenth century American colleges.[24]

Critics of these two new developments soon emerged. Yale president Thomas Clap and eventual Princeton president Jonathan Edwards expressed concern about how this new approach to moral philosophy resulted in a subtle theological shift. Whereas Puritans understood that humans had a greater need to rely and depend upon God's revelation for insight into moral truth because of our fallen human nature, this new approach to moral philosophy rested upon a more optimistic attitude toward the ability of human reason to discover God's moral truths through the study of human nature and the natural world. It also rested upon a more optimistic understanding of the ability of humans to choose the good.

Despite the concerns of critics, this new approach to ethics continued to grow in popularity because it satisfied most sides in that time period's tournament of moral traditions. For influential Deists and Unitarians such as Thomas Jefferson, it meant religious revelation could be understood as superfluous. Likewise, minority Christian sects that opposed moral teachings tied to the dominant Christian sect's theology appreciated this common ground approach.[25] Even for the dominant Christian confessions this method did not appear to threaten their identity, community, and tradition. As George Marsden remarks, "This audacious yet plausible project seemed entirely complementary to Christianity, since most of the moralists assumed that such a rationally discovered ethic had to originate with the creator, and so could not contradict truly revealed religion."[26]

This new moral philosophy, in fulfillment of the fears of its critics, soon took over the place held by theology. Frederick Rudolph claims that "between 1700 and 1850 [the moral philosophy course] took its place in the curriculum as 'the semisecular way station between the great era of theological dominance' of the Middle Ages and the twentieth century, when objective science presses so hard on all other modes of experience"[27] Harvard, Yale, William and Mary, and other new colleges adopted the practice of making a moral philosophy course the capstone of the required curriculum. The course, usually taught by the college president, focused less on abstract questions and more on practical matters concerning one's obligation to God and fellow humans.[28] Or as D.H. Meyer remarked in his study of such courses that proliferated in the early eighteenth century, "It was intended to produce not the analytical mind but the committed intellect, the pious heart, and the dedicated will."[29] Such courses fit under what we today would label moral or character formation. "The most important end to be secured in the education of the young," Francis Wayland, the president of Brown in the early 1800s wrote, "is moral character. Without this, brilliancy of intellect will only plunge its possessor more deeply in temporary disgrace and eternal misery."[30] Wayland himself would write one of the first American texts on moral philosophy, *The Elements of Moral Science*, which would sell over 100,000 copies.[31]

The attempt to downplay certain contentious elements of the Christian tradition did not necessarily involve its abandonment. "The basis of moral authority," Norman Fiering notes, "shifted slowly to 'reason' and 'nature' from Scripture and revelation, but it was a Christianized reason and a Christianized nature that came to the foreground, albeit well camouflaged."[32] When reason appeared to show particular limitations, these thinkers often referred to Scripture or God's moral law. Meyer concludes his study of these American moral philosophers by noting, "Although they dealt dutifully with the logic of ethics, and realized that God's naked will is not a proper basis for a rational theory of duty, they all relied ultimately on their faith that God's will and the moral law coincide."[33] In other words, the moral philosophy presented in most American colleges still drew from the Christian tradition and was considered compatible with it.

Of course, the moral philosophy course was meant to serve only as one part, albeit the capstone, in the overall character formation of students. Other parts of the curriculum, such as the study of classics, the mental discipline of studying Latin and mathematics, the evidence of God's design in nature presented in science classes, were meant to foster moral formation. Likewise, college chapels, daily prayers, and moral rules that enforced *in loco parentis* served to moral ends as well. As Douglas Sloan notes, "The entire college experience was meant, above all, to be an experience in character development and the moral life as epitomized, secured, and brought to a focus in the moral philosophy course."[34]

2. *The Democratic Identity and Moral Tradition*

Another advantage of the new approach to ethics exemplified in the moral philosophy course is that it proved consistent with another emerging source of moral guidance, America's democratic tradition of political thought. The creation of America and the Constitution produced a national identity, communal narrative, a new political community, and a set of moral ideals and particular practices that not only supported a political arrangement, but also began to be used as the justification for various forms of moral education. Noah Webster agreed with Montesquieu that "the laws of education ought to be relative to the principles of the government."[35] He argued for an education more suited to a democracy than a monarchy and suggested an approach to education that would "...implant in the minds of the American youth the principles of virtue and of liberty and inspire them with just and liberal ideas of government and with an inviolable attachment to their own country."[36] Understandably, the founders of the new nation were quite concerned with the arrangement of students' identities and loves. Benjamin Rush would likewise argue, "Our country includes family, friends and property, and should be preferred to them all."[37]

The emerging emphasis upon natural, rational ethics had already proved quite compatible with the new democratic tradition. It helped provide a source of moral authority and knowledge in an increasingly diverse set of colonies that had different religious establishments and even some colonies without an established religion. After the American Revolution, the new country rejected the establishment of a national church. As a consequence, many of the intellectual leaders sensed that Americans needed to find common moral beliefs held by all groups.[38] Views of Biblical authority differed among Christian traditions. Non-Christians would not draw upon the Bible for their moral views. As a result, the Bible could no longer be counted upon to provide a common source of morality in America. Finding common moral beliefs through nature or universal reason instead of revelation avoided controversial sectarian arguments about Biblical interpretation and provided a common moral foundation upon which democracy could be built. In particular, what we call character education, but what at that time would be labeled education in virtue, became a common moral language and focus in the new republic.

3. The Plurality and Mixture of Moral Traditions

Which of the three traditions, Christian, Enlightenment, or Democratic, might be emphasized and prioritized at various American colleges, of course, varied depending on the college and the faculty. At Harvard and Thomas Jefferson's University of Virginia, one finds less emphasis upon the Christian tradition and more focus on the other two traditions while Yale demonstrated more commitment to the Christian tradition. Princeton, under the influence of John Witherspoon, gave emphasis to all three with Christianity or "true religion" serving as the foundation.[39] The Princeton pattern would prove the dominant one in the early eighteenth century colleges. In William Smith's study of forty-eight teachers of moral philosophy courses, he noted that almost all of them shared a belief that God's moral law served as the foundation of a moral order that demanded duty and righteousness from us.[40] Second, Smith found these teachers also looked to Scottish common-sense philosophy, propounded by Witherspoon, for the belief that we all possess a moral sense or conscience that could guide us even apart from revelation. Third, Smith found a "common ground of discussion, even exhortation, until inundated by the tides of extreme sectionalism, was an aggressive yet pliable nationalism."[41] Despite these agreements, however, various differences always lurked underneath. As Smith notes, "Theology was the heart of the college professor's ethical assumptions" and sectarian theological differences colored moral philosophy teachers' views of cosmology, human nature, and history.[42] The attempt to find a "common" moral tradition only proved successful for a time until moral conflicts and disagreements would expose its weaknesses.

The Demise of Natural Theology and American Moral Philosophy

The merging of the Christian Natural Law, Enlightenment, and Democratic traditions in early American colleges, especially as found in the moral philosophy course, lasted for most of the nineteenth century. The decades surrounding the end of the nineteenth and early-twentieth centuries, however, saw a radical transformation in American higher education as well as approaches to moral education. Scholars have traced these changes as they relate to moral education at both the curricular level and at the larger institutional level.[43] What we will point out in this brief overview is how the synthesis of the three above mentioned traditions of moral education, especially as combined in the moral philosophy course, deteriorated due to a number of internal and external challenges. Although reformers holding to these traditions hoped, according to Reuben "to create new institutional forms that would embody their belief that truth incorporated all knowledge and was morally relevant, and also provide the basis for scholarly progress," they ultimately failed to do so.[44]

In addition, other attempts to fashion a common secular moral tradition compatible with democracy also failed. Even more limited moral traditions rooted in the emerging concept of the professional did not make permanent inroads into the curriculum. The result for moral education was its eventual marginalization from the curricular into the co-curricular realm of the university. This new co-curricular realm was understood to include all functions or activities which took place beyond the formal parameters of the classroom. Faculty members still retained responsibility for these activities even if they were beginning to feel more and more uncomfortable with the theoretical rationale for doing so. Eventually, this level of discomfort grew to the point that faculty retreated back into the classroom over the course of the mid-twentieth century and made room for a new class of administrators to enter the university—student life professionals. These professionals became responsible for the moral education of students with perhaps the exception of matters of academic dishonesty. However, even in a now formalized co-curricular realm, the increasing secularization and nationalization of higher education resulted in students exerting their moral freedom in more radical ways.[45]

The Decline of the Moral Philosophy Capstone

The last few decades of the 1800s saw the decline of the moral philosophy course as capstone classes, as can be evidenced by the fact that the last text for a moral philosophy course of the traditional type was published in 1892.[46] Scholars identify various reasons for this decline. Sloan and Smith argue that the weaknesses were primarily related to internal deficiencies with the course itself.[47] First, the moral philosophers were so consumed with finding common ground that they avoided moral controversy and conflict. Unitarians, such as James Walker at Harvard, who was reluctant to commit himself on public moral issues, represent for them the fading power of the American Enlightenment and natural theology to secure moral agreement. Moral philosophers such as Walker focused on teaching and supporting shallow moral truisms on which all Americans could agree. Only a few, such as Francis Wayland, the eventual president of Brown University, even addressed the controversial issues of the day such as slavery.

Second, the moral philosophy course could no longer serve as a capstone course in light of the burgeoning growth of knowledge, part of which the moral philosophy course had helped to nourish.[48] The ethical and scientific study of various social problems required increased precision and greater delineation of the various fields of study. The discipline of ethics, despite certain attempts at Harvard, proved unable to respond to this explosion by developing into its own separate university department or discipline which could house these separate branches of study. Sloan observes that this led to three important results:

> First, moral philosophy became an important source for the origin and development of what later developed as political science, economics, philosophical ethics, psychology, anthropology and sociology. Second, as these subjects split out of moral philosophy, they based many of their claims for autonomy on the very scientific status moral philosophy accorded them. Third, as these subjects became fields of study in their own right, they often carried with them the moral and ethical imperatives of moral philosophy.[49]

The first two developments would lead to a further explosion and fragmentation of knowledge.

Consequently, the standardized classical college curriculum in which every student took the same course of study began to be critiqued as being too basic and confining. It prevented specialized study and thus America's intellectual and moral advancement.

Julie Reuben identifies another external problem that led to the course's demise. She argues that the natural theology that supported the unity of truth began to be undermined by new developments in science. The old approach to moral philosophy relied on Francis Bacon's understanding of science that proved more compatible with religion. When the new scientific theories began to undermine support for the belief in divinely created moral order, establishing ethics instruction on the foundation of natural theology began to prove problematic. For instance, evolutionary theory helped to undercut the perceived unity of truth between revealed religion and reason/natural theology. As a result, ethics began to be separated into two types: faith-based and reason-based.[50] This separation of faith and reason in ethics merely reflected the overall methodological secularization that was taking place in other disciplines.

This methodological secularization was furthered by new scientific proposals, such as Darwin's theory of evolution, which gave rise to new, secular views about the relationship between religion and science and the emergence of biblical criticism. Now, writers began contending that a fundamental conflict existed between science and religion. Natural theology began to be discredited and with it the belief in a divinely established moral order—the view promulgated in moral philosophy courses. In this manner, progressive views of science began to undermine both natural theology and belief in a natural moral law.

We would also add other political factors that are usually not identified by scholars. The first development concerns the growth of state-funded universities. Before the end of the nineteenth century, over ninety percent of universities could still trace their origins to Christian denominations, and many of them still shared direct links to their Christian churches.[51] The Morrill Federal Land Grant Act of 1862, however, began increasing the role of state government in higher education while also increasing the value of higher education as a means that served the more immediate needs of a seemingly ever expanding nation. As higher education grew, state education grew faster than private religious education and eventually overtook private education in the 1950s as the dominant form. Unlike church schools, leaders of these institutions often had less interest in synthesizing religious moral traditions of education with science or other competing moral traditions. Instead of being concerned with forming Christian saints or Christian gentlemen, they focused on producing educated and productive citizens for the United States.

This development also influenced the growing area of student life. Students at state schools showed less inclination to be guided by moral rules and regulations that emerged from a religious tradition. For instance, Lincoln Steffens, a student who entered the University of California at Berkeley in 1885 described how he encountered upper-class students protesting the university president's attempt to guide their "private lives and...public morals" by putting a ladder through the front door of the president's house and "to the chant of obscene songs, swung it back and forth, up and down, round and round, till everything breakable within sounded broken."[52] Thus, it is no surprise that in her study of the history of student life, Helen Horowitz concludes, "Nineteenth-century colleges may have had regulations against drinking, card playing and profanity, but these rules were honored only in the breach. Except for strongly denominational schools, colleges increasingly left students to their private lives."[53] The autonomy that the democratic tradition celebrated began to be expanded and defended by the students in the schools the state funded.

The Rise of Less than Human Moral Traditions and the Failed Curricular Search for a Common Moral Tradition

1. *The Rise of the University and the Professionalization of Higher Education*

Some leaders saw the rise of the modern university in the 1870s as a means by which to address some of these new trends. Universities, they dreamed, should be scientific and expansive. Each individual specialist would add to the encyclopedia of knowledge through research. Educated experts could also apply their specialized knowledge to the moral problems of the day. To aid this process students would not be taught a set curriculum but would begin to choose their own areas of specialization. President Charles Eliot's reforms at Harvard exemplified this approach. He dismantled the required academic curriculum and introduced the elective system which resulted in the growth of new academic disciplines and specializations. In these new disciplines, students and professors began focusing more on learning the academic skills and knowledge associated with particular professions.[54]

This emphasis upon scholarly disciplines eventually had an important influence on approaches to moral education in the new university. Gilman's quote cited at the beginning of the chapter, while attempting to describe the old consensus actually reveals the new direction. Gilman called not for the molding of Christians or even educated Christian gentlemen. Instead, he called for the university to produce moral professionals. Not surprisingly, the 1880s and 1890s in particular saw the increased growth of professional societies based around particular disciplines or fields of knowledge. These professions began to assume a larger role in the emerging universities that also increasingly set the standards for the smaller colleges.[55] Within these societies particular professional aims slowly began to be substituted for general moral aims rooted in a Christian or democratic tradition as the disciplines began to become more and more specialized.[56] The professions themselves, especially in the early 1900s, also began to formulate their own moral codes.[57]

The power of the professional movement is evidenced by the fact that moral concerns outside this tradition would eventually be abandoned. Sloan claims that along with the fragmentation of knowledge, professionalization led to a situation where "the ethical, social, and character concerns, once central to higher education, were giving way to an emphasis on research and specialized training as the primary purpose of the university."[58]

2. Failed Attempt at Synthesis

Most university officials, including those advocating reform, still believed that the new universities and colleges, should be involved in broader forms of humanistic character formation and that religion provided the best foundation for such education. Again, the complaint arose that what was at fault, these leaders contended, was that the old synthesis was still too infected with denominational sectarianism. It was not common and universal enough. For instance, Charles Eliot disliked the way religion hindered scientific and professional approaches to knowledge as well as the running of a university in general. He criticized philosophy, the place where moral education was most related to the curriculum, as being "full of disputed matters, and open questions, and bottomless speculation."[59] Instead he thought it should merely be taught as a history of ideas and not certain knowledge. He also criticized the hiring of clergy to run colleges and the dogmatic teaching associated with them. "The notion that education consists in the authoritative inculcation of what a teacher deems true may be logical and appropriate in a convent or a seminary for priests, but it is intolerable in universities and public schools, from primary to professional."[60] Eliot wanted a professional university.

For Eliot a professional university, even one with a divinity school, would avoid sectarianism or denominationalism. A denominational school does not produce "openness of mind, liberality of sentiment, and breadth of sympathy," he lamented. The irony, of course, is that while Eliot recognized the need for a professional commitment in the study of other subjects, he did not think such a commitment was important in the religious profession. Eliot so successfully promoted and defended his vision against challengers that the nonsectarian approach became the norm for new private universities such as Stanford University and the University of Chicago. It would even influence the Carnegie Foundation's decision to initially exclude denominational schools from the retirement pension program for faculty that it introduced in 1906.[61]

Eliot and other university reformers also proved instrumental in disbanding the moral philosophy and natural theology courses that created the old synthesis. New universities such as Johns Hopkins,

Chicago, and Stanford never established courses in natural theology or evidences of Christianity. All of them implemented new courses in the scientific study of religion. For the religious liberals promoting this trend, science provided the methods that could be transferred to all disciplines to help discover truth. In the end though, this approach failed to gain student interest. Major programs in religious studies failed. The study of religion declined and religious worship and study became, at best, a co-curricular activity.[62] In addition, the old practices associated with the Christian religion became the tools by which to promote other moral traditions. As Reuben noted, "Christianity as presented in university chapels, became little more than appeals to clean living and good citizenship."[63] In trying to alter the old synthesis between the Christian, Enlightenment, and Democratic traditions, the reformers ended up largely abandoning the Christian moral tradition.

3. The Rise and Fall of the Secular Scientific Approach to Moral Education

This abandonment of Christian humanism proved particularly problematic for moral education because liberal Protestants had the damaging tendency of equating religion with morality. As a result, Reuben observes, "During the early twentieth century educators gradually backed away from the position that there was no morality without religion and began instead to emphasize secular sources for moral development...."[64] Sensing the need for a new and different foundation, university reformers turned to science as the possible means by which to secure common agreement about moral knowledge. As already mentioned a moral contribution of science, noted by advocates of this approach, included the virtues acquired when engaging in the practice of the scientific profession, proponents claimed, developed characteristics such as "a passion for knowledge, the love of truth, honesty, patience, single-mindedness of mind, simplicity of character, humility, reverence, [and] imagination."[65]

While this approach was merely an extension of the professional tradition of moral education, proponents also argued that science offered more. They insisted the evolutionary story actually supplied a metanarrative with a comprehensive view of life.[66] Science, through the technological advances it supplied, was revealed to be our coming savior. Edward Bellamy's *Looking Backward* helped popularize the scientific good news and professors from a wide range of scientific disciplines proclaimed it.[67] For example, some claimed scientific advances in agriculture could lead to world peace and developments in biology could help us understand history and foreign policy. Eugenics research, university leaders contended, was one of the ways the university could contribute to the progress of a nation and humanity. In this view, the scientific method would lead to increased knowledge of both the true and the good.[68]

Practitioners of the new social sciences that arose from the old moral philosophy course proved especially interested in using their scientific findings for moral ends. Early economists, political scientists, psychologists, and sociologists, Reuben observes, debated not about the objectivity of their results but the moral ways that science should be used.[69] Initially the work of the social sciences was meant to be a compliment to religion but in the end it replaced religion. John Dewey and James Tufts even set forth a scientific conception of ethics rooted in evolutionary theory instead of a supernatural belief in God.[70]

The scientific moral tradition, however, eventually stumbled under the weight of critiques from its own practitioners who claimed that science exceeded its authority when it tried to answer moral questions that went beyond its methods. The root of the problem was that science could not provide a unified view of the world any more than philosophy or theology. As Reuben observes:

> intellectuals had advocated the scientific study of humans as a way to solve the perennial contests between different schools of theologians and philosophers. Because they rejected dogmatic presuppositions in favor of free and open inquiry, they expected these new sciences to break through interminable debates about a priori principles and gradually establish a factual understanding of human nature and society. But in the end social scientists found themselves embroiled in as many conflicts as their dogmatic predecessors.[71]

Social scientists themselves actually proved surprisingly insensitive to the philosophical and theological presuppositions they brought to their research. For instance, one of these presuppositions concerned the idea of historical progress. Scientists often exhibited an uncritical and utopian belief that scientific progress would necessarily result in moral progress and that producing better knowledge would lead to better people. This optimistic and unrealistic hope would soon give way to a more powerful outlook that led to the marginalization of ethics from the sciences and social sciences.

Advocates of scientific forms of knowledge and methods began to place increasing emphasis upon a researcher or teacher being objective or value-free.[72] This approach, it was argued, was needed to arrive at an accurate knowledge of the facts. The scientific method, however, could not discover what "ought" to be. Because moral claims were merely issues of value and not fact, ethics began to be seen as subjective. Consequently, by the 1920s two things had occurred. First, natural and social scientists believed that practicing the scientific method required objectivity and ethical detachment. Second, this attitude effectively undermined attempts to create a secular approach to moral education based on science.[73]

Humanism's Last Stand: Religious and Secular Humanists Fight for General Education

Since the sciences could not provide answers to moral issues, university officials interested in maintaining a place for ethics had to look elsewhere. They turned to the humanities since they provided a place to explore issues of ethics and the good life without reliance upon religious foundations or presuppositions. The general education movement, in particular, provided a staging ground for this new effort.[74] The movement grew out of attempts to reshape the curriculum at Columbia, Bennington, Reed College, the University of Wisconsin, Harvard and Yale. Its leaders saw their efforts as attempting to provide the curriculum with some unity and moral purpose. As Douglas Sloan writes, "the major advocates of these experiments all indicated that their central concern was moral education, the turning out of persons with the breadth of knowledge, intellectual discipline, and ethical sensitivity needed to grapple with the personal and social problems of the modern world."[75]

Anthony Kronman claims that these innovators spawned not merely a curricular movement but also a particular moral tradition, the tradition of secular humanism. For Kronman secular humanism was a tradition because:

> It had central texts and abiding themes. It had a history and an internal life of its own. It could be taught in an organized way. It offered students a common set of references, a shared lexicon of works, and a fund of developed ideas with which to formulate their individual judgments and express them to others. It provoked in the way that any living tradition does, a feeling of reverence for its previous contributors, a sense of responsibility for promoting their achievements, and the

experience of freedom in being able to build something uniquely one's own from these inherited materials.[76]

Kronman claims three other common assumptions supported the tradition. First, adherents believed that despite the plurality of religions and worldviews, humans share certain conditions deriving from our common human nature. We all share mortality, needs and certain facts of life: "that we are physical beings with recurrent bodily needs; that we possess the capacity to form and use abstractions; that we are limited and yet relatively equal in our powers, so that cooperation among us is both possible and required; that we create laws and live in political communities; that we take pleasure in knowledge for its own sake...."[77] These commonalities link humans together across times and cultures. For example, Woodrow Wilson believed history was beneficial for helping train students in moral perception and even argued, "The facts of history may escape our memory, but the morals of history, the operations of character, the play of motive, the distinction of integrity, may leave their lasting impression upon us.[78] History proved morally beneficial, because we still shared a common human nature with those who lived that history. Second, adherents accepted that there are a variety of ways to human fulfillment and that some of these are incompatible with others. The task of the humanities, within the framework of secular humanism, was to help us identify the various paths and understand them. Third, according to Kronman, secular humanists rejected the idea that human life must be directed toward God and a divine end, but they also affirmed the importance of larger social structures, communities, and identities (e.g., families, nations, etc.) as necessary components in any meaningful life. These frameworks of meaning are not eternal or established by God, indeed they are human creations, but they last beyond the individual lives of humans.

Kronman's generalities, however, miss some important nuances about this movement. Despite the supposedly broad humanistic impulses of these efforts, a majority of them were largely motivated by an interest in forming citizens. Thus, one finds language about being "concerned with education for effective citizenship in a democratic society."[79] The innovators wanted citizens with certain virtues such as "excellence of behavior" and "the ability to think, to communicate, to make intelligent and wise judgments, to evaluate moral situations, and to work effectively to good ends with others."[80] Beyond a concern with forming citizens, however, most proposals lacked a common integrating identity or metanarrative.

Instead, four different types of proposals existed. Two of the approaches, one advocated by Alexander Meiklejohn and the other by John Dewey, focused more upon finding unity in the methods for dealing with cultural or life problems. Another two approaches sought to make substantive curricular changes. One of these approaches, fostered at Columbia University, attempted to find commonality in "our" identity as products of Western civilization. It involved requiring students to take courses in Western Civilization. Later, however, it become increasingly difficult to defend a metanarrative of Western civilization that can support a common understanding of moral order, prized virtues, moral heroes, wisdom, and more. Thus, Sloan points out, that when the moral outlook supporting these courses was challenged, "the general education based on them had little defense to fall back upon."[81] The last approach supported by University of Chicago president, Robert Maynard Hutchins, also promoted the study of Great Texts. Yet, it advocated a broader form of humanism similar to that of Christian humanism from the past. Not surprisingly, Kronman does not include this example in his list of secular humanist programs, since it belonged to a tradition opposed to secular humanism. In fact, Kronman's claim that the secular humanist tradition supported the Great Texts approach provides an astounding example of rewriting history. Leading secular humanists such as John Dewey and Sydney Hook ardently opposed Hutchins' project. Hutchins believed that the best education should "draw out the elements of our common human nature."[82] After all, Hutchins argued, "These elements are the same in any time or place. The notion of educating a man to live in any particular time or place, to adjust him to any particular environment, is therefore foreign to a true conception of education."[83] Hutchins' approach, however, could not be considered "secular" because it relied upon the old belief, rooted in the Thomistic tradition of natural law that we can find a common rational foundation for our conception of the moral order undergirded by theism.

According to Kronman, the humanities movement, and the golden age of secular humanism in particular, became corrupted by the same serpent which tempted universities and colleges with the modern research ideal or what we have been calling the professional tradition. When humanities departments at universities consumed the modern research ideal, the ideal worked to undermine three values that had sustained both the classical tradition and secular humanism. First, it elevated originality, especially future originality, over the value of repetition and recurrence that led thinkers to commune with the giants of the past. Second, it also emphasized that one cannot acquire the knowledge one needs in four years, such as the knowledge to explore life's meaning. Consequently, larger human questions, such as the question of life's meaning, began to be seen as unprofessional, because it led one to focus on one's own life and mortality instead of the larger narrative of one's discipline. Finally, it particularly undermined the humanities whose specialty is not new research but the enrichment of our humanity.

The failure of such approaches, however, cannot merely be placed upon the research ideal, although it clearly played a part. Infighting among religious and secular humanists, including debates between religious humanists such as Hutchins and Mortimer Adler and secular humanists such as John Dewey and Sydney Hook, proved detrimental as well. They could not find a nonsectarian humanism.

In the end, Hutchins' vision of a humanism grounded in natural law lost ground to a less than human approach to moral education. This approach "associated morality with the emotional appeal of beauty, rather than with the cognitive authority of knowledge."[84] Consequently, it served to undermine the objective status of ethics and associated ethics with aesthetics. It also supported the emerging theory of emotivism, the view that ethical judgments are merely emotional claims and not cognitive claims to truth.

Removing Moral Education from the Curriculum

Turning to the Faculty

These developments only served to further marginalize moral education from the curriculum in both philosophy departments and general education.[85] For universities, administrators began to view ethical formation less as something to do with the content of the curriculum and more to do with the character of the professor. Reuben quotes Otis Randall of Brown University as a representative of the view that ultimately prevailed, "There are no courses of study yet devised nor are there likely to be which in themselves are going to build character in our young men."[86] Instead, Randall argued, "The great contributions toward character building are made by those teachers who through the influence of their own lives and characters, who by their personal touch and magnetism are able to mould [sic] the life of the young man."[87] Nonetheless, the professionalization of higher education led university administrators to focus less on the moral character of professors and more on their professional qualifications. For instance, whereas in the 1800s, the presidents of Harvard and Yale considered the character of a prospective faculty member as being perhaps even more important in hiring than their quality of scholarship or teaching, a 1939 Harvard committee would declare, "Personal characteristics should not be considered as a primary criteria [in hiring]. A faculty made up wholly of amiable and attractive men, or even of saints would not as such serve the purposes of a college or university."[88] Moral education became marginalized not only from the curriculum but also from the standards and expectations held for professors.

The overall result of these trends during the middle of the twentieth century would be the eventual marginalization of moral education from both the curriculum and the mission of many universities and colleges.[89] By the mid-twentieth-century moral education in general disappeared from the requirements and catalogues of most research university curricula. In addition, many liberal arts colleges and universities diminished curricular attempts to provide moral education, though catalogues and public relations guides still referred to moral education. These aims were largely seen as being accomplished by the co-curricular side of the university that began to grow in importance in the mid 1900s.[90]

Professionalizing the Co-curricular: The Rise of the Profession of Student Development

The one moral tradition in higher education that survived the early twentieth century ended up being the professional tradition. Its survival was inescapable. After all, professors had to pass along the moral purposes and virtues associated with their particular fields. Yet, the professional tradition also permeated the growing co-curricular dimension of student life. Since faculty advisors began to be seen as insufficient in helping students find their way through college life, universities and colleges began to add professionals to help students choose courses and find jobs. The vocational guidance movement supported by the scholarship of Frank Parsons began to grow throughout the early 1900s to meet this need. Soon, universities began hiring personnel to take care of other student needs. Yale created a Dean of

Students position in 1919 to "deal with all the collective problems of public morals and public order which confront the University as a whole."[91] Advocates claimed that these new specialized experts, the forerunners to those who would eventually serve as student life professionals, were required to address the physical, intellectual, moral and religious needs of students, since faculty could no longer handle this complex task.

The leaders of this new movement began arguing for the need to admit students according to character. Thus, although Harvard would stop applying the category of character when looking for faculty applicants, they would begin using student admissions to "test character and personality, as well as mental power."[92] Other universities with a surplus of applicants, such as Yale, Columbia, Stanford, Chicago, Johns Hopkins, and Michigan, joined Harvard in employing restrictive admissions.

Universities also built more dormitories as a way to establish moral community for students. Proponents of building more dormitories believed that by controlling students' living environment they could create a moral atmosphere conducive to building students' character. Lyman Wilbur, president of Stanford, espoused a common sentiment, "When students are housed together there is developed a strong cooperative sense of loyalty and enthusiasm called 'college spirit' which has a profound effect upon the development of the character of the students and upon the welfare of the institution."[93] In this way, they hoped to harness peer-pressure for noble moral purposes.

Universities also began to try and take back the expanding co-curricular realm of student life already run by students and alumni and use it for their own moral purposes. Student life professionals and university-hired coaches were placed in charge of fraternities and athletic contests that already existed. Administrators hoped that student life professionals could harness fraternities through various rules and regulations meant to improve their moral influence and help them take academics and community service seriously. Moreover, "By instituting changes in athletics," Reuben observes, "university educators hoped that they could reshape students' community life to make it a force for moral improvement."[94] Overall, she concludes "'Student life' replaced the classroom and the chapel as the locus of the moral mission of the university. This institutional arrangement reflected the intellectual division between fact and value, and reduced morality to campus morale."[95]

A 1937 report commissioned by the American Council on Education on personnel practices in colleges and universities, *The*

Student Personnel Point of View, articulated the authority of the new student life professionals over the moral lives of students. The report insisted that universities had the moral obligation "to assist the student in developing to the limits of his potentialities and in making his contribution to the betterment of society."[96] These potentialities included not just intellectual potential but social relationships, physical condition and moral and religious values. The report assumed that colleges and universities could agree upon the improvement of things such as "personal appearance" and "manners" as well as "progression in religious, emotional and social development."[97] It also claimed that "an effective educational program" would include student personnel engaged in "supervising, evaluating and developing the religious life and interests of students" and "maintaining student group morale by understanding and evaluating student mores." The new profession quite quickly and officially tasked itself with doing the moral tasks no longer addressed by the faculty or the curriculum.

The student life profession now needed a moral tradition for guidance since it could not talk about "those individual and social responsibilities which are essential to the common good" without some kind of larger framework than "individual development." Thus, the American Council on Education eventually revised its 1937 statement in 1949. Their new statement drew directly upon the democratic tradition. For instance, it articulated its goals as "education for a fuller realization of democracy in every phase of living" and "the application of creative imagination and trained intelligence to the solution of social problems and to the administration of public affairs."[98] Democracy no longer existed as a mere political philosophy but it became a whole approach to education and life. Ironically, the writers of the statement actually saw themselves as countering the nationalist rise "of the modern research-centered German university" that steered American universities toward "intellectualism" and connecting with the pre-modern university and college tradition where there was concern for the "spiritual, social and personal development of students."[99] In reality, of course, they were doing no such thing, except in relation to the scope of focus. The political rationale for focusing on the whole student was very much in keeping with the political way of thinking propounded by the modern research universities of Germany. Thus, the student life movement justified its approach by claiming, "Our way of life depends upon a renewed faith in, and extensive use of, democratic methods, upon the development of more citizens to assume responsibilities in matters of social concern, and upon the active participation of millions of men and women in the enterprise of social improvement." Colleges and universities, therefore, needed to inculcate in students "a firm and enlightened belief in democracy."[100]

The emerging student life profession approached religious and ethical beliefs much differently than political thought and participation. Under the heading, "The student discovers ethical and spiritual meaning in life," the statement recognized that students will have to adjust to the lack of firmness or the reality that "the time-honored teachings of organized religion may lose their effectiveness both as explanatory and guiding principles. The resultant disturbance may have deep and far-reaching ramifications into personal as well as family, and even broader, social conflicts. In his new search for values which are worthy of personal allegiance in a time of social conflict, the student needs mature guidance."[101] Who would provide this new guidance? Not the faculty or even great texts. "The religious counselor and the religious-activities program with a broad social reference may assist the student in developing an understanding of proper concepts of behavior, ethical standards, and spiritual values consistent with his broadened horizons resulting from newly acquired scientific and technical knowledge."[102] The new student life professional would guide students through the soft sand of religious and moral doubt with the help of "newly acquired scientific and technical knowledge." Since science was value-free, however, it was unclear how this knowledge was to provide any normative guidance.

Conclusion

From the beginning of Harvard in 1636 to the mid 1900s colleges and universities in early America changed from being concerned with the moral formation of good Christian gentlemen to the character formation of good Americans. In the late-nineteenth and early-twentieth centuries, with the rise of the professions and research universities, higher education institutions eventually began to understand the formation of American men (and later women), as Gilman's quote indicates, as pertaining less to a broader humanistic and democratic tradition and more related to the limited task of making good professionals. Interestingly, even this emphasis declined over time, particularly in the curriculum. It eventually ended in failure at the curricular level with most research universities and many liberal arts colleges eventually marginalizing most formal offerings of moral education from the curriculum. Thus, for the first two-thirds of the twentieth century, colleges and universities largely abandoned humanistic forms of moral education from both the college curriculum and the purposes of higher education.

The reason for this marginalization involved the failure of moral education courses to meet the purposes for which they were originally given such a high importance in the curriculum. Moral education based upon more inclusive approaches to knowledge, it was hoped, could provide a source of common agreement about human ideals, character, and behavior in a new country fragmented by sectarian divisions. Moral philosophy courses could help form humans, Americans or professionals and not particular types of Anglicans, Presbyterians, Methodists, Baptists, Lutherans, or Catholics. What became clear, however, as both religious and secular forms of ideological pluralism expanded in America, is that the answers to important foundational ethical questions always involved questions and answers about human nature and the good life that are connected to particular traditions of moral thought rooted in different aspects of human identity. Differences between these moral traditions could not be easily resolved by appeals to the Bible, reason, or even scientific methods. In this respect, the story of moral education in American higher education from 1636 to the 1950s can be understood as an attempt to escape from particularistic moral identities, narratives, communities, and traditions to more inclusive and universal moral identities, narratives, communities, and traditions. The rising dominance of state-funded universities would reflect and also reinforce the demise of humanistic moral education. While in the 1940s, there were still more students in private higher education than in public, by the mid-1950s public enrollments would overtake private enrollments.[103] Understandably, state institutions would face additional constraints that would limit their ability to set forth a broad vision for moral flourishing.

Ultimately, the failed quest undermined moral education in many universities and colleges and left it largely in the co-curricular realm of university life where it resided under the ambiguous area of moral development. For all their progress in knowledge, universities stood farther away from agreeing upon what it meant to be a fully developed moral human being than when Harvard College opened in 1636.

Chapter Three

The Rise of Less than Human Moral Education

Courses in Ethical Reasoning teach students to reason in a principled way about moral and political beliefs and practices, and to deliberate and assess claims for themselves about ethical issues.

—*Report on the Task Force on General Education,*
Harvard University, 2007[1]

It's not rationality that I lack but mercy, compassion, and forgiveness.
—Uma Thurman as The Bride in *Kill Bill I*

The 1960s would prove to be a turning point for moral education in higher education. Instead of leading university presidents proclaiming that the object of the university was to develop character, they set forth visions devoid of major moral goals. In the curricular realm, ethics teaching continued to be marginalized. Moreover, in the co-curricular realm, the university abandoned many of the old behavior codes and enforcement efforts in the belief that students in a free society must learn to develop morally on their own without guidance from the university. Student life professionals thus became attracted to new theories of moral development that mapped changes in the cognitive reasoning ability of students. Although they still claimed a responsibility for nurturing the moral lives of students, it often remained unclear what role student life professionals could or should play in terms of moral development.

From the 1970s to the 1990s, moral education would eventually be revived, but it would be a very limited revival. In the curricular realm, moral education revived in, of all places, the disciplines that had first rejected it—the sciences. New technologies required professionals to face difficult new moral problems. Consequently, ethics education in the curriculum began playing a greater and greater role in forming good professionals. In student life the political turmoil of the 1960s would produce new forms of consciousness about race, class, gender, and eventually sexual orientation that would become the basis for certain segments of behavior codes oriented less to a person's humanity and more to moral obligations linked to particular social identities. By the turn of the century, moral education in higher education would lose its focus on humanity and settle for less than human forms of moral education.

The 1960s and Ethics in the University

"By the mid-1960s the teaching of ethics was in big trouble," concludes Douglas Sloan in his article summarizing the state of ethics education from 1876 to 1976.[2] He cites three particular reasons for the crisis. First, ethicists continued the futile quest to find a common rational grounding for ethics or as Sloan puts it, they sought "to establish and secure 'the place of value in a world of fact.'"[3] Second, ethicists largely focused on metaethics to the exclusion of normative matters and concrete social problems. Finally, due to the first two factors, ethics became increasingly isolated and marginalized within the curriculum. One study, which Sloan claimed was "probably fairly representative," found that only a miniscule number of students even took an ethics course.[4]

At the same time, college and university leaders began to rethink the university's place and purpose. Interestingly, their new visions no longer saw universities as places that shape and cultivate humans. Instead, they focused on more narrow academic ends and elevated virtues that dealt solely with the mind. Creating critical thinkers who can navigate a complex and free world became the goal of the new, modern university.

Despite or perhaps because of the absence of ethics education in the 1960s curricula and university visions, students played pivotal roles in the major moral protests of the period: the civil rights movement, the women's rights movement, and resistance to the war in Vietnam. College campuses became arenas in which these efforts were launched. Demonstrations ranged from the peaceful to the chaotic, and finally even to the tragic.[5] Closings were issued for "the entire University of California and State University of California systems, encompassing 325,000 students. All of the schools in Boston's massive university complex were on strike; the eighteen Pennsylvania State University campuses were closed indefinitely."[6] In total, somewhere "between 550 and 600 schools were either shut down or on strike."[7] Finally, the shootings of students at Jackson State and Kent State speak to an ultimately tragic turn.

College campuses did not simply serve as arenas for these efforts. In time, students began to turn the level of social criticism on their own institutions. Colleges and universities were criticized by students for their unequal treatment of ethnic minorities and women as well as their involvement in the military-industrial complex. They wanted the university to engage in creating a more just, human society.

Limiting the University's Purpose: Jacques Barzun and Clark Kerr

Leading university leaders, however, did not always share the views of student protesters. Nonetheless, they did propose rethinking the purposes of the university, albeit in very narrow ways that downplayed the moral dimension of student learning and development. Two leading voices amongst these efforts emerged from two of the institutions which perhaps faced the most intense demonstrations and criticisms—Columbia University and the University of California at Berkeley: Jacques Barzun a historian who also served as dean of faculties and provost at Columbia and Clark Kerr an economist and former president and chancellor at the University of California, Berkeley.

In 1968, Barzun published *The American University*. His own university, Columbia, witnessed one of the most explosive forms of protest when students occupied five buildings, some leaving only under exhibitions of significant force by New York City police officers. Students walked out of commencement that year only to hold a counter-commencement of their own. His book, in some respects, sought to address this moral crisis.

The subtitle of *How It Runs, Where It Is Going* says something of how Barzun organized this book. The first part offered a descriptive account of the organization of the research university as it had emerged by the 1960s. The second part of the book provided a philosophical analysis of the challenges and the opportunities facing such a university. Of greatest concern to Barzun was the unbounded growth of the university which inevitably leads to what he identified as an absence of a unifying center. Barzun claimed that the university "will in slumber dream of itself as a great national force and call itself a multiversity, which at first only a few will see as a contradiction in terms."[8] Without a center, Barzun predicted the parts of this multiversity will begin to go their own separate ways. In one sense, he claimed that the autonomous faculty member who sees him or herself as a self-employed member of a guild is a symptom of this dilemma. In another sense, he claimed that student riots are a different symptom of this same problem. As in an earlier work entitled *The House of the Intellect*, Barzun saw the pain incurred by such symptoms as being self-inflicted. The bottom line was that the university, by virtue of its very lack of definition and understanding of its own identity, brought these problems on to itself.

Barzun concluded his work by offering a host of practical recommendations—68 in total—of how a university can "make fresh choices affecting all parts."[9] While voluminous in nature, these recommendations all revolved around an aspiration to possess a common center. According to Barzun "a university should be and remain One, not Many, singular not plural, a republic, not an empire; and that no matter how old, large, rich, or conceited, it should from time to time join with other universities to introduce ripened innovations."[10] The key to the latter portion of this assertion is not so much Barzun's focus on the introduction of innovations but ripened innovations. Such attempts are not the byproduct of fashion or even fleeting wants but of the master virtues that flow from the center of the university. While the formation of the intellectual virtues may take place within such a context, moral formation remained marginalized in Barzun's proposals. For example, when discussing "social responsibility to neighbors" Barzun applauded a university that did not ask professors to engage in using urban redevelopment funds since the university "cannot, except badly and dangerously, do things—however good— for which it is not equipped and organized."[11] Likewise when it comes to students solving urban problems, Barzun advised, "The all-purpose man in an all-purpose college negates education. If a youth feels a vocation for social work, let him either prepare for it through study or drop studies and go use his talents in the midst of life."[12] Although intellectual and moral virtues are not entirely separable from one another in Barzun's account, moral formation in Barzun's ideal university would occur more by default than by intentional design.

Although living through the same disconcerting era in American life, Clark Kerr came to some very different conclusions concerning the nature of the university than Barzun. In *The Uses of the University* (the title itself beckoning some of those differences), Kerr wrote of Barzun as establishing his house from an "inward looking and idealistic point of view, as opposed to the 'corruption' of science, to modern art, to foundations with their interdisciplinary projects [perhaps referencing the enemy of philanthropy], and so forth, regretting that the 'House' is no longer 'a company apart.'"[13] Referencing Robert Maynard Hutchins in the same work, Kerr concured with the former president of the University of Chicago in that the university "needs a purpose, 'a vision of the end.' If it is to have a 'vision,' the president must identify it; and, without vision, there is 'aimlessness' and the 'vast chaos of the American university.'"[14] Yet, Kerr possessed a very different vision of the university than Hutchins or Barzun.

Instead of denouncing the idea and impending existence of the multiversity, Kerr opened *The Uses of the University* with an attempt to revise, conceptualize, and defend such a reality. In his introduction to this concept, Kerr acknowledged that the research university in America is "a new type of institution, it is not really private and it is not really public; it is neither entirely of the world nor entirely apart from it. It is unique."[15] Unlike Barzun's ideal of the university, Kerr claimed that the multiversity is an imperative thrust upon the American educational landscape by the logic of history. At its best, such an institution is British in terms of how it dispenses undergraduate education, German in terms of how it dispenses graduate education, and "as American as possible for the sake of the public at large."[16] Finally, Kerr made an unexpected observation in the sense that he referred to the multiversity as an institution that is "as confused as possible for the sake of the preservation of the whole uneasy balance."[17] While Barzun's university's had a definitive center focused on cognitive formation, Kerr's multiversity and its varied forms of cognitive formation are the products of a well-managed tension that prohibits any one expression of a university to come to dominate the others.

In such an institution, Kerr claimed that students possess a considerable amount of power. The elective system gives them a chance to select courses and thus dictate where the university may grow and where it may constrict. The same may also be said of a system where students select majors. Kerr thus openly acknowledged in this sense that the students are consumers who purchase particular goods and services from the university. Kerr then goes on to claim that such a system is preferable to "a more rigid guild system of producer determination."[18] In addition, Kerr noted that students also select who does the actual teaching. By virtue of how patterns of course registration develop, the faculty whose courses students populate most frequently may account for approximately 25 percent of the total number of faculty members on campus. However, these same faculty members may carry as much as 50 percent of the student load. Likewise, Kerr estimated that these same registration patterns leave approximately 10 percent of the faculty with little to no students.

While students may possess real power in such a context, Kerr also openly acknowledged that "The multiversity is a confusing place for the student. He has problems of establishing his identity and sense of security within it."[19] The compensation which comes for students within the context of the multiversity is the range of choice such an institution affords them. Kerr quantifies this range of choices as being staggering. He claimed, "The casualty rate is high. The walking wounded are many."[20] However, he also claimed that "Lernfreiheit—the freedom of the student to pick and choose, to stay or move on—is triumphant."[21]

While Kerr celebrated how adaptive and responsive the multiversity can be to a diverse and changing American society, he also acknowledged its neglect of some of its most distinctive characteristics. This form of neglect includes the moral imprint such a university leaves on the student. The ideas that Barzun extolled are designed to leave a heavy imprint upon the intellectual formation of the student—even if it comes at the price of moral formation. Regardless, moral formation of some form or another takes place even if such formation is not intentional. The multiversity, and its staggering array of choices, is one which rewards students who reflect what Friedrich Nietzsche referred to as the will to power. If so, the only downside is that the remaining students become part of the casualty rate that Kerr referenced as nothing less than being high. Perhaps it should come as no surprise then that student protesters would see universities such as Kerr's as "moral wastelands."[22]

Both understandings—one where the university serves as a forum for liberal learning and one where the university serves as a forum for choice—perpetuate a particular conception of moral order linked to an underdeveloped anthropology. In essence, these approaches only see the cognitive qualities of life as being relevant to what it means to be human. In other words, both of these visions of the university view students in relation to the powers of their minds. Although the co-curricular arena of the university may exist, it proves to be insignificant to the curricular arena. Risking hyperbole, one could think of students in these environments as being brains on sticks. One set of brains may be formed to face challenges necessitating critical thinking. The second set of brains may be formed to face the need to make choices amid boundless opportunities. As different as the goals and the means may prove to be, the range of the formative impact is still limited to the cognitive abilities of the student. Not surprisingly, student radicals would use Kerr's work to criticize the university as a "soulless 'knowledge factory'" where "students were no more than raw material for the mass production process."[23]

Cognitive Conceptions of Moral Development: Perry and Kohlberg

With the marginalization of morality to the co-curricular realm, the faculty came to think of themselves as only being responsible for the production and dissemination of facts and perhaps professional or scholarly development. As a result, the new class of administrators known as student life professionals continued to manage the growing co-curricular realm. The era of the 1960s also brought with it, however, a rebellion against the behavioral expectations enforced by those in charge of this co-curricular realm. The successful rebellion brought down a whole range of rules governing the lives of students outside of class relating to issues such as curfews, chapel attendance, and sexual behavior.

In the area of moral development, however, student life professionals were not content to ignore moral issues. Not surprisingly, a 1968 report on *The Student in Higher Education* lamented the narrow focus on intellectual development since "it becomes virtually impossible to separate intellectual from moral and emotional growth."[24] This report argued for developmental education since "even technicians cannot be trained unless it is recognized that they are something more than functionaries—that they are also human beings..."[25] Thus, student life professionals now needed a new set of tools by which to understand and engage students as the university encouraged them to develop on their own In particular, the report contended that "the knowledge of human development from the behavioral sciences now makes possible a wider vision of what the school can accomplish and of more effective ways of teaching. American higher education has not paid enough attention to human development as part of its mission..."[26] Science still provided the hope for humanity.

Emerging developments in cognitive psychology, in particular, provided help with a vision for a more human developmental education. These attempts still aspired to provide objective and tradition-free ways of understanding moral development. Two such theories included William Perry's work on *Forms of Intellectual and Ethical Development in the College Years*[27] and Lawrence Kohlberg's theory of moral development. Perry's theory is really less a theory of ethical development than a theory of intellectual development. Using qualitative analysis from interviews with young men at Harvard University, Perry outlined a theory that showed how students' intellectual reasoning moved from simple dualism, to complex dualism, to relativism, to commitment in relativism.

Perry claimed a universal and scientific status for a theory developed in qualitative analysis. Nonetheless, Perry acknowledged that his descriptive theoretical framework of college students' development could not be considered morally neutral or objective in that it clearly prized certain virtues:

> For example, since each step in the development presents a challenge to a person's previous assumptions and requires that he redefine and extend his responsibilities in the midst of increased complexity and uncertainty, his growth does indeed involve his courage. In short, the development resembles what used to be called "an adventure of the spirit." One psychologist dubbed it an "epistemological *Pilgrim's Progress.*"[28]

The *Pilgrim's Progress* terminology reveals one of the ways in which Perry's theory provides an alternative map or narrative of moral development as compared to those maps rooted in the Christian tradition.

While Bunyan told his story as a dream to visualize an ideal of how a Christian can develop successfully through life, Perry's scheme attempts to be a sort of secular *Pilgrim's Progress*. For instance, Perry admitted that the scheme reflects both Deweyian pragmatism as well as existentialism and that "at the highest point of development in our scheme, the majority of our students are portrayed as addressing the world in the very same general terms as our scheme's own philosophical outlook."[29] Along his secular pilgrim's progress, Perry's pilgrim faces temptations to retreat into simplistic dualism. Instead, the pilgrim must close his or her ears to those temptations and run with courage toward complex dualism, relativism, and then "complex commitment." Moreover, instead of Vanity Fair the pilgrim must avoid "escape" from commitment.

Perry also saw the university, especially the faculty, as needing to take a moral stand in light of his findings. The university must seek to guide students from relativism, which in its failure "to provide orientation for the individual makes its structure highly unstable"[30] to commitment. In fact, he believed this responsibility should rouse the scholar from any neutral, objective stance. He argued, "...it is no longer tenable for an educator to take the position that what a person does with his intellectual skills is a moral rather than intellectual problem and therefore none of the scholar's business."[31] Scholars should be committed to taking students toward commitment. The

role of the university in actually suggesting there might be better commitments than others or in differentiating among commitments, however, is not addressed by Perry. Following his theory merely leaves
universities valuing commitment in general instead of alienation or
escape.

The map of moral development supplied by Perry's scheme
proved quite limited. According to Perry's theory, the university's
lack of commitment may at times move students toward intellectual development. For instance, one Harvard student noted that
when he asked his freshman advisor for guidance the advisor
responded, "Well you've got to decide that for yourself." The student told Perry, "I just couldn't understand it. Then, you know,
that, that here I was completely lost and he wouldn't help me."[32]
Moreover, Perry actually saw students looking for such guidance
as perhaps misguided. He categorized the student who claims
"you're left to cope too much on your own" as a student who
wished to escape complexity and retreat to dualism.[33] At an institutional level, Perry's theory merely reinforced Michael Novak's
critique of the university at the time:

> It may be that the American consensus has forced a "commitment to
> nothing" upon our universities; we are a pluralist people, and it seems
> very difficult to discover a way to teach about those differences on ulti-
> mate questions that muse us so. The colleges make a "commitment to
> noncommitment," have a "faith in non-faith." They demand perpetual
> re-examination and have nowhere to rest.[34]

The 1968 report on *The Student in Higher Education* echoes
Novak's concern that the university's commitment to noncommit-
ment failed to help students. This report lamented, "We do little to
help students in their search for commitment, despite our knowledge
that they are at precisely the age when commitment is of crucial
importance. Instead, we stand idly by while young people search
fruitlessly for propositions and commitments which will explain the
chaos and confusion of life, and worse, we fail to indicate the possibility of a meaningful bridge between the private and public
conscience."[35] Unfortunately, Perry's theme could provide no answer
to this problem.

Perry's work would come under criticism from a number of fronts.
Perhaps the most pronounced and insightful concerns were raised by
Mary Field Belenky and her colleagues in *Women's Ways of Knowing*.
In the introduction, they note that "While a few women were included
in Perry's original study as subjects, only the interviews with men

were used in illustrating and validating his scheme on intellectual and ethical development."[36] In addition, Perry concluded that when he did look at the limited data he received from women, that data conformed to the data he received from men. As a result, Belenky and her colleagues focused "on what else women might have to say about the development of their minds and on alternative routes that are sketchy or missing in Perry's version."[37] Belenky and her colleagues subsequently uncovered that women do differ from men in terms of their cognitive development and their development in terms of self concept.

In the realm of moral development, Lawrence Kohlberg's approach provided more specific guidance, at least for student life professionals. Kohlberg proposed a theory of moral development that outlined the six cognitive stages of moral reasoning through which individuals may proceed.[38] Similar to Perry, Kohlberg's study did not focus upon the actual moral content of individual's choices but upon the form and basis of reasoning used to arrive at certain moral commitments. Kohlberg's theory provided a map by which student life professionals could measure moral development by claiming that individual's progress through these stages of moral reasoning. "The educational goal," according to Kohlberg, "is the eventual attainment of a higher level or stage of development in adulthood, not merely the healthy functioning of the child at the present level."[39]

Kohlberg, however, admitted that his scheme did not actually provide specific normative guidance. Moreover, he recognized the limitations imposed by the is-ought gap developed by the positivists. He wrote, "Factual statements about what the processes of learning and development *are* cannot be directly translated into statements about what children's learning and development *ought to be* without introduction of some value-principles."[40] Thus, Kohlberg admitted that he founded his theory on what he calls "the value postulates of ethical liberalism."[41] Kohlberg hoped his theory would educate individuals who will emerge from schools "free and just" and able "to defend [their] own rights and the rights of others."[42] Kohlberg's "scientific" solution ended up being an appeal to the liberal-democratic tradition. In this respect, Kohlberg also took liberalism from a political theory that allows communities with competing conceptions of the good to live together to its own comprehensive vision of the good. Overall, he promoted an end that divorced moral theory from any connection to the perfection of the human soul or the final human purpose.

It comes as no surprise then that the universality of Kohlberg's theory would be challenged on a variety of different fronts. Carol Gilligan argued that Kohlberg's scale does not accurately account for the unique ways that women reason about moral issues.[43] Women, she argued, rely less upon the application of abstract moral principles and demonstrate more sensitivity to what might be the caring response in a particular situation and context. Richard Schweder called Kohlberg's approach "the ideal of an articulate liberal secular humanist."[44] Certainly, Kohlberg's model was also limited in other respects. It only dealt with human reasoning and not other dimensions of humanity. It was, in other words, a less than fully human approach to moral education. Don Browning summarizes some of these problems with Kohlberg:

> Kohlberg's thin view of moral thinking finds no place for ethics as the pursuit of the goods of life, no place for our pleasurable, self-actualizing kin-altruistic, or attachment needs and aspirations....Furthermore, Kohlberg finds little place for tradition and the narrative classics that give broader meaning to our ethical strivings.[45]

It also gave little attention to how we order our loves and identities and neglects to address other dimensions of the moral world we have discussed such as virtue, wisdom, moral models, narrative, and the role of moral tradition.[46]

Despite these limitations and critiques, both Perry and Kohlberg would continue to serve as some of the primary theories of developmental guidance in the moral domain for many student life professionals. They held out the hope and the illusion for student life professionals that they could engage in the science of objective, tradition-free moral development.

Resurrecting the Professional Moral Tradition in the Curriculum

One of the marks of Kohlberg's theory was the use of moral dilemmas to uncover different forms of moral reasoning. During this time, however, real life moral dilemmas began to emerge in the medical field due to technological advances and the moral pluralism promoted by the fact-value distinction. Thus, one of the ironies in the history of moral education in higher education curriculum is that the scientific professionals who proposed the fact-value distinction that led to the marginalization of ethics from the curriculum in the first place actually helped produce what Michael Davis labels the ethics "boom" of the late twentieth century[47] As scientific professionals ill-equipped to handle ethical questions, they turned to the professional ethicists who still remained in philosophy and religion departments and began to engage in joint conversations. Slowly, courses began to develop with the first medical ethics text appearing in 1976.[48]

At the same time, some evidence of a change also emerged in other fields such as law. Scholars identify Watergate as an important event since it led to several states requiring courses in legal ethics in 1974.[49] Other professions, such as business and engineering, had similar developments around this time. Slowly this trend spread to the universities. For instance, a Hastings Center's study searched one-fourth (623 out of 2,270) of all accredited college and university catalogs for the 1978–1979 academic year for courses in ethics, which the authors defined as "the study of good and evil, of right and wrong, of duty and obligation in human conduct and of reasoning and choice about them."[50] Their research staff found that only 14 percent of institutions did not have an ethics course and that half of the ethics courses were in applied ethics (e.g., "bioethics, business ethics, the morality of war or ethics and human experimentation"). In contrast, a sampling of ethics catalogues and texts between 1950 and 1965 found few courses devoted to concrete issues. Not surprisingly, they concluded, "There has been a resurgence of teaching ethics at the college level."[51] Nonetheless, the vast majority of colleges still fell far short of the Hastings Center recommendation that every school require at least one ethics course.[52]

Derek Bok attributed the increased interest in professional ethics to major issues such as Watergate, the emergence of medical issues such as abortion and physician-assisted suicide, and revelations of emerging corruption in the corporate world.[53] Davis, however, argued that much deeper changes in society led to the contemporary ethics boom.[54] Urbanization fostered less reliance on personal social relationships as a means of social control and the decline of religion left people without common religious standards. Without these two controls, laws and the market proved insufficient sources of common standards of conduct. It left us with this question, *"How can large numbers of people without strict regulation by law, without personal knowledge of one another, and without a common religious tradition coordinate conduct in the complex ways necessary to make life in this society good or, at least, bearable?"*[55] The recent professional ethics boom emerged, Davis claims, as an answer to this question, at least in efforts to settle upon the goods, virtues, and rules that will further the profession. Not surprisingly, this new ethics boom emerged from the professions largely with the help of philosophers instead of religious leaders or theologians. If they could not find a nonsectarian human ethics, philosophers hoped to find nonsectarian professional ethics.

The new professional ethics attempted to avoid "indoctrination," and placed a high confidence in reason to help students solve moral dilemmas. Following the lead of Kohlberg, most of the new ethics instruction offered in classrooms took a case study approach to ethics. Difficult ethical issues were analyzed through the lens of general moral principles. For instance, medical ethics students were encouraged to examine dilemmas in light of the supposedly nonsectarian values of beneficence, nonmaleficence, autonomy, and justice.[56] The ways that different moral traditions understand and apply these virtues or principles were not addressed. In this respect, the moral education proved quite limited. It focused solely upon exposing students to various moral arguments and positions pertaining to professional practices.

The professional moral tradition continues to dominate higher education. In hundreds of ethics books and classes students are usually expected to learn the various positions related to recent controversial professional issues although they are not usually encouraged to take particular types of stands on these moral issues.[57] Professional ethics has been subject to numerous critiques but few professions have resisted this approach as a whole. Since universities have embraced the professions, they must address what it means to be a good engineer, nurse, social worker, journalist, teacher, et cetera. This approach also provides one of the surest foundations in light of the rejection or failure of the other historical traditions. In *The Moral Collapse of the University*, Bruce Wilshire claims, "Professionalism emerges as a quasi-religion, our only way, apparently, of holding ourselves together after the disintegration of religious myths and pre-industrial traditions."[58]

Teaching Ethics from Nowhere: Fostering Commitment to the Liberal Tradition of Moral Education

The surge in teaching professional ethics also created a renewed interest in teaching ethics beyond the professions. Thus, even though half of the 1980 book *Ethics Teaching in Higher Education* focused

on professional ethics, the authors did offer broader recommendations for other areas of the curriculum.[59] Interestingly, the authors
offer no guidance to student life professionals.

The advice offered supposedly can apply to any institution or educator. From the authors' perspective, ethics education needs no moral
orientation. Teaching ethics can be disconnected from the identity of
the institution and the student. Moreover, it should focus primarily
on cognitive abilities such as "stimulating the moral imagination,
developing skills in the recognition and analysis of moral issues, elic-
iting a sense of moral obligation and personal responsibility and
learning both to tolerate and to resist moral disagreement and
ambiguity."[60] While indoctrination is of course frowned upon, the
recommendations themselves create a certain kind of moral order
filled with various values and goals linked to the liberal tradition.
Students are to learn how to "wrestle with problems" and engage in
"careful and serious moral reflection." Ethics courses, however,
should not seek to change behavior or alter one's affections. Ethics in
the curricular realm should only seek to shape the mind or one's cognitive abilities.

Overall, *Ethics Teaching in Higher Education* reflected the dominant understanding of the age. Universities, presidents and scholars
believed, should primarily concern themselves with the cognitive
moral development of professionals. Even in the areas where one
might expect a broader focus, such as student life, focus was placed
less on holistic forms of moral development and more upon cognitive
moral development. This trend would then be transferred to the new
curricular approaches to ethics that began to revive in the late 1960s
and early 1970s.

Laments for Humanism

Of course, students are so much more than just future professionals
or moral reasoners within liberal democracies. Thus, it should be no
surprise that with the growth of less than human forms of moral
education, we should find the emergence of a new crop of books
lamenting humanism's demise. We will mention two contemporary
examples. First, in *A University in Ruins*, Bill Readings argues that
the university may not literally be in ruins but what we may now
inherit as the university may prove to be philosophically frayed.[61]
Amidst its prosperity are definitive signs of its confusion and thus
impending demise.

At the heart of this problem is what Readings identifies as a funda-mental shift in the social role of the university and thus key internal systems. What concerns Readings the most is the uncertain place of the humanities. According to Readings, these disciplines have stood at the center of academe's efforts for a number of generations. In essence, disciplines such as history, philosophy, and literature are being pushed to the periphery while other more practical, professional efforts such as business, education, and nursing are drawn closer to the center. Echoing Jacques Barzun's concerns, Readings now believes that "What counts, and what marks the tone of contemporary dia-tribes, is that the grand narrative of the University, centered on the production of a liberal, reasoning, subject, is no longer available to us."[62] At the root of this dilemma is what Readings identifies as a shift in seeing the overall nature of the university as "corporate rather than cultural."[63] The university is now an integrated industry with service providers and customers. The humanities are in their current position due to the fact that they are perceived as possessing little to no bear-ing in this emerging paradigm. Absent a larger understanding of the good, customers are interested in more immediate returns than those that can come from reading the definitive texts of disciplines such as literature and philosophy. They seek coursework that is relevant to what one can only define as more near-sighted timetable than the one employed by previous generations. "As a result, the contemporary university is busily transforming itself from an ideological arm of the state into a bureaucratically oriented and relatively consumer-oriented corporation."[64] Perhaps one can only imagine this predicament is the logical result of the triumph of the multiversity Clark Kerr sought to describe.

Part of what makes it possible for Readings to see this predicament in this manner is that he served in a university, the University of Montréal that resides beyond the American border. This transforma-tion of the university is something Readings refers to as its Americanization. Seeking to be service providers to customers with a variety of wants and needs, universities are seeking to provide ways to claim their uniqueness. In the end, this shift leads all universities to say the exact same thing. While American society is becoming more heterogeneous, the universities which populate it are ironically becom-ing more homogeneous. What makes one service provider different from another is difficult, if not impossible, to identify. Readings sees this process beginning with American consumerism and then eventu-ally being exported to a host of other nations, including his own. The only remaining thread that unifies a culture is our common participation in the production of various goods and services. The fabric of that culture is left to fray, as no one is capable of seeing and thus caring for the whole. Universities simply train students to excel in relation to previously determined choices, to learn to make better choices. For Readings, a university in ruins ultimately leads to the ruin of a host of liberal-democratic states.

Anthony Kronman's *Education's End: Why Our Colleges and Universities Have Given Up on the Meaning of Life*, provides another example of a contemporary lament for humanism. As mentioned in the last chapter, Kronman argues that the secular humanist tradition flourished at one time in colleges and universities. According to Kronman, the humanities' embrace of the "research ideal" associated with professional liberalism led to the downfall of the original secular humanist tradition. He also claims that the humanities most recently tried to respond to the research ideal by embracing "the ideas of diversity and multiculturalism, and the theory that values are merely disguised acts of power."[65] Student life professionals also bought into this emphasis. Yet, by overly supporting diversity, multiculturalism, and constructivism, what Kronman labels as expressions of political correctness, the humanities found themselves unable to produce a justification for the necessity of Western literature and values. By granting admission to these factors of correctness, professors in the humanities no longer have the confidence to argue their ideas on truth. Now, every source has to be considered equal and pertinent, and a balance has to be achieved by compensating the formerly persecuted minority. As a result, dialogue becomes group representation. Lost is "the notion of an old and ongoing conversation that gives each entrant a weighted and responsible sense of connection to the past."[66] Instead, we now find "the egoistic presumption that we can start a new and freer conversation on our own, engaging all the works of the world's great civilizations in a colloquy we invent for ourselves."[67]

We find such laments understandable, although in some cases the stories they tell are at times inaccurate or problematic. For instance, to claim, as Readings does, that the historical project for humanity is a legacy of the Enlightenment is highly questionable. We also question whether a humanities program designed with the ends of liberal-democratic state in mind is really one that makes people more fully human. Moreover, we wonder whether some of the laments fail to recognize that part of the problem may stem either from the liberal-democratic or secular humanist traditions they espouse. These traditions have left the university committed to outlooks that perhaps exacerbate our very problem.

Generation Me

In *Generation Me*, Jean M. Twenge attempts to define the marks of the current generation passing through late-adolescence. More shocking than the title of her book is the subtitle, *Why Today's Young Americans Are More Confident, More Assertive, Entitled—and More Miserable Than Ever Before*. The underlying argument Twenge makes is that the fall of larger social norms is proportional and perhaps even directly related to the rise of the individual.[68] The lack of social norms has created the possibility that anything is, in fact, possible. However, the unrelenting busyness which defines this generation is more indicative of an unrelenting void in their lives than an unprecedented level of industriousness. Extremity has now replaced moderation in any number of ways. In the end, we are still left to ponder, as the subtitle to *Generation Me* beckons, why are today's young Americans more confident, more assertive, entitled, and more miserable than ever before?

Is there a correlation between the limited ethical commitment in universities and the nature of young adults today? For example, in *Unhooked: How Young Women Pursue Sex, Delay Love and Lose at Both*, Laura Sessions Stepp, a Pulitzer-Prize-winning journalist argues that the growing investment in spontaneous sexual activity, activity lacking any form of commitment, produces an inability to commit in other areas of one's life.[69] As a result, students' inability to commit in terms of interpersonal relationships is then replicated in terms of their inability to commit in matters such as family, employer, and community. The origins of the generation me phenomenon may not be the result of efforts made by college faculty members and administrators. However, the cultures we both create and tolerate may exacerbate the impulses readily present in generation me. Donna Freitas observed similar phenomena in her study of college students, "Many students seem afraid of realizing they have chosen poorly or acted wrongly. So they remain in limbo, committing to no one and nothing—a difficult place to be."[70]

Despite our ability to quantify the developmental capacities of our students in a host of interesting ways, we are perhaps now more uncertain than ever as to whom we should be helping our students become. While we speak of excellence and development, perhaps one reason we may do so is because the vapid nature of such terms allows us to sound ambitious without the possibility of being held accountable for our inevitable shortcomings.

Chapter Four

The Quandary Facing Contemporary Higher Education: Moral Education in Postmodern Universities

> The mission of Yale College is to seek exceptionally promising students of all backgrounds from across the nation and around the world and to educate them, through mental discipline and social experience, to develop their intellectual, moral, civic and creative capacities.
> —Yale College Mission Statement[1]

> I'm all for moral, civic, and creative capacities, but I'm not sure that there is much I or anyone else could do as a teacher to develop them.
> —Stanley Fish, *Save the World on Your Own Time*[2]

At the end of her book on the marginalization of moral education within universities from the eighteenth to the middle of the twentieth century, Julie Reuben summarized a dilemma.[3] Modern universities, she observed, never abandoned their traditional moral aims. Despite moral pluralism, they continue to claim that they "should prepare their students to live 'properly' and contribute to the betterment of society."[4] The problem, she argued, is that they "no longer have a basis from which to judge moral claims."[5]

We believe the situation should be summarized in a slightly different way. Colleges and universities do find and use some basis by which they orient their moral ideals. The difficulty is that universities as a whole do not share a *common* basis for moral education or a common understanding of human flourishing. Only the quest to find a *common, universal* foundation for moral education and cultivating humanity failed. The use of reason and modern scientific methods has not proved more successful in providing common moral knowledge. As Christian Smith observes, "There *is* no secular, universal, indubitable foundation of knowledge available to us humans."[6]

The advent of postmodernism helped clarify the problem facing universities regarding moral education that actually had already plagued them for over a century. Jean-François Lyotard, considered to be the originator of the term "postmodernism," defines it simply as "incredulity toward metanarratives."[7] Without a general agreement within the academic community upon a larger metanarrative that supplies an understanding of the basic human purpose or the common good, universities do not share agreement upon moral knowledge. They possess no universal scheme by which to prioritize individual and institutional identities and ends as well as the virtues and practices that would define and shape a fully developed human or a better society.

While we outlined the historical source of this development in the last two chapters, this chapter presents three contemporary suggestions about what universities should do in light of this situation. Stanley Fish argues that universities should accept this situation and focus on narrow professional goals. It is not the job of universities or professors, Fish argues, to engage in the moral formation or education of students unless that formation or education involves practices related to the academic ends of the university. In contrast, Derek Bok still expresses hope in the Enlightenment ideal. He argues that through the use of reason we can still help students identify moral problems, find common moral principles by which they can be solved and discern common virtues for character education.

We argue that the above two visions, while certainly possible and maybe even preferable in some publicly funded university settings, harbor important weaknesses. As a result, we need a third vision that recognizes the benefits of universities engaged in more human forms of moral education.

The Contemporary Search for Common, Tradition-Free Moral Education

Stanley Fish's Professional University

Although the effectiveness of academic classes to produce virtuous behavior has often been questioned, there is rarely any question that universities set forth moral and not merely technical ideals regarding what it means to be a good student, a good professional (e.g., teacher, social worker, business person, engineer, journalist, etc.) or even a good scholar (e.g., historian, philosopher, sociologist). Since universities make this claim, they must affirm the authority to engage in a certain kind of professional formation. The critical question is whether universities or professors should move beyond these limited forms of ethics education.

Stanley Fish does not believe they should. According to Fish, "No university, and therefore no university official, should ever take a stand on any social, political or moral issue."[8] Of course, Fish does not mean that the university should not claim to know what a good student, social worker or teacher is or should do. That would put universities out of business. Instead, he argues that universities and the professors employed by them should not offer answers to moral questions or shape students' character in accord with some larger vision of the good beyond a vision associated with student or professional identity.

The moral authority for Fish's normative claim stems from what he thinks should be the purposes of the academic profession and the university. He summarizes the two purposes as follows:

> (1) introduce students to bodies of knowledge and traditions of inquiry they didn't know much about before; and (2) equip those same students with the analytical skills that will enable them to move confidently within those traditions and to engage in independent research should they choose to do so.[9]

For Fish these are the goods internal to academic practice.

Those who join universities, therefore, should pledge a monastic type of commitment to abide by these missions and form their professional lives accordingly. Fish writes, "It is the professional, and in some sense moral, obligation of faculty members to check their moral commitments at the door."[10] Fish applies the same approach to thinking about the moral education of students. He believes the university should only promote a specific moral vision, rooted in a student's vocational identity and the university's limited vocational mission. "No doubt, the practices of responsible citizenship and moral behavior should be encouraged in our young adults," Fish admits, "but it's not the business of the university to do so, except when the morality in question is the morality that penalizes cheating, plagiarizing and shoddy teaching, and the desired citizenship is defined not by the demands of democracy, but by the demands of the academy."[11]

As the above points reveal, Fish still sets forth a vision of moral formation for the university and its faculty and students. The moral role of the university, Fish believes, is to promote those principles and virtues among faculty and students that are necessary to realize the internal academic goods of the academy. Fish writes regarding the assessment of professors:

> Job performance should be assessed on the basis of academic virtue, not virtue in general. Teachers should show up for their classes, prepare lesson plans, teach what has been advertised, be current in the literature in the field, promptly correct assignments and papers, hold regular office hours, and give academic (not political or moral) advice.[12]

Likewise, Fish is still morally demanding of universities and their expectations of students. He insists that universities must take moral stands on issues such as "the integrity of scholarship, the evil of plagiarism, the value of liberal education."[13] He also believes that moral training involves promoting particular intellectual virtues such as "thoroughness, perseverance, [and] intellectual honesty."[14] In this respect, Fish's approach would be quite comfortable with efforts to promote and teach professional ethics across the disciplines.[15]

Fish does not think, however, that professors teaching professional ethics courses, such as business, communication, or engineering ethics, should defend certain moral views on controversial issues. "Analyzing ethical issues is one thing, deciding them is another, and only the first is an appropriate academic activity."[16] Thus, even discovering and discussing what it means to be a good engineer, journalist, or scientist in controversial moral situations, in Fish's view, should be limited to exploring options and not coming to conclusions. Fish's position represents the logical outcome of the centuries-long search for a tradition-free approach to moral education in the university.

Derek Bok and the Reasonable University

In his many books on moral and civic dimensions of higher education, Derek Bok consistently defends a different approach. In *Our Underachieving Colleges,* he contends, "Notwithstanding professor Fish, it is perfectly possible to teach moral reasoning or prepare students to be enlightened citizens without having instructors impose their personal ideologies or policy views on their students."[17] While acknowledging the presence of moral diversity, he still believes that human reason, instead of merely illuminating our fundamental ontological differences, can be used as the basis for finding common moral ground beyond professional goods. Colleges and universities can then use this common ground, without reference to foundational or narrative differences, as the basis for character education that reaches beyond professional formation. They should not, however, move beyond matters of reasonable agreement.[18]

In his chapter on "Building Character" one might expect to find clear character qualities that serve as goals, but Bok largely avoids listing substantive moral goals. In fact, he approvingly points out that the new emphasis upon ethics no longer involves professors "delivering authoritative answers to moral and political questions of the day."[19] Instead, "professors try to teach their students to think more carefully about ethical problems by having them discuss dilemmas that arise frequently in personal and professional life."[20] What Bok describes as building character really turns out to be an attempt to resurrect Kohlberg's cognitive approach to moral education. It also merely extends the goal of critical thinking into the moral domain in ways quite compatible with what Fish proposes.

Interestingly, despite the research questioning Kohlberg's approach,[21] Bok expresses genuine puzzlement at why faculty might wonder whether this approach might be necessary or appropriate. He does not even answer the question of the effectiveness of professional ethics classes—of whether such courses make students more virtuous or even more consistent moral reasoners. Instead, he implies that professors should shed their doubts in light of the range of statistics indicating a possible prevalence of cheating, lying, and stealing among college students and graduates. For some odd reason, the crisis provides the answer to doubts about the solution.

For Bok, the university can primarily solve the problems of cheating, lying, and stealing by improving moral reasoning or helping students make "thoughtful judgments." Again, Bok does not suggest that it is the role of the university to suggest substantive moral traditions which could guide a student's ethical thinking or to help students acquire habits that lead to certain virtues. At one point he does suggest that certain common moral beliefs about "lying, cheating, breaking promises, and using violence against others" can form a basis from which conclusions can be drawn, but he quickly moves from these substantive proposals to the conviction that "further thought" can help solve moral problems.[22] For Bok it is most important that responses to moral issues are "thoughtful," "reasoned," and "principled." He rarely discusses the substantive basis of the reasoning or the narrative tradition guiding the interpretation of the principles.

Bok does admit, "Moral disagreements do occur in which all attempts at reason fail to yield an acceptable result," but he goes on to caution, "Classes devoted exclusively to such problems could actually discourage students from thinking carefully about ethical questions by persuading them that all moral arguments are inconclusive."[23] Bok places more value upon the modern hope of finding "universal agreement," instead of the postmodern recognition that such disagreement derives from different guiding metanarratives and different forms of rationality.

Improving students' moral awareness and reasoning should have some positive effect on behavior, Bok suggests, although he admits that the research supporting such views can only establish weak connections. In this respect, the title to Bok's chapter appears rather odd, since forming character is usually associated with using habituation to develop certain virtues or habits of acting. In contrast, Bok does not want faculty to convince students that they should acquire certain virtues.

Nonetheless, Bok also recognizes that helping students reason about ethical issues is not enough. He also proposes ways that colleges and universities can strengthen the wills of students to act morally. He suggests that university administrators can provide a moral example themselves, explain the reasons for certain actions or rules, and attempt to be morally consistent in enforcement of principles or rules. Requiring classes with readings from great works of literature, holding workshops on diversity, and encouraging students to engage in community service, he claims, can also help shape the moral will of students.

Evaluating the Visions

Although both Bok and Fish largely write about their differences, they actually share more agreement than they acknowledge. Both assume that universities as a whole should be guided by common purposes that require moral education. Both also believe that universities should preserve and promote those ends, virtues, and principles required to preserve the academy and keep it functioning. Thus, they both emphasize that universities should form honest students who do not plagiarize or cheat. Both would also agree that universities should show moral consistency and should not let their practices be corrupted by external goods such as athletic success, outside business interests, the interests of state legislators, et cetera. The key difference is that

Fish thinks moral formation should only be guided by agreed upon *academic* ends while Bok thinks we can find broader agreement about basic ends.

Second, both support limited forms of ethics education that avoid touching upon the affective or behavioral dimensions of students' lives or institutional commitment. As already mentioned, Fish claims only analyzing ethical issues, and not deciding them, is an appropriate academic activity.[24] Bok would appear to agree with this distinction as he contends that faculty members should not prescribe to students what is virtuous but argues that the university should help students reason about moral issues. Thus, although Fish would argue that universities should not pursue "building character" through the curriculum and Bok makes it a central purpose, what they actually believe teachers should do through the curriculum appears quite similar and largely defends the status quo.

One important difference between Fish and Bok primarily concerns how each one approaches the co-curricular arena of the university. Fish largely focuses on the university's curricular arena and the things for which students can and should receive credit. Fish wants to both celebrate and preserve the marginalization of broader forms of moral formation from the curriculum that Reuben chronicles. Bok thinks universities should not only shape students' moral reasoning abilities in the curricular realm, but also strengthen students' moral will through various activities in the co-curricular realm. Consequently, he faults Fish for equating "what an undergraduate education should accomplish with what professors can achieve in the classroom," an approach he calls "a cramped and excessively faculty-centered point of view."[25] He notes, "Fish overlooks all that admissions policies, residential living arrangements, and extracurricular life can contribute to an undergraduate's development."[26] In this area, Bok correctly identifies one of the major weaknesses with Fish's approach.

To better evaluate the visions of Fish and Bok, however, we must return to the issue of moral identity and moral orientation. Charles Taylor points out the importance of this point for individuals:

> People may see their identity as defined partly by some moral or spiritual commitment, say as a Catholic or anarchist. Or they may define it in part by the nation or tradition they belong to, as an Armenian, say, or a Québecois. What they are saying by this is not just that they are strongly attached to this spiritual view or background; rather it is that this provides the frame within which they can determine where they stand on questions of what is good, or worthwhile, or admirable, or of value.[27]

Taylor's observation about the way identity shapes the moral orientation of an individual also applies to institutions as well as scholars who talk about the moral purposes of higher education.

By uncovering the identity community or communities that Fish and Bok propose that the university serves, we can gain better insight into each author's vision. The reasons why an individual or institution elevates a particular identity or even excludes the moral norms from another identity usually stems from value commitments associated with a particular moral identity. They then draw upon the larger story connected to that identity to order the institution's ends and determine what kind of moral order to promote (or not promote). Once we uncover this point, we can also better understand the limits of their visions.

Stanley Fish and the Limits of the Professional Academic Moral Tradition

Stanley Fish clearly believes the university serves the professional scholarly community and the ends of various professional disciplines. More importantly, he not only wants the professional community to be the major identity community served by the university, he wants it to be the only one. Fish makes two arguments for why this should be the case.

First, Fish argues that when a university is not single-mindedly committed to the professional moral tradition, the university becomes corrupted, because its "resources have been appropriated for a nonacademic purpose."[28] This problem presents those who wish to discredit or take over higher education with opportunities to do so. Fish uses the democratic tradition as an example. Promoting a moral education guided primarily by the liberal-democratic identity and tradition, Fish argues, distorts the purposes of the academy since "democratic values and academic values are not the same and that the confusion of the two can easily damage the quality of education."[29]

Second, Fish thinks the purposes he proposes are the only ones universities can actually achieve. "Teachers cannot," he claims, "except for a serendipity that by definition cannot be counted on, fashion moral character, or inculcate respect for others, or produce citizens of a certain temper."[30] Moreover, he argues that you cannot find such tasks in their contracts. We find three basic problems with this approach.

1. The Illusory Independence of the Professional Academic Tradition of Education

For Fish, the university can remain uncommitted or neutral in relation to all other commitments except its professional commitments. This approach proves impossible in practice. For instance, while we agree with Fish that one end of the university should be to "introduce students to bodies of knowledge and traditions of inquiry they didn't know much about before," the obvious question to ask about his end is: which "bodies of knowledge" and whose "traditions of inquiry" should students encounter and learn?[31] If an institution chooses to require students to learn Church history instead of European or African history, it makes a moral decision, not merely an educational one, about the importance of a particular identity community and its story. It chooses to enrich one element of a student's identity and to promote one community's story over others. Of course, how those identities, stories, or traditions are taught will also involve similar choices.

This point applies not only to how the university shapes the curriculum but also academic fields themselves. One's interpretations of phenomena or data will always be influenced by one's worldview and not merely one's professional tradition.[32] This influence will occur at a variety of levels. At the most basic level, the conceptualization of important terms cannot escape this influence. For example, writing about psychology, David Myers and Malcolm Jeeves note that terms such as "mental and sexual health" or "self-actualization and fulfillment" cannot be interpreted without implicit assumptions about human well-being that are usually informed by one's worldview.[33] Likewise, George Marsden notes how the term "public good" often carries a host of worldview assumptions.[34] Second, the language of interpretation will carry ideological weight. As Myers and Jeeves point out, "Whether we describe those who favor their own racial and national groups as 'ethnocentric' or as exhibiting strong 'group pride'; whether we view a persuasive message as 'propaganda' or 'education'" will depend upon one's worldview.[35] Third, the presuppositions guiding one's interpretation will be influenced by one's worldview. Myers and Jeeves cite as an example the question, "Is it better to express and act on one's feelings, or to exhibit self-control?"[36] How psychologists answer this question is not merely informed by professional opinion.

2. *The Two-Way Influence of Other Traditions*

Second, Fish appears to believe that the influence of nonprofessional moral traditions upon the life of the university will primarily be negative. Just as universities threw off the shackles of the various Christian stories which both guided and constrained universities, Fish claims universities must now throw off the shackles of the various versions of the liberal-democratic story that compete to control it in order to realize its purposes. Of course, this move also requires that the university place shackles on faculty who wish to espouse nonvocationally derived moral views. In this respect, Fish demonstrates the common need of all moral traditions to place limits upon the individual community member's moral autonomy in order to be faithful to a tradition.

Fish is certainly correct that universities can be corrupted by political or other ideological traditions. The institutions of higher education in post-communist countries are notorious for their academic corruption.[37] Fish might argue that they do not have a tradition of professionalism and neutrality because they have been ideologized for such a long time. The Soviet academy never developed a strong commitment to academic freedom and integrity. It was used to spread a particular moral agenda at the cost of good scholarship and professionalism.

Nonetheless, what is a professor supposed to do when it is the university that needs saving and not the world?[38] Saving post-communist universities, according to Fish's perspective likely involves recovering professional academic ideals without the help of other traditions. Within Fish's world there remains no other place for professors to find help, since importing other moral traditions in the university may be corrupting.

What Fish fails to recognize is that while certain moral traditions may corrupt the academy, other moral traditions may enhance it (of course, judgments about corruption and enhancement will vary by tradition). For example, Mark Schwehn, in his book *Exiles from Eden*, contends that a solution to what ails the contemporary academic vocation, and thus the modern academy, must involve recognition of what was lost from the original religiously inspired and informed universities.[39] Schwehn notes, "The practice of certain spiritual virtues is and has always been essential to the process of learning, even within the secular academy."[40] The virtues he has in mind are those such as humility, faith, self-sacrifice, and charity that were originally prized within a Christian context.

Schwehn's argument may also apply to other contexts and to other virtues such as integrity and honesty. Ukrainian Catholic University (UCU), the only major institution of Christian higher education in Ukraine, provides a helpful example of this point. From the start UCU's stated aim has been to become a model for the reform of post-Soviet higher education. In other words, they want to save higher education in Ukraine. As part of this aim, UCU seeks to preserve the basic aims of the university that Fish prizes. According to UCU's literature, "The first goal of the Ukrainian Catholic University has been to provide students with a normal academic life, free from concerns of bribery and cheating." They appear to have had some success. As an administrator related to one of us, "UCU is known to be a corruption-free zone."[41] This claim is likely more than an administrative boast as the Ukraine's prime minister has declared it one of only two higher education institutions without significant corruption (the other being an Orthodox seminary).

UCU's efforts to provide an example of a corruption-free university in Ukraine stem not merely from deep and abiding commitment to the professional tradition, although the results are quite consistent with it. Even the professors who are not part of the dominant moral tradition have recognized this point. Olena Dzhedzhora, a humanities professor at UCU, has noted how when the university began, they had trouble finding Christian humanities professors. As a result, they hired a number of non-Christian professors. When these professors began to be treated with dignity, did not have to deal with bribes, found clean classrooms, and were paid decently, a number progressed on a faith journey to the Church, since "these values were soon seen as Catholic."[42]

What makes it possible for some semblance of the idea of the university to be "saved" in Ukraine is much more than a tradition-free commitment to professional academic purposes and virtues. It involves a communal commitment to broader human goods, such as human dignity, that are cultivated in the basic practices of the worshipping community that makes up UCU. Perhaps, it is no surprise then that at UCU the mentally handicapped from the community join with the university community for worship once a week or that the president, Father Borys Guziak, seeks to provide and maintain clean bathrooms and well-kept buildings and grounds. Respecting human dignity, he told one of us, starts with providing clean bathrooms.[43] Perhaps one could tell the cleaning and grounds staff to "just be professional," but if the surrounding ethos and community lack an overarching narrative that motivates and reinforces respect for human dignity, there remains little motivation or imagination for achieving goods internal to professions.

If hopes for returning virtues to a corrupted professional environment often require communities of people concerned with larger human goods and virtues, we may at times need a vision for moral education in higher education that goes beyond the professional tradition. At the very least, we need one that opens the door for universities sustained by moral traditions other than the professional tradition suggested by Fish.

We also believe that Fish needs to recognize that the corruption begotten by the professional tradition can also occur. Our concern with such universities is that they condition students and faculty to think of ethics primarily in terms of professional identity. A good example of the distorting effect of reasoning in the professional moral tradition comes from an article by Alan Wolfe. In an article addressing Wheaton College's required Statement of Faith for faculty, Wolfe considered the requirement to sign the statement problematic, despite the fact that signing the statement was purely voluntary. Wolfe claimed, "When careers are at stake it is hard to take seriously [Wheaton president] Litfin's insistence that signing Wheaton's declaration is a purely voluntary act."[44] For Wolfe, losing one's professional identity is the ultimate sacrifice and appears even more problematic than an individual losing his or her identity or an institution losing its identity. This outlook stems from a particular moral orientation toward the profession instead of the integrity of the self or an institution.

3. Moral Education beyond the Professional Tradition

Fish's pragmatic claim that moral education will not work in a university is simply not true. As the next three chapters will make clear, a plurality of colleges and universities currently promote a variety of moral visions of what it means to be fully human while some also promote limited or restricted moral visions based on the agreement reached regarding the ends associated with particular aspects of human identity (e.g., ethnic identity, political identity).

These colleges and universities recognize what James Davison Hunter found regarding social science evidence. Character thrives when young people "inhabit a social world that coherently incarnates a moral culture defined by a clear and intelligible understanding of public and private good."[45] Hunter describes this *comprehensive moral culture* as a milieu: "...where the school, youth organizations, and larger community share a moral culture that is integrated and mutually reinforcing...where intellectual and moral virtues are not only naturally interwoven in a distinctive moral ethos but embedded within the structure of communities."[46] In another place, Hunter describes such cultures as "totalizing learning environments" which do not separate education from "the concept of what constitutes a good life and good community."[47] Thus, it should be no surprise that universities with these kinds of totalizing environments (e.g., Christian universities, military academies, private universities of a certain kind) are the ones often cited for their attention to character and moral education.[48] Whether these institutions are good for the students will vary upon one's understanding of what it means to be fully human. The reality of the advancing postmodern era means we should not expect agreement about this question.

4. *The Cognitive and Conservative Nature of Fish's Vision*

Finally, the fact that we have fundamental disagreements about what it means to be fully human does not mean that some universities associated with communities should not experiment with proceeding in life as if their answers to questions of human goodness were actually true. In this respect, we believe Fish does not take his own stated purpose of the university seriously enough. He wants to approach moral disagreement by merely having professors discuss it. We contend that if universities are actually serious about exploring possible moral answers, they may need to be moral laboratories themselves.

Thus, if Fish was offering his vision as an ideal for a particular university or set of universities, we would find it an interesting and creative idea. It would be fascinating to see if it gained support from individual donors and groups who support the vision. It would also be interesting to see the moral results. What he describes would probably be best tried at a place such as the University of Phoenix or online colleges without extensive student life programs or residence halls. Yet, it appears that Fish believes his unencumbered vision of the university should be the ideal to which all true universities aspire. In this respect, the university landscape Fish envisions lacks diversity, imagination, and openness to experimentation.

Bok and the Limits of the Enlightenment Tradition

Like Fish, Bok believes that state and secular, private universities can avoid promoting a set of special beliefs or behaviors justified by a particular moral tradition. The reality, however is that universities orient students morally by the very environment they create, the identities they use to orient students morally (e.g., professional, citizen, human) and the types of moral formation they believe are most important and those that they believe should be left to student choices.

If Bok defended a broad humanistic approach to moral education by pointing to the findings of philosophers and positive psychologists who claim we can identify particular individual and social virtues that lead to general human flourishing, his argument might be more original and convincing.[49] He might then propose substantive moral goods which the university could use to guide its practices and form students. Since Bok does not take this approach, we will discuss this strategy in the next chapter.

Instead, Bok defends his understanding of moral education by making general moral appeals grounded in what we label the Enlightenment tradition. As previously indicated, this tradition elevates both human reason and autonomous choice as the sufficient instruments by which to discover moral knowledge. Thus, throughout Bok's argument he makes appeals to how "careful analysis" and "further thought" will help students develop principled moral reasoning. In fact, similar to Kohlberg and contrary to positive psychology, Bok appears to downplay encouraging students to acquire certain virtues and instead exalts autonomous choice and the power of unguided human reason apart from particular identities, worldviews, traditions, or narratives.

Bok, in keeping with the Enlightenment tradition, believes the supposedly autonomous individual should make "rational" choices from a buffet of moral options. His subtle embrace of this approach is revealed by his welcome acceptance of the sociological finding that Americans do not see themselves as looking for moral knowledge in a transcendent moral order but instead coble together their own personal standards. Instead of suggesting that this trend may be a problem or that universities should expose students to alternative traditions or perhaps even challenge this American approach, he suggests universities should adapt to it. Sounding like an outdated values clarification manual, Bok notes, "It is not the place of faculty members to prescribe what undergraduates ought to consider virtuous. But surely faculties should do whatever they can to prepare their students to arrive at thoughtful judgments of their own."[50]

Bok's approach, far from being neutral, still poses a challenge to other moral traditions. A former values clarification advocate, Howard Kirschenbaum, had this brought home to him while trying to promote values clarification to Israeli educators. Understandably, the Israeli educators wondered why they should use an approach that might undermine Israeli identity and values. Kirshenbaum had often answered such questions, he claims, a hundred times. What made this situation different was that Kirschenbaum, a Jew, felt more sympathy with the Israeli educators because he identified with their identity and story.

> As the Israeli educators sat waiting for my answer, I realized what the stakes were. As a salesman for values clarification, I realized that if I said "Values clarification will make it more likely your children will emigrate" or "I don't know what effect values clarification will have on your young people's patriotism" I knew what their response would be "Thanks, but no thanks!" because this was a life-and-death issue for them. If too many young people left the country or refused to serve in the armed forces, the country would not survive. It was that simple. And, to my surprise, values clarification theory aside, I found myself sympathetic to their concern and, in turn, with the premise or hidden assumption behind the question that there are some things in life that are more important to us than maximizing people's free choices.[51]

Bok appears not to recognize what Kirschenbaum understood. Modernity and its exaltation of reason and autonomy can be competitors with other moral traditions that place more value on creating an environment that enriches a particular aspect of human identity. In this case, Israeli educators wanted to enrich students' knowledge of and commitment to the flourishing of the Israeli nation-state. The Enlightenment liberal arts tradition seeks to liberate students from particular traditions while other more classical approaches to liberal arts moral education seek to deepen a student's understanding of and commitment to a particular moral tradition.

To Bok's credit, he does recognize that approaches to moral education that only focus on principled moral reasoning are rather limited. As scholars of higher education are now beginning to recognize, moral education must also devote attention to "moral sensitivity (being aware that a situation has a moral dimension to it and how one's action could affect others involved), moral motivation (prioritizing moral considerations relative to other situations), and moral character (the capacity to implement and persist in one's moral course of action)."[52] Bok then makes an extended argument as to how college and moral reasoning courses may help in these areas. What Bok does not tell his readers is what Ernest Pascarella and Patrick Terenzini admit in their review of research, "Unfortunately, compared with principled moral reasoning, we uncovered little or no systematic evidence concerning the influence of postsecondary education on these other three enabling precursors of moral behavior."[53]

Part of the reason for these findings, we believe, is that researchers have been too preoccupied with Kohlberg and the Enlightenment paradigm of moral education promoted by figures such as Bok. Proponents of the modern tradition tend to focus primarily on moral reasoning while ignoring these other important dimensions of the moral world. Thus, little research exists regarding the influence of larger moral traditions, worldviews and narratives guiding moral outlooks or the role of motivation, identity, virtues, wisdom, moral mentors and models, moral practices, and the moral setting. It should also be noted that it is much easier to measure changes in moral reasoning than moral sensitivity, character, and motivation.

The Postliberal University: Education from and for Moral Commitment

On the last page of Julie Reuben's book about the history of moral education in the early research university, she sets forth what she believes might be a condition for bringing moral education back into the curriculum of such universities. She contends that scholars may need to rethink the idea that agreement "is the proper standard by which to identify 'truth'."[54] In contrast to what Derek Bok might say, she proposes, "If universities can learn to tolerate more conflict, we may be able to define cognitive standards by which we can address moral questions. Since it has proved impossible to completely separate fact and value, we should begin to explore ways to reintegrate them."[55]

How universities might tolerate more conflict or reintegrate fact and value are two questions Reuben never answers. We argue that in his various works, particularly *After Virtue* and *Three Rival Versions of Moral Enquiry*, Alasdair MacIntyre provides some possible answers that we contend can help us better understand moral education in higher education. MacIntyre argues in *After Virtue* that the reintegration of fact and value always requires some degree of agreement about human or institutional purpose or functionality linked to basic understandings about human nature or the nature of an institution.[56] If we agree upon those purposes or functions, it becomes possible to then identify and rationally discuss what we consider good (e.g., a good person, a good citizen, a good student, a good university, etc.), as well as the moral motivation, virtues, practices, and mentors and models required to help us achieve those goods. Consequently, universities always require a certain level of agreement when they engage in preparing future historians, teachers, scientists, or social workers regarding the goods internal to those professions. Fish would likely agree.

For MacIntyre, however, the university should not be content to engage in less than human forms of moral inquiry in the university. Of course, he recognizes that more human forms of moral formation will require particular communities that shape individuals according to more comprehensive moral ideals. Thus, for individual universities to make progress in moral inquiry or education, they will always require less and not more tolerance. MacIntyre explains the reason why:

> But the institutional tolerance of limitless disagreement encounters in the areas of morality and theology standpoints which by their very nature cannot accept the indifference presupposed by such tolerance, standpoints which invite rejection rather than toleration. And thus such standpoints have to be at best exiled to the margins of the internal conversations of the liberal university.[57]

Here MacIntyre's argument coheres with our explanation in chapter one of why moral education eventually became marginalized to the co-curricular arena.

Yet, Macintyre also helps us think about possible ways that moral inquiry and education can be and indeed are integrated into both the curricular and co-curricular arenas of university life. In contrast to Bok he argues we must recognize that there is no universal reason that can lead us to a common understanding of what it means to be fully human or common agreement about the good society. He also rejects Fish's vision of the university that is shorn of any larger metanarrative (the genealogical tradition). In fact, MacIntyre argues that participation in the practices that Fish believes should characterize the university necessarily involves membership in a certain kind of moral community sustained by a particular tradition and not merely a particular set of practices. It requires, in MacIntyre's words, a postliberal university.

MacIntyre's postliberal university is "a place of constrained disagreement, of imposed participation in conflict, in which a central responsibility of higher education would be to initiate students into conflict."[58] Unlike Fish's ideal university, professors in this university would advance teaching and moral inquiry from a particular viewpoint while also presenting and engaging rival viewpoints. Thus, in public lectures, a professor would not pretend to speak to every reasonable person or even the profession but would instead acknowledge commitment to some particular partisan standpoint. Of course, professors would also need to play a role in ordering the conflicts and sustaining institutionalized forums for such conflicts to occur.

This approach would prove particularly helpful, MacIntyre believes, in advancing systematically conducted moral and theological inquiry. The liberal university ended up excluding substantive moral and theological inquiry from academic conversations, because such inquiry required settling fundamental disagreements in order for progress to be made. Liberal universities sought to abolish any moral or religious tests which attempted to secure such agreement. In contrast, a postliberal university could require moral or religious consensus in order to advance inquiry.

MacIntyre realizes that attempts to establish postliberal universities will result in different interpretive traditions creating rival universities "each advancing its own inquiries in its own terms, and each securing the type of agreement necessary to ensure the progress and flourishing of its inquires by its own set of exclusions and prohibitions, formal and informal."[59] There would also then need to be forums where rival universities could engage in debate, especially about the moral and theological underpinnings of their views. In this respect MacIntyre suggests we need more tolerance and thus more conflict among different types of universities rather than tolerance for moral conflict or reduction of moral conflict within a uniform set of liberal institutions (as Bok and Fish seem to suggest).

In the end, we agree with MacIntyre's assertion. Universities and professors need to be clear about how they understand and order their various identities and the role of their various identities in shaping their moral outlooks. Fish's approach requires hiding or submerging such realities and limiting the university to the advancement of moral inquiry only in matters of professional and academic training. In contrast, MacIntyre's vision shows greater openness to the plurality of visions of human flourishing that exist in the world by recognizing the need for a greater diversity of universities with constrained disagreement.

Although MacIntyre does not discuss institutional policy toward moral education or the co-curricular arena, one might also assume, in keeping with MacIntyre's earlier arguments, that such universities would also seek to be "local forms of community within which civility and the intellectual and moral life can be sustained..."[60] In other words, rival universities with their rival moral traditions would sustain very different forms of moral education. The moral virtues would not be cultivated merely by students' participation in various academic practices, although such participation would play a part. The cultivation of virtues would require two other important elements. First, it necessitates the university acknowledging "a concept of a self whose unity resides in the unity of a narrative which links birth to life to death as narrative beginning to middle to end."[61] Second, the university would recognize that the story of a person's life is always embedded in the story of those communities from which a person derives his or her identity.[62] These communities embody living traditions, which MacIntyre defines as encompassing a "historically extended, socially embodied argument, and an argument precisely in part about the goods which constitute that tradition."[63] Thus, in contrast to both Fish and Bok, MacIntyre argues that moral education requires more than academic practices and more than generally agreed upon virtues disconnected from particularistic traditions. In fact, MacIntyre concludes *After Virtue* by arguing that the political traditions within our culture all share a type of moral exhaustion when it comes to the cultivation of the virtues. Thus, he famously concludes, "What matters at this stage is the construction of local forms of community within which civility and the intellectual moral life can be sustained through the new dark ages which are already upon us."[64]

We would argue that universities can fulfill this goal in two particular ways. First, a university could allow, and perhaps even encourage, the creation of smaller communities of character, and in fact, one can argue this is what many secular universities do in their particular co-curricular arenas. Of course, they remain agnostic about whether such communities actually cultivate character, or what type of character they cultivate, until perhaps legal issues become involved. Bart Pattyn points out one problematic feature of such a university.[65] It may reinforce the belief that "everyone should be able to cultivate the illusion that the life he or she leads is as justified as the life of anyone else."[66] The problem with this approach, Pattyn notes, is that "we are embarrassed when someone with a distinct moral view or cultural ideal disturbs the concommittal nature of our modern understanding."[67] In other words, a certain ethos is created whereby students are not expected to address moral conflict. Yet, "By refusing to examine the importance of moral and cultural virtues more deeply, we create an atmosphere that makes it seem inconsequential how someone chooses to organize his or her life."[68]

If a university were to try to cultivate communities of virtue or character, it would need to do something more in these areas. The university itself would need to be consciously connected to a particular social identity and its related moral tradition. Institutionally, we argue, that level of connection also involves an ordering of identities and traditions that necessarily results in constraining the individual autonomy of those who live in that academic community. In other words, this type of character formation requires constrained disagreement at the institutional level. We discuss what exactly this might entail for university life in the rest of the book.

Conclusion

Narrow prescriptions concerning the role of education may eschew the impact which institutions of higher learning have on the moral formation of their students. However, such a posture is difficult to maintain and is fraught with more illusion than reality. Education is not a neutral endeavor. Universities choose to engage in less than or more human forms of moral education. Based upon these choices, for better and for worse, colleges and universities orient their students in moral spaces and thus shape the moral identities of students. As a result, the larger challenge looming on the horizon is how educators think through this orientation process. In the work of Alasdair MacIntyre, we find the possibility of initiating and even framing such an understanding. The next few chapters will demonstrate this point by looking at universities noted for their efforts in relation to moral education.

Part II

*A More Human Education: Moral
Identity and Moral Orientation*

Chapter Five

Who Are We? The Identities Universities Use To Provide Moral Orientation

> Underlying our modern talk of identity is the notion that questions of
> moral orientation cannot be solved in simply universal terms.
> —Charles Taylor, *Sources of the Self*[1]

Although Stanley Fish argues that encouraging moral commitments beyond those related to being a good student or scholar should be avoided by universities, most universities actually defend and promote moral ideals or standards beyond those required to form professionals. For instance, one recent study of 110 nationally ranked liberal arts colleges found that 80 percent expressed both academic *and* nonacademic behavioral expectations.[2]

The most serious attempt highlight these efforts can be found in Anne Colby and her coauthors' work, *Educating Citizens*. They document the extensive attention given to moral and civic education at a wide range of American universities. In addition, they draw upon their research at twelve exemplary institutions to provide an in-depth understanding of best practices. According to their findings, while all exemplary colleges or universities encourage the acquisition of certain moral competencies, each institution usually focuses on certain moral themes. Universities that emphasize what they call the community connections approach focus upon "connections with and service to particular communities."Universities specializing in the moral and civic virtue approach emphasize personal virtues and values such as integrity, courage, and responsibility. Finally, universities that nurture the social justice or systematic social responsibility approach teach students how to contribute to social change and advance public policies that will address various economic, political, or social injustices.[3]

While we believe this categorization provides insight into the way different universities emphasize various aspects of a moral order, Colby and her coauthors do not emphasize the importance of the moral identity used to frame these moral themes. Service to particular communities, the development of various virtues and the promotion of social justice or responsibility become transformed when undertaken for specific identities and moral traditions. The next two chapters attempt to identify the various ways that colleges use identities to orient moral education on campus.

As mentioned in chapter one, moral agreement beyond that related to academic practices is achieved in two different ways. First, due to the failed attempt to find a universal ground for moral education, and the need to respect diversity, most universities can only support a vision of the good related to a particular aspect of human identity (e.g., what it means to be a good citizen). Institutions then suggest students acquire moral knowledge, affections, and practices relevant to the particular ideals associated with the identity. Usually, the agreement reached using these identities does not serve as a comprehensive vision of what it means to be human. Therefore, we call them less than human forms of moral education. We will discuss the nature of these approaches as well as their limitations in this chapter.

Second, some colleges and universities also attempt to promulgate broad agreement about what it means to be a good human. Scholars or institutions that promote secular humanism, common ground humanism, or some form of religious humanism fall into this category. These approaches will be described in more detail in the following two chapters.

Less than Human Forms of Moral Education

Most contemporary American universities undertake less than human forms of moral education. By employing this term we do not mean that these approaches are necessarily inferior to humanistic education. After all, many universities limit the scope of moral education for legal and moral reasons. For instance, most state universities choose to promulgate less than human forms of education out of respect for the First Amendment as well as the plurality of worldviews that their students profess. We should not expect to find many state-sponsored universities with well-developed moral orientations in pluralistic liberal democracies.

Nonetheless, some state universities and secular private institutions support moral education that extends beyond professional moral formation. When these universities seek to promote moral education they also set forth and defend some form of constrained disagreement that results in a unique moral culture. In other words, they find moral agreement not through appeals to a common rational foundation but through the functional moral ideals associated with a particular moral identity. In the sections below we attempt to provide examples of these different approaches based upon our own research and the research of other scholars.[4] We will also discuss the possible strengths and weaknesses of these approaches in an attempt to highlight the unique qualities of the efforts in place at such institutions.

Political Moral Formation

With the demise of humanist forms of moral education and the rise of state-sponsored education it only seems natural that moral discourse in universities would now be oriented by political identity. Numerous scholars now argue that universities should be engaged in preparing good citizens or furthering the "public good," sometimes also labeled the "common good."[5] When unpacking these terms, one finds the advocates are not concerned with the good of humanity but rather the good of a particular politically defined community, usually the American nation-state. In other words, these authors believe we can find common moral ground when we focus upon our common identity as citizens of liberal democracies[6] and the tradition, narrative, virtues, principles, wisdom, and models associated with that identity. In fact, some of the advocates are quite explicit about how this approach will reject liberal education's past concern with developing a broadly humanistic approach to knowledge.[7]

This moral orientation is exemplified in Harold Shapiro's, *A Larger Sense of Purpose: Higher Education and Society*. In a chapter entitled "Liberal Education, Liberal Democracy, and the Soul of the University," Shapiro argues, "To me, a liberal education is directly connected to the nature of the society we wish to sustain. When I think about education, I think about the ideal human types for the society we envision."[8] Although one might mistake Shapiro for a humanist at this point, what becomes apparent is that the society Shapiro has in mind is a particular type of political society or community. Thus, he argues that a university's vision of liberal education in America or Europe should be primarily connected to the "particular educational needs of contemporary Western liberal democracies."[9] According to his view, the university's "role in the moral development of its students is one vehicle through which it can contribute to our national life, especially because many of its students will be in a position to exercise power and influence."[10] Shapiro especially emphasizes, "We must remember...that the university experience of many of our nation's future leaders will influence their moral development and, thus, their ethical judgments and their behavior as leaders."[11] For Shapiro, a particular student's or a particular university's political identity becomes the primary identity by which the university's moral agenda and outlook should be shaped.

In *Educating Citizens* by Colby et al. the title gives evidence of a similar approach.[12] Like Shapiro they also want to argue that despite moral pluralism, we can agree about the qualities necessary to sustain our life together in a liberal democracy such as "mutual respect and tolerance, concern for both the rights and the welfare of individuals and the community, recognition that each individual is part of the larger social fabric, critical self-reflectiveness, and a commitment to civil and rational discourse and procedural impartiality."[13] Not all the campuses they study use civic or political identity to orient their moral education, but of course the state institutions do. They note that Portland State University uses the motto, "Let Knowledge Serve the City," California State University at Monterey Bay asks faculty to sign their mission statement each year that "the campus will be distinctive in serving the diverse people of California,"[14] and, the U.S. Air Force Academy describes its mission as seeking: "To educate, train and inspire men and women to become officers of character, motivated to lead the United States Air Force in service to our nation."[15]

On campuses that make extensive use of a political moral orientation, one may find a form of a moral tradition similar to that described by Jeffrey Stout in *Democracy and Tradition*. The institution "inculcates certain habits of reasoning, certain attitudes toward deference and authority in political discussion, and love for certain good and virtues, as well as a disposition to respond to certain types of events or persons with admiration, pity, or horror."[16] Of course, the democratic tradition, like any well-developed identity tradition, includes sectarian approaches to this form of moral formation.

Institutions promoting the liberal version tend to support certain ideals such as equality and social justice. For example, California State University, Monterey Bay (CSUMB) not only declares that the campus will serve California, but "especially the working class and historically undereducated and low-income population."[17] CSUMB also requires new faculty to come to an opening ritual where leaders display the college's mission. New faculty are then asked to sign the displayed mission "as a symbol to support the values and culture of the campus."[18] Professors largely focus on social ethics pertaining to political arrangements. Learning outcomes include areas such as "Ethics, Democratic Participation, Community Participation, Culture and Equity."[19] According to the culture and equity requirement, students should be able to "analyze and describe the concepts of power relations, equity and social justice and find examples of each concept in the U.S. society and other societies" and "analyze historical and contemporary cross-cultural scenarios of discrimination, inequity and social injustice."[20] Emphasis is also placed on ethical communication that is defined as "exchanges characterized by individuals' cooperative, responsible attempts to understand each other's points of view, with 'open-heartedness' and with non-manipulative intent, as opposed to efforts to win the argument or gain control over others, subjugating alternative points of view."[21]

The conservative version of democratic moral education can be found in military academies or the rare conservative university. It especially succeeds at military academies, because one finds a common adherence to the nationalistic story, a coherent moral culture (duty, honor, country) and a clear end for education (defending the American nation-state). The United States Air Force Academy provides a helpful example in its commitment to the core values of "Integrity First, Service before Self, and Excellence in All We Do."[22] These core values permeate every dimension of a cadet's life. As one administrator told us, "We tell them, 'If you don't believe that, just go home, because you are making a big mistake.'"[23] Little distinction is made between how the curricular and the co-curricular arenas fit together. At the Air Force Academy, all of these efforts are designed to serve the larger goal of forming Air Force officers with both cognitive skills and particular character qualities.

To reach their moral ends, the Air Force Academy also seeks to cultivate within each cadet a moral compass that it views as being synonymous with character. The Air Force Academy defines the moral compass as "'the sum of those qualities of moral excellence which compel a person to do the right thing despite pressure or temptations to the contrary.'"[24] Such qualities include responsibility, selflessness, and self-discipline.

The nature of the moral formation cadets undergo proves more holistic than any other nonmilitary educational institution. As one administrator shared with one of us, "But when we start them out here, we tell them exactly how to do everything: 'You don't know to walk, talk, eat, anything. You are going to do it our way.' And then from there as freshmen we get them to start thinking more independently and more creatively."[25] In order to cultivate the particular moral qualities mentioned above, the Air Force Academy established the Center for Character Development that is then broken up into three divisions.

The first division is the Honor Division that works with groups such as the Cadet Honor Committee. With a group selected from each squadron, this committee assumes responsibility for implementing the institution's Honor Code that simply reads "We will not lie, steal, or cheat, nor tolerate among us anyone who does."[26] For example, they guide their fellow cadets facing possible infractions through the review process. These cadets also aid in the instruction process concerning the honor code, a process that continues all four years. "In the first two years, instruction focuses on understanding and living under the Code, and in the final two years, emphasis is placed on cadets living an honorable life, while helping others to do the same."[27] The second division, the Character and Leadership Education Division, supervises the required seminars that each cadet must take every year related to character education. The third division, the Excellence Division, "organizes symposiums, conducts seminars, and offers a variety of forums for cadets to pursue their own character development."[28]

The virtues promoted at the Air Force Academy are not generic "universal" character traits but are understood as virtues given meaning, importance, and priority because of a particular political and professional tradition and narrative. In fact, as part of the character education seminars sponsored by the Center for Character Development, the Center chooses moral models to come mentor younger officers in how to make moral decisions or exemplify particular virtues in light of this tradition.[29] Other rituals and socialization strategies reinforce a homogenous moral culture. Overall, this identity and its associated homogenous moral tradition then socially and structurally constrain all elements of campus faculty, curriculum, and culture.

Race, Ethnicity, Gender, and Sexuality

Many moral claims associated with ethnic, racial, or economic identity often rely on the liberal political tradition for their moral force. For example, American women, African-Americans, or Native Americans make moral claims based upon past and present failures to uphold the moral ideals in the democratic tradition. Yet, these identities increasingly serve as a source of moral orientation or education. For instance, in a response to John Mearsheimer's claim, mentioned in the introduction, that universities do not provide moral guidance, John Lyons from the University of Virginia, offered this counter, "It looks to me as if the university, and particularly the faculty, is more involved collectively, in providing moral guidance to students than at any time in the last century."[30] The moral authority for the guidance, Lyons claimed, no longer stemmed from the idea that we can find objectively agreed upon moral knowledge about what it means to be fully human. Instead, it sprang from faculty members' "perception of their own identity as a person of color, a particular gender, ethnicity, sexual orientation, etc."[31] Increasingly, campuses and not merely faculty members take this approach. For example, Colby and her coauthors detail how Miami University frequently uses Native American cultures to help students "appreciate the value of diversity. In other years other cultures and perspectives have been highlighted by summer reading books such as Cornel West's *Race Matters* (1993), Julia Alvarez's *How the Garcia Girls Lost Their Accents* (1991), and Abraham Verghese's *My Own Country* (1994)."[32] Although respect for different cultures and diversity could be fostered by looking through other identity lenses, in this case racial, ethnic, and gender identities were the context for teaching a particular virtue.

Certain institutions draw upon a specific ethnic, racial, economic, or sexual identity for substantive moral agreement more than others. For instance, Colby et al. mention that Kapi'olani Community College focuses "on Hawaiian and Asian-Pacific values."[33] They do not specify what these values are. Nonetheless, they point out, "Nearly half of the Kapi'olani faculty incorporates Hawaiian and Asian-Pacific emphases into their teaching, and the campus as a whole is infused with a strong Hawaiian identity."[34] Turtle Mountain Community College specializes in "creating an academic environment in which the cultural and social heritage of the Turtle Mountain Band of Chippewa is brought to bear throughout the curriculum."[35] In fact, in ways that sound similar to religious colleges that talk about the integration of faith and learning, the faculty are asked to practice the integration of Chippewa Indian identity and learning. As Colby et al. note, "Faculty are asked to infuse the culture into every course offered, and this has been achieved in most courses."[36] Even the ethos and co-curricular activities of the campuses also reinforce a particular moral tradition. For example, Turtle Mountain Community College's building "was designed to reflect the college's commitment to Native American values."[37] Colby et al., go on to describe the details:

> The 105,000-square-foot building is designed in the abstracted shape of a thunderbird, and an interpretive trail encircles it. All the design elements—even the railings—reflect the college's efforts to integrate tribal culture into the education of its students. From a distance a large skylight behind the entrance gives the impression of a turtle's back. In front of the entrance is a circle of seven columns each of which has one of the seven 'teachings of the Chippewa Band that are central to the Ojibway heritage: Wisdom, Love, Respect, Bravery, Honesty, Humility, and Truth....[38]

Similar to the way that religious campuses seek to use architecture and symbolism to shape the identity of students, Turtle Mountain seeks to pass along a distinct identity that orients students morally.

One of the most unique trends regarding moral appeals to identity pertains to the transformation in appeals to gender as an identity construct to guide moral education. In the past, when men dominated higher education, college presidents articulated one of the purposes or functions of universities as forming men or gentlemen. As President Gilman confidently proclaimed at the opening of the Johns Hopkins University, "The object of the university is to develop character—to make men."[39] Likewise, when women's colleges started, the rhetoric of forming "young ladies" communicated certain moral expectations associated with gender.

While there are far more private women's colleges than men's colleges, they no longer associate the moral education of women with traditional ideals attached to gender (e.g., forming ladies).[40] Instead, gender-related moral ideals emerge largely from feminist scholarship that both seeks to exalt the equality and status of women while also pointing out the unique moral insights offered by female experience and perspective.[41] Women are taught to view their female identity as one of the most important, if not the most important, prism by which to analyze knowledge and life. This identity has become so important, in the academy that its study is perhaps, "the most powerful single force breaking up disciplinary partitions."[42]

Interestingly, men have been slower to replace the old moral language of "gentlemen" or to formulate a contemporary alternative to the feminist movement with moral ideals unique to men or manliness.[43] Nonetheless, as the next section will indicate there is still at least one campus that defends the masculine tradition of being a gentleman.

Less than Human Characteristics
and Challenges

The identities used for moral orientation mentioned above provide a way of fostering moral agreement and calling upon a particular moral tradition and its specific virtues, principles, models, and wisdom. Moreover, in all these cases the moral tradition associated with the identity extends beyond academic boundaries. The extended nature of this influence means that these less than human approaches to moral education will still face unique challenges.

1. The Challenge of Blending Traditions

For less than human approaches to moral education, questions will always be raised about how a particular identity tradition should relate to other identity traditions. For example, some sources mentioned above that are derived from ethnic identities actually appear to involve a particular religious worldview (the Native American and Hawaiian colleges). What relationship will this tradition have to other religious identities? Such forms of exclusion may also prove to be in conflict with other prominent religious traditions (e.g., Christianity, Islam), and it is not clear that adherents to some of those traditions would find the moral tradition taught compatible with their meta-physical or moral beliefs. Nonetheless, most institutions emphasizing less than human approaches to moral education will likely seek to blend these commitments together in some pragmatic fashion. In our own study, we found two examples of colleges that blended traditions together with some success.

Hampden-Sydney College
Located southwest of Richmond in a relatively remote yet pastoral segment of the Virginia countryside, Hampden-Sydney College offers a liberal arts education to an all male student body. As one of only three remaining all male colleges in the country (Morehouse College and Wabash College being the other two), Hampden-Sydney has remained steadfast in its commitment to the tradition of educating gentlemen since 1775. With an enrollment of approximately 1,120 men, its mission remains "to form good men and good citizens in an atmosphere of sound learning."[44] It also still "expects its students to be gentlemen of good moral character and to be active and informed

participants in the life of their communities."[45] As these quotes reveal, there are actually multiple moral orientations at Hampden-Sydney.

In the curricular realm, the liberal arts tradition combines with the civic orientation. Thus, their "atmosphere of sound learning" is defined by "the belief that a liberal education provides the best foundation not only for a professional career, but for the great intellectual and moral challenges of life."[46] As a result, the liberal arts curriculum at Hampden-Sydney "introduces the student to general principles and areas of knowledge which develop minds and characters capable of making enlightened choices between truth and error, between right and wrong."[47]

In the co-curricular realm, this spirit of democracy and self-governance permeates living-learning opportunities such as traditional residence halls, apartments, and even fraternity houses. Students at Hampden-Sydney also:

> serve as members of the faculty's Academic Affairs, Student Affairs, Lectures and Programs, and Athletic Committees. In addition, students are named to various task forces, ad hoc committees, and often, to search committees seeking key College officers. All students are expected to participate in the self-government which is prized so highly on our campus.[48]

Students are thus expected to take an active role in not only taking responsibility for their own well-being but also the well-being of their fellow members of the larger college community. This active role is not simply evident in the efforts made by Student Government but by the approximately 30 student organizations active on campus.

At the heart of this spirit of self-governance is what is referred to at Hampden-Sydney as "Upon these Two Commandments: A Compact Guide to Standards of Behavior for the Hampden-Sydney Man." The first commandment is the Code of Conduct. Although the Code of Conduct has grown to include a variety of details in the student handbook, one principle dating from the 1800s still defines this code, "The Hampden-Sydney student will behave as a gentleman at all times and in all places."[49] When asked the exact nature of what the ideal of a gentleman, one administrator noted,

> I think if you talked to our students, there would be almost universal agreement that part of what we are after at the conclusion of a four-year education is their perhaps overly idealized vision of a southern gentleman. And when you had to start defining what that meant,

there'd probably be more agreement among our students and less agreement among our faculty about what that is.[50]

The second commandment is the honor code. Like the Air Force Academy, the Honor Code simply reads, "The Hampden-Sydney student will not lie, cheat, or steal, nor tolerate those who do."[51] As an expression of the College's commitment to self-governance and democracy, the details of the honor code are administered by students. In this particular form:

> The judicial power of Student Government is vested in the Student Court, a body composed of members elected by classes. The Court tries cases arising from breaches of the Code of Student Conduct and Honor Code violations, assisted by a corps of student investigators and advisors.

These positions are elected by the student body and thus vested with the collective wisdom of that community. As a result, students are prosecuted by their peers, defended by their peers, and receive hearings before their peers. First-year students are introduced to the Honor Code through an orientation. They are then asked to sign a document affirming their adherence to the Honor Code, and the signed document is posted at the entrance to the dining hall as a reminder of students' commitment. Importantly, both the honor code and the code of conduct are considered to apply both on and off campus. At Hampden Sydney one should not only show honor and be a gentleman in class but also in every area of life.

Mary Baldwin College

Located in the city of Staunton in Virginia's Shenandoah Valley, Mary Baldwin enrolls approximately 850 female students in the Residential College for Women and another 1,450 students in its adult and graduate programs. Although Mary Baldwin in the past and even today uses gender as one source of moral orientation, it also uses a variety of identities to orient its moral language and ideals. For example, it lists "citizenship" as one of its goals and proclaims that one of the outcomes it seeks of students is that: "They are responsible citizens. They act within a consistent set of values and ethical principles, apply those principles in their dealings with society and its members, and take responsibility for their decisions and actions."[52]

In fact, what makes Mary Baldwin comparable to service academies such as the Air Force Academy is that it houses the only all-female corps of cadets in the world. While not all Mary Baldwin students are required to participate in the Corps of Cadets, all are exposed to Mary Baldwin's pervasive commitment to cultivate female leaders. Such a commitment is echoed in Mary Baldwin's mission statement when it professes the institution's "commitment to the liberal arts as preparation for life, for careers, for graduate and professional studies, and for leadership."[53]

Central to Mary Baldwin's mission of cultivating leaders is its Virginia Women's Institute for Leadership (VWIL). The origins of this Institute can be traced back to the legal challenges that the Virginia Military Institute was facing in relation to its status as an institution that served male students. The initial request for the development of such a program came from the Virginia State Legislature in 1993 with seed money provided by the Virginia Military Institute Foundation.[54] One Mary Baldwin administrator commented that such an effort was "to establish a parallel military program at a women's college."[55] Although the Virginia Military Institute would lose in its effort to maintain its all-male enrollment, the vision for Institute and the Corps of Cadets at Mary Baldwin would persist. "In March 1996, the VWIL Corps of Cadets presented its first public parade, using recorded music. Since then the corps has grown to its current size of approximately 125 and now includes a marching band unit, a staff, a color guard, four rifle platoons, and an honor guard."[56] Admission to the Institute and the Corps is competitive and is dependent upon not only one's test scores and grade point average but also one's commitment to leadership and physical fitness. As a result, one administrator commented that "there is a strong commitment to service in that program and adherence to standards and accountability and integrity."[57]

Via the honor code, these same commitments can be found throughout the Mary Baldwin community. All students at Mary Baldwin are asked to adhere to the following honor pledge.

> Believing in the principles of the Student Government, I pledge myself to uphold the ideals and regulations of the Mary Baldwin College community. I recognize the principles of honor and cooperation as the basis of our life together. I shall endeavor faithfully to live my life accordingly. I will not lie, cheat, steal, plagiarize, or violate my pledge of confidentiality. I will not fail to report others who lie, cheat, steal, plagiarize, or violate their pledge of confidentiality. I will encourage others to fulfill the ideals of the Honor System.

Although longer than the pledge in place at the Air Force Academy and Hampden-Sydney College, the two pledges share many common

details in the sense that abstinence from lying, cheating, and stealing are foundational to both. Both also ask students to pledge to hold their fellow students accountable. Mary Baldwin adds abstinence from plagiarism and a commitment to confidentiality. Although prospective students are introduced to the concept of the honor code in the variety of materials they receive from Mary Baldwin, Charter Day is the point in time when students are formally introduced to the honor code and then are asked to offer their commitment to it by virtue of their signature. Describing Charter Day, one administrator offered:
That is the day on which the Honor Code is laid out.

> We have a full academic procession. We have a speaker for that day who will talk about honor, and talk about moral commitment and ethical behavior. And at the end of that speech the students from Student Government will usher the first-year students who had just arrived on our campus, will usher them to these tables to sign their name to the pledge to uphold the Honor Code.[58]

Violations of the Honor Code are brought before the Honor Council. Elected by their student peers, members of the Honor Council are guided by the purpose to: "promote the spirit of honor throughout all aspects of campus life…[and deal] with infractions of the honor system, which include lying, cheating, stealing, plagiarism, violation of a pledge of confidentiality."[59] In this manner, leadership and the cultivation of character are woven into the student body through not only the ideals but also the process and the outcomes of the judicial system.

In terms of the core curriculum required of all students in the Residential College for Women, Mary Baldwin's commitment to cultivating female leaders can be found in its gender studies requirement where a student can choose from over thirty courses concerned with women and religion, communication, philosophy, politics, sports, et cetera.[60] Yet, Mary Baldwin also offers unique majors in areas such as leadership and minors such as peacemaking and conflict resolution, global poverty and development, and United States poverty analysis.

Perhaps the most fascinating dimension of the Mary Baldwin experience is not the way it represents any one particular ideal in a pronounced way but how several different ideals are woven together. In no overriding way does Mary Baldwin reflect the aspirations of a women's college, a liberal arts college, or a service academy. In contrast, it seeks to bring all three together to provide a unique experience that the school proudly announces as being "Boldly Baldwin."

2. The Challenge of Fostering Integrity and Limits

Although, the previous two colleges successfully use and integrate different moral orientations, the potential for conflicts will lead to a second challenge, or perhaps more appropriately labeled a limit, for less than human approaches. It is not always clear that these identities will help a student develop integrity, the virtue associated with being able to have one's loves, one's numerous identities, and thus one's life rightly ordered.[61] Nonetheless, merely because we classify these approaches as less than human does not mean that certain advocates do not try to make them more comprehensive ways to be human.

Advocates of moral education for the liberal-democratic tradition provide a good example. Liberal democracies emerged in order to allow the flourishing of individuals, institutions, and communities that believe one's primary moral identity and obligation does not necessarily belong to the political community. In this view, we are more than citizens and our responsibilities extend to a variety of identity groups. Although some higher education scholars clearly understand students' national citizenship as a penultimate moral identity that will necessarily need to accommodate and be merged with others (e.g., Colby et al.),[62] other authors and leaders (e.g., Kezar et al.; Shapiro)[63] appear to elevate liberal democracy from a political philosophy to a guiding identity that shapes the whole liberal arts curriculum. Shapiro believes universities supported by the state that shape the curriculum according to the state's needs can actually prevent its abuse of power, although to his credit he does recognize that this view is "quite novel."[64] We think it also remains quite dangerous. Unfortunately, nation-states and state-funded institutions, even in liberal democracies, are quite adept at either reducing our humanity to our citizenship or claiming that our national identity deserves our first love. As John Robinson astutely notes, "Even the well-intentioned state tends to homogenize its citizens, delegitimizing all loyalties except those that bind the individual to the state."[65] The end result is the promotion of a controversial and reductionistic vision of what it means to be human in a context where pluralism and diversity are supposed to be prized and respected.

Yet, we are more than just citizens. Any compelling and comprehensive vision of what it means to be fully human must both address all of these facets of identity and, most importantly, help us order them properly. To be fully human requires that we learn how to best order our virtues in relation to these identities. By primarily emphasizing the story and needs of liberal democracy or a particular liberal democratic nation-state universities face the danger of focusing less on making students more fully human and more on making good liberal democrats or good Americans, Canadians, or individuals with certain political sympathies and views. In addition, even authors who appear to recognize the need to acknowledge, for example, the "tribalisms of ethnicity and religion," are not always clear that political identity is merely one more identity and an identity, according to liberal political theory, that recognizes its people may have other ultimate commitments.[66]

Ultimately, democracy often becomes elevated to the level of guiding metanarrative for all human life outside of the political sphere—including family life and other forms of society. Yet as Fish reminds us, "Democracy, we must remember, is a political not an educational project."[67] This distinction is vitally important for the political well-being of democracies. As Alasdair MacIntyre notes:

> the shared goods of the modern nation-state are not the common goods of a genuine nation-wide community and, when the nation-state masquerades as the guardian of such a common good, the outcome is bound to be either ludicrous or disastrous or both. For the counterpart to the nation-state thus misconceived as itself a community is a misconception of its citizens as constituting a *Volk*, a type of collectivity whose bonds are simultaneously to extend to the entire body of citizens and yet to be as binding as the ties of kinship and locality. In a modern, large scale nation-state no such collectivity is possible and the pretense that it is always an ideological disguise for sinister realities.[68]

We believe that such sinister realities are already at work in universities that are attempting to make all other local forms of community into communities that follow the democratic tradition.

One such example is the current church-state controversy in public higher education concerning leadership qualifications for student religious groups on campus. A number of colleges and universities have started to enforce nondiscrimination policies against Christian groups and fraternities. The colleges and universities that have engaged in this action include: Georgia, Rutgers, Southern Illinois, Penn State, Minnesota, Washburn, Arizona State, San Diego State, Wisconsin-Superior, Wisconsin-Madison, and North Carolina.[69] These institutions take this stand because leaders for the group are expected to be Christians and abide by a certain lifestyle. For example, in 2006 the University of Georgia refused to grant official recognition to Beta

Upsilon Chi, Brothers Under Christ because they only allowed Christians to be officers. Christian Legal Society and Alliance Defense Fund sent a letter and the University changed its policy. In February of 2008, the Christian Legal Society brought suit against the University of South Carolina's School of Law challenging its prohibition of granting funds to religious student organizations, arguing that it is unlawful viewpoint discrimination. In June 2008, the university agreed to lift its restriction. In a number of these cases the group is actually derecognized. For instance, the University of Montana derecognized the Christian Legal Society because it required voting members and leaders to refrain from sexual activity outside of marriage, a standard the university claimed perpetuated "discrimination." Instead of using discrimination laws to protect identity classes from past injustices suffered for illegitimate reasons, universities are using such laws to enforce the Democratic tradition upon Christian communities.[70]

Conclusion

Too often, the challenges facing schools in terms of moral education come in the form of those narratives held to be so true that too often we fail to even note their existence. As a result, they simply operate as cultural defaults versus serving as a means of strengthening and even advancing the moral fabric of our campuses. Stanley Fish contends that such defaults are problematic and thus beyond the scope of what institutions of higher education should pursue. Yet, the reality is that many universities promote moral ideals beyond those required to form professionals. By virtue of our very nature to be more human, such pursuits are likely unavoidable. As a result, perhaps the question that needs to be asked is not whether colleges and universities should promote moral ideals beyond professional standards but what identity narrative or tradition should give shape and focus to those ideals. Moreover, what will hold the disparate identity traditions together for an institution or a student within the institution? The next chapter explores universities that answer these questions by taking what we describe as more comprehensive human approaches to moral education.

Chapter Six

Searching for a More Human Moral Education: Three Approaches

When American universities became officially secular, a century ago, the problem of defining the human was not foreseen.
—H. John Sommerville, *The Decline of the Secular University*[1]

Despite our inability to solve matters of moral orientation in universal terms, this failure has not stopped all attempts to set forth a vision of education grounded in some form of humanism. For example, in a previous chapter, we critiqued Derek Bok's approach, but other options also exist. These next three proposals are much more realistic about their possible limitations. The three approaches we will review in this chapter are what we call common ground humanism, secular humanism, and religious humanism.

Common Ground Humanism

An emerging group of scholars argue that we can find common ground regarding the human virtues that lead to human flourishing, whatever our different identity backgrounds and commitments. There are two versions of this form of common-ground humanism, although we would argue that one is a more genuine humanism.

Types of Common Ground Humanism

The first version of common ground humanism attempts to establish its appeals in academic findings that identify what human character qualities lead to human flourishing. The scholars behind this movement possess confidence in the various methods of the social sciences, particularly psychology, and are quite clear that they believe we can find substantive moral virtues which we agree are essential for human flourishing (both individually and socially). Two scholars, Christopher Peterson and Martin Seligman (2004) have argued that while psychologists currently have a classification manual, the *Diagnostic and Statistical Manual of Mental Disorders* (DSM) to determine what is plaguing humans, we do not have a manual to evaluate what is right or good.[2] As a result, Peterson and Seligman's book, *Character Strengths and Virtues: A Handbook and Classification* attempts to fill that vacuum. They hope that their classification could be used for "the deliberate creation of institutions that enable good character."[3] Their book sets forth ten criteria by which to identity character strengths and then goes about identifying six general classifications of character qualities (wisdom and knowledge, courage, humanity, justice, temperance, and transcendence). Within these categories they also place other virtues or character qualities.

Most universities, by their very nature, encourage those qualities listed under wisdom and knowledge: creativity [originality, ingenuity], curiosity [interest, novelty-seeking, openness to experience], open-mindedness [judgment, critical thinking], love of learning and perspective [wisdom]. Other universities would also insist that they seek to demonstrate and encourage virtues listed under other categories (e.g., integrity, gratitude—especially encouraged by alumni associations, fairness, appreciation of beauty and excellence, etc.).

Our question is whether colleges and universities should be expected to encourage these virtues beyond particular identity contexts. For instance, will integrity be encouraged merely as a professional virtue of students and scientists with regard to their work, or is it a virtue to be prized in all of life as something that contributes to human well-being? To move beyond encouraging character qualities outside of certain professional practices would require a commitment to a broader vision of human well-being. Currently, there are universities demonstrating such a commitment, a few of whom we will discuss in the next chapter, but these universities share a particular moral tradition. We thus question whether Peterson and Seligman's project holds promise for promulgating some form of common ground humanism in universities. Nonetheless, we remain hopeful.

The second version of common ground humanism derives agreement about moral virtues or principles through a political process such as voting or meetings that attempt to come to a consensus. The goal in these instances is to find common moral agreement from which moral education can then proceed. Much of contemporary primary and secondary character education proceeds in this manner. Some degree of moral agreement can be reached with this method

although the range of moral virtues prized is also quite diverse.[4] As
the following example suggests, this approach may be successful,
although the shallow nature of the agreement may limit its appeal.

Case Study: Common Ground Humanism and Colorado State University

The potential strengths and challenges to taking a common ground
humanism approach to moral education can be found through an
examination of one unique experiment in character education at
Colorado State University (CSU). Established by the signing of a ter-
ritorial bill by Governor Edward McCook in 1870, today the university boasts approximately 25,000 students which come from every
state in the United States and approximately 85 foreign countries.[5]
With such a diverse population, there might be some question as to
whether the university could undertake an approach rooted in common virtues. Nonetheless, CSU did. The story of why it did, however,
reveals that its origins were anything but common.

In 2001 the city of Fort Collins entered into an agreement with
Character First International based out of Oklahoma City to become
a city of character. To further this goal, the city and other community
leaders formed Character Fort Collins, a community wide initiative
to extend this effort to promote good character to various sectors of
the city.[6] Character Fort Collins asked Colorado State University to
further this initiative as part of the education sector. Consequently,
the President of CSU asked the Vice President for Student Affairs to
implement the Character First approach to character education on
campus.

What makes this partnership and request unusual is that Character First is an organization affiliated with Bill Gothard ministries,
a fundamentalist Christian ministry that has developed an approach
to character education that they believed would be suitable for public
schools.[7] The CSU administrator in charge of the initiative
observed:

> So we took this very structured approach from Character First and tried
> to implement it here. It was not successful because it's faith-based, and so
> that's challenging at a public institution. It was 49 character traits that
> were polar opposites like obedience versus rebelliousness. How do you say
> that obedience is a character trait at a public higher education institution?
> You can't. That's not a value that we would uphold.[8]

Consequently, the CSU student development office negotiated with Character Fort Collins and told them, "You know, we can't follow exactly what you are doing, but if you are patient with us, we are going to be doing the same kinds of things, but in a different way. A way that fits our culture." The city agreed. Interestingly, at the same time, Front Range Community College, the local community college in Fort Collins, decided to roll out the 49 traits as they were. They made big banners and unrolled the first one, which was "Obedience," and as one CSU administrator described it, "The institution, I mean the faculty, just went nuts. And it crashed, and they were not able to do anything again."[9]

CSU's student development office took a different approach. A committee spent the next two years looking at every trait and deciding whether it fit higher education and CSU's culture. An administrator described some of the process:

> It was just grueling to go through all of those traits and realize that some of the character traits that we really uphold were not even on the list. Like respect, service.... Some pretty foundational traits that we would look for in helping students to develop weren't on this list. So what we came up with were—and you can have this—ten traits, or not ten, I think twenty traits. Yeah, twenty traits—two per month—and this was painful to get to. But it was fascinating conversations... pride was one of them... [according to the curriculum] it was a bad thing, and from the Black student services office that pride is a good thing, and from the Native American student services that pride is a bad thing. So how do you come together? It was just fabulous conversations, but it took us a long time.[10]

Once they developed the list,[11] they started trying to come up with programs and initiatives around the character traits. They helped host Erik Weihenmeyer, a visually disabled mountain climber as a joint CSU/Fort Collins event. "The idea was that persistence is a character trait, persistence is important, and determination, and how we highlight that trait so that students think, 'How does this relate to my life?'"[12] In addition, during other events that they held, such as a food drive, they would highlight the character quality being emphasized. They also placed character traits and quotes, chosen by the project committee, in the student government handbook. The Assistant Director of Apartment Life even integrated it into his division by writing articles about different character traits. Another administrator in charge of relationships between CSU and the city integrated the character qualities into their efforts to help CSU students learn how to live in the community and be good neighbors, "She advised students that when you are working with your neighbors, you need to show open-mindedness, and here is a way to do that out in the neighborhood. Invite your neighbors and learn about their stories."[13] Through these efforts and others CSU became known as a campus of character.[14]

In this case, common ground forms of character education, despite the controversial origins of the program, actually provided a workable framework. When asked if the broad nature of the character qualities caused any problems, one administrator noted that it actually helped. She observed, "I think if we had tried to dive down into real specific language, we could not create buy-in. So I think we have buy-in because people can take it to the depth that they would like to, but it starts at a pretty common language."[15] In the case of CSU, a limited form of common ground humanism determined through a democratic process within the student life department, advanced a certain moral framework and language on campus. Nonetheless, despite the success of the initiative, it was largely promulgated by the student development office and has since its initiation lost some steam. Moreover, the fact that few other state universities have replicated these efforts may indicate its limited potential. Today, CSU focuses more upon other initiatives such as being an environmentally-friendly or "green university."

Recovering a Secular Form of Humanism

In *Education's End: Why Our Colleges and Universities Have Given Up on the Meaning of Life*, Yale law professor Anthony Kronman does not necessarily propose a comprehensive approach to moral education. Nonetheless, his idea that colleges and universities should educate students about the meaning of life reaches beyond the professional academic tradition propounded by Fish and attempts to open the door to at least a minimalist form of moral education across the curriculum. Even more intriguing, Kronman offers a vision for moral education that is grounded not merely in professional liberalism but in a broader tradition of secular humanism.

Kronman believes that secular humanism, as expressed through the humanities in the university, can save us from the damage inflicted by the research ideal and political correctness. The scientific tradition cannot provide our lives with meaning since it only allows us greater control over nature while fostering ignorance about ourselves.

Kronman does not believe religion can help because it claims we understand ourselves by understanding God (here Kronman is clearly referring to theistic religions). "The answer is that we need the humanities to meet the deepest spiritual longings of our age..."[16] The humanities can help us understand ourselves and give us the courage to face the crisis of meaning plaguing our lives.

Yet, it is not necessarily the humanities that provide the answer for Kronman, as does a particular type of humanities curriculum, a core curriculum focused on the great books of the Western tradition, and the conversation contained within these books. He particularly holds out as exemplary the elective Yale Directed Studies program in which he teaches. Since Kronman's solution primarily relates to the curricular arena he does not discuss whether he thinks questions about life's meaning are addressed in the co-curricular arena of Ivy League universities, state universities, and secular liberal arts colleges. Interestingly he claims that "the question of life's meaning is monopolized by the churches, to whom our colleges and universities have relinquished all authority to ask it."[17] He fails to mention the ways that colleges and universities, especially faculty, supported this arrangement by banishing issues of meaning and morality to the co-curricular arena. Moreover, like Fish, he neglects the whole co-curricular arena of colleges and universities.

Overall, Kronman's effort demonstrates one of the more ambitious efforts to revive a secular form of humanism with spirit. His last chapter almost serves as a sort of revival sermon calling colleges and universities to throw off the shackles of the research ideal and political correctness in order to embrace the saving role of the humanities as embodied in secular humanism. He ends his book by proclaiming, "Let our colleges and universities be the spiritual leaders they once were and that all of us, teachers, students, parents, citizens of the republic, need for them to be again."[18] In this respect, Kronman echoes the past hope held by university administrators for the humanities.

A Case Study of the Secular Humanist Tradition? Yale University

Since we have examined Kronman's argument in various chapters and Kronman lists one program in Yale as an example, we believe it would be more beneficial to examine whether Kronman's narrative about secular humanism perhaps reflects Kronman's particular setting at

Yale University. Chartered in 1701, Yale University is the third oldest institution of higher learning in the United States. Yale was initially established by Congregationalists who believed that Harvard College had lost its commitment to orthodox forms of Puritan theology. Consequently, it was initially charged to be a place "wherein Youth may be instructed in the Arts and Sciences [and] through the blessing of Almighty God may be fitted for Publick employment both in Church and Civil State."[19] Today, Yale has now grown into a secular research university with over 5,000 undergraduate students and over 6,000 graduate students.

While Yale's gradual secularization might initially fit within Kronman's narrative mentioned in chapter two, Yale leaders did not see their gradually secularizing institution as fitting within the secular humanist tradition. For example, in the mid to late-1800s, Yale's president, Noah Porter, faced the growing pressures within American colleges and universities to succumb to the mounting challenges posed by theological liberalism. Many believed modern science provided a more advanced means of explaining the world than reigning theological models. Others such as Porter were concerned that such an empirical approach would limit the relation of humans to God in a number of ways. To this day, some view Porter as a leader unwilling to accept change. Others view him as someone with a depth of thought which allowed him to see the shortcomings of scientific naturalism long before its postmodern critics. Despite Porter's influence, in the 1900s Yale would move closer to the secular humanist vision described by Kronman, although even as late as the 1960s when William Buckley published *God and Man at Yale*, leaders would deny seeing Yale as bastion of secular humanism.[20]

Today, Yale stands as an interesting mix of Congregationalist past along with a more secular present. The University Church and the Divinity School are the two most noticeable architectural symbols of the campus's religious heritage. In a more symbolic manner, the names of Yale's Congregationalist past dot the campus and the city of New Haven. However, a more secular impulse now dominates the heart of the institution. For example, while the University Church recognizes its connection to the United Church of Christ (Congregationalism), it also seeks to be a place which welcomes the religious practices of people stemming from a wide variety of faith traditions. In addition, the latter portion of the mission of the Divinity School reads:

> Ecumenical and university-based, the School recognizes as indispensable to its mission a communal environment which combines rigorous

scholarly inquiry, public worship and spiritual nurture, practical involvement with the churches' ministries, and mutual regard among human beings across the diversities of gender, sexual orientation, race, class, nationality, and culture.[21]

In essence, Yale University's more recent historical story mirrors the secular humanist vision that Kronman sets forth.

Yale's contemporary investment in the moral formation of its students reflects a similar approach and comes through two interrelated means. First, Yale's liberal arts curriculum bears the imprint, albeit now a secular imprint, of its earlier generation of Congregational leaders. As students in Yale College, the curriculum which most undergraduates encounter is "a liberal arts education, one that aims to cultivate a broadly informed, highly disciplined intellect without specifying in advance how that intellect will be used."[22] Echoing the intentions of the Yale Report of 1828, the preface to the Undergraduate Curriculum from the Yale College Bulletin detailing programs of study offers that the:

main goal [of the curriculum] is to instill knowledge and skills that students can bring to bear in whatever work they eventually choose. This philosophy of education corresponds with that expressed in the Yale Report of 1828, which draws a distinction between "expanding [the mind's] powers, and storing it with knowledge."[23]

As a result, Yale College maintains its firm commitment to requiring that students fulfill a wide variety of distribution requirements such as two course credits in the humanities and arts, two course credits in the sciences, two course credits in the social sciences, fulfillment of a skills requirement in a foreign language, fulfillment of a skills requirement in a quantitative reasoning, and fulfillment of a skills requirement in writing.

More unique than the course requirements Yale has in place is their students' co-curricular experience. Little distinction exists between the curricular and the co-curricular at Yale. As a result, efforts such as moral formation at Yale really do take place in an environment that can arguably be labeled as seamless. The definitive component of this experience is the Yale's system of residential colleges. In 1930, Yale accepted Edward S. Harkness' "plan to construct and endow the undergraduate residential college system to develop closer student-teacher relationships and create communities composed of cross-sections of the student body."[24] Inspired by the college systems of the University of Oxford and Cambridge University, the college system would become the foundation of the Yale undergraduate experience. Reuben observes of this development, "University officials hoped that students would develop identities as members of a particular house/college...By building university-run housing, educators tried to replace the existing student culture with what they expected would be a more morally uplifting community life."[25]

Although Yale has largely lost its religious identity, a strong commitment to fostering residential identity continues. Although each entering class of students at Yale College is primarily housed in a common area known as Old Campus, these same students are also assigned to one of Yale's twelve residential colleges. While residence halls on most campuses are administered by student life professionals, each college at Yale receives leadership from a master, usually a full professor with an appointment somewhere within Yale University. The daily affairs of each college are then tended to by a dean. This official usually possesses a nontenure track appointment somewhere within the university and carries some form of a teaching load. The physical plant for each college not only includes lodging for the master (as well as his or her family) and the dean (as well as his or her family) but also the students. These students take most of their meals in their appointed colleges. Many activities ranging from intramurals to service projects are organized by the colleges.

Along the same lines, some of the residential colleges also host what they call Melon Forums. These forums, developed with the generous support of the Andrew W. Mellon Foundation, bring members of the college together for a formal dinner and then to hear the details of the research being conducted by a senior. One administrator offered that "The seniors rotate presenting their research to the other students, in part it's to help them with their public speaking skills, but also to talk about their research."[26] The same administrator also offered that the other students who participate in such events learn a lot about how to interact in such formal academic settings—skills which prove indispensable to students who go on to graduate or professional school. The dimension which makes these experiences different for Yale students is that they take place with the students in their particular residential college—students who they live with but students who also represent a host of disciplinary interests. As a result, one Yale administrator referred to the fact that the residential college system "sets the tone for how service, scholarship, and leadership relate to one another."[27]

If Yale's approach to intellectual and moral formation represents a form of secular humanism, it appears to prioritize student commitment to its own identity, or perhaps, the Yale educational experience. For example, the types of student formation that an institution will not compromise when facing a conflict with other identities always provides a window into identity prioritization. A revealing test of Yale's commitment to forming students' residential identity came in the form of a law suit initially filed in the late-1990s by five Orthodox Jewish students. These students, who came to eventually be referred to as the "Yale Five," claimed "that Yale's housing policy, which requires unmarried freshmen and sophomores to live on campus, was discriminatory against Orthodox Jews and violated the Sherman Anti-Trust Act because it tied together two businesses—education and housing."[28] The students also argued that the university's long-standing relationship with the colony and then the state of Connecticut precluded the university from claiming that it was a private institution. In the spring of 1996, three Yale students, Elisha Hack, Batsheva Greer, and Rachel Wohlgelernter, filed for exemptions from Yale's policy that first and second-year students must live in campus housing. The students "claimed living in coed dorms was a violation of the Jewish notion of modesty between the genders, and thus, untenable for them as religious Jews."[29] Yale refused to grant the exemption but did offer to allow the students to live on single-sex floors and in suites with bathrooms. The students claimed that this offer on the part of the university was still discriminatory against their religious beliefs.

In the end, these three students, joined by two others, Lisa Friedman and Jeremy Hershman, retained legal counsel and eventually filed a law suit against Yale. By this point in time, this controversy had become the focus of national media attention with several outlets running stories concerning the impending legal action. In 1998, a U.S. District Court decided in favor of Yale and offered that the plaintiffs "could have chosen to attend another university if they felt Yale's housing policy violated their religious convictions."[30] The plaintiffs then appealed to the Second Circuit Court of Appeals but received the same decision. In the end, the critical question which never seemed to be resolved was whether Yale's secular tradition of residential identity formation as embodied by not only its housing policies, but also its curriculum, was neutral in nature or whether it at times did discriminate against other traditions. Questions both on and off-campus concerning that matter appeared to never come to a conclusion. Some argued that the compromise that the university offered was insufficient and thus still fostering a spirit of discrimination. Others argued that the students were motivated by factors beyond simply their religious convictions. Regardless, the concerns raised by the "Yale 5" offer an interesting window into what can happen when particular secular and religious humanist traditions collide.

The Limits of Kronman's Secular Humanism

While we believe Kronman's vision can prove helpful for institutions such as Yale, Kronman's vision appears to be more a sectarian Ivy League perspective than a vision readily transferable to other university contexts. Our reason for making this claim stems from Kronman's assumed identity orientation as well as some weaknesses with his argument.

First, empirically speaking it is not at all clear that "our" universities have given up on the meaning of life. It all depends upon which universities a person wishes to claim are associated with one's identity. Kronman likely means American universities but even then this claim is suspect. It is doubtful that American religious universities or colleges such as those we have studied in the past[31] or we review in this volume would acknowledge the title's assumption. Compounding this concern, Kronman provides little empirical evidence to support his claim. What becomes clear in Kronman's generalized narrative is that he is referring to the secularized Protestant institutions that once dominated American intellectual life such as his own Yale University.

This point raises a second problem with Kronman's historical narrative. Kronman fails to acknowledge that secular humanism may have actually contributed to our current problem regarding academic attention to the meaning of life.[32] Instead of replacing the old antebellum college's Christian vision for one that welcomed colleges and universities with various types of constrained disagreement (both religious and secular), the secular humanist model that he proposes denigrates agreement based upon religion. Yet, in his book, *The Decline of the Secular University*, C. John Sommerville argues that secular universities now have trouble defining what makes us human precisely because of their secular nature. Sommerville contends:

> When American universities became officially secular, a century ago, the problem of defining the human was not foreseen. Much of a traditional Christian intellectual culture was taken for granted. Mistaking their habits of thinking for rationality itself, those founders thought

religion was redundant and could be ignored without loss of sub-stance. It has taken a century to discover the intellectual void that results when religious categories are systematically rejected wherever they are discovered. Thoughtful commentators now speak of "secular inhumanism."[33]

Thus, it is clearly contested whether secular humanism moved the university forward in its effort to define essential human ends.

Third, Kronman wants to claim that the secular humanism that he sets forth represents a milder, more inclusive form than iterations embraced by other users of the term or even past signers of secular humanist manifestos. Yet, it is hard to see how secular humanism can be embracing of all approaches to life, particularly religious human-ism. "Secular" is not a neutral term or tradition. While we are all human, we do not share a "secular" identity (as the story of the Yale Five would reveal). In fact, there is a great deal of confusion about what the term secular actually means,[34] and we believe it is often used as a less offensive term for other moral traditions. In this case, what Kronman proposes is an argument grounded in Enlightenment agnos-ticism and a curriculum that is really what we would call Western humanism (a point we explore below).

Fourth, it remains unclear why a particular curriculum will encourage education, reflection, and commitment about life's meaning (although it is not at all clear that Kronman ever wants students to make commitments). Cognitive efforts alone are insuf-ficient in terms of moral formation. As James Engell and Anthony Dangerfield observe, "Like the uses of all knowledge, the uses of literature *guarantee* nothing. Its knowledge acts as an instrumen-tality. Like a scalpel or laser, it can heal or lance a cavity swollen with prejudice. It can also destroy, kill or justify killing. Many SS officers were well educated."[35] Similar to moral educators from Plato to Kohlberg, Kronman places great faith in the possibility that knowledge will shape a person's affections and will. In con-trast, we would argue that such a limited cognitive approach to moral education is neither holistic, nor effective and bears the atti-tude of the secular humanist tradition which helped marginalize ethics from the curriculum.[36]

Fifth, his narrative fails to appreciate how each of the "problems" or things that undermine secular humanism are attempts to do what those teaching the humanities must necessarily do. They must choose to order the importance of certain identities in a particular way and to enrich those particular identities at the expense of others. A true form of humanism cannot rest merely upon acknowledging "the broad social structures that provide meaning." It also must, out of necessity, make choices. Which history do we study? Which literature do we assign? What music should students learn? Whose dramas do we perform? Education always takes place in a tradition that makes curricular choices based upon an ordering of identity priorities. A curriculum will always enrich one's understanding of certain identities, and perhaps even attract students to certain identities, at the expense of other identities. Understandably, schools from a particular tradition will want students to come away with a better understanding of the particular identities valued by the institution. One finds this true even when Kronman must finally make some choices. Kronman's choice of curriculum is not "secular humanist," since secular humanism is largely a rather limited tradition with few classic texts. Instead, his reading list of great books includes a variety of ideological perspectives in the Western tradition. It would be more accurate and appropriate if Kronman used the term "Western humanism" for this is actually the broader tradition and identity from which the reading list springs. Such a curriculum, of course, could be used by a variety of colleges and universities that do not seek to defend the secular humanist tradition. This point is exemplified by the fact that Kronman cites St. Olaf College as an example of a university taking the kind of approach he's proposing.[37] In reality, St. Olaf College, as we will discuss later in this book, represents an example of an institution promoting a broad form of Christian humanism. Its connections to the Lutheran Church, in particular the Evangelical Lutheran Church in America or ELCA, speak to its continuing support for a Luther-informed Augustinian outlook that affirms ultimate meaning is found in relationship with a transcendent God.

Overall, it appears that Kronman believes that his form of secular humanism could be implemented at numerous research universities and liberal arts colleges; although he admits the programs he mentions should not be "copied with mechanical precision."[38] Nonetheless, he makes no distinctions among different types of universities where unique identities related to religion, gender, class, ethnicity, or even professional purpose may significantly shape a university's mission and ethos. In fact, neither his diagnosis nor his solution make any distinctions between various types of colleges and universities. Kronman's narrative and even the title speak in universal and general terms, lacking attention to the diverse nature of these institutions. Kronman's proposal ultimately fails to give attention both to the plurality of universities and identities that currently exist in America and the fact that any humanities curriculum always involves particular choices related to how one orders one's identities.

Religious Humanism

Contrary to Kronman's argument, a set of universities still exist that share a commitment to a particular way of thinking about the meaning of life as well as the good life in general. These institutions stand as representatives of the belief that any effort to be more fully human must involve one's relationship to God and a certain quality of relating to one's fellow human being. Moreover, although they have also been influenced by larger cultural pressures regarding the role of moral education in the academy, they still set forth particular visions of human flourishing. For example, although the story of the marginalization of moral education applied initially to the major research universities and eventually spread to smaller liberal arts colleges, colleges and universities connected to a sponsoring religious body still proved to be exceptions. Protestant, Roman Catholic, and Jewish institutions, continued to offer religion courses whereas many state schools and secularized private colleges excluded such courses. A 1936 study of religion in American colleges and universities found that all Catholic students and one in two students at Protestant schools received religious instruction.[39] In contrast, at private secular colleges only one in eight students received such instruction. At state institutions it was only one in twenty students. Ethics and doctrine were the two major subjects for Catholic schools while in Protestant schools the major courses addressed Biblical Studies, the life, and teachings of Jesus, ethics, and religious education.[40]

After World War II there was a dramatic growth in religion departments at state and private, nonsectarian colleges and universities. While ethical and moral questions began receiving increased emphasis in the curriculum during this time, this emphasis eventually dissipated due to the increased secularization and professionalization of the academy described in chapter two.[41] As one Hastings Center report summarized the situation, "In denominational schools only, courses on ethics often retained their central role, but by the early sixties, even those schools sharply reflected the general trend toward specialization and professionalism, usually at the expense of traditional emphasis."[42] A series of self-studies by thirteen Christian colleges in 1986 would appear to confirm this fact. Arthur Holmes summarized the findings, "Apart from the occasional course and professor in religion or philosophy few claimed any competence or any preparation, and most departments admitted that little if anything was being done other than occasional moralizing or consciousness raising."[43] Thus, while a college or university's religious affiliation perhaps slowed the marginalization of ethics, it did not totally exempt them from the marginalization of ethics.

The contemporary situation, however, at least according to various studies, appears much different. The knowledge gleaned from studies comparing moral education at different kinds of religious and secular institutions now reveals the distinct uniqueness of Christian colleges and universities when it comes to moral education. The nature of the distinctiveness can be divided into five areas: (1) faculty attitudes; (2) ethics in the curriculum; (3) measured or reported impact on character or moral attitudes; (4) students' moral reasoning; and (5) alumni views about moral education. In addition, a survey of colleges that encourage character also sheds light on this matter.

With regard to recent faculty attitudes, surveys of faculty in North America identify a significant gap between "public" institutions and Christian institutions with regard to their concern for moral and civic education.[44] Less than half of the faculty at public universities thought it was very important or essential for students to develop moral character, whereas close to seventy-five percent of faculty at Catholic or other religious (largely Protestant) institutions affirmed this view (see table 6.1).

Faculty members at religious colleges also clearly placed greater importance upon moral and civic concerns when compared to other nonsectarian and public colleges as well as private and public universities. In addition, they perceived matters related to moral and civic education to be higher priorities at their institutions. For instance in a 1998–1999 survey only 34.5 percent of public universities saw helping students understand values as a high or the highest priority at their institution while over 80 percent of Catholic and Protestant universities took this view. According to these surveys, the closer a school is to being a private liberal arts religious college the more seriously faculty perceive matters of moral or civic education. Interestingly, another study of religious research universities also found considerable levels of support for moral and civic education comparable to the levels found among religious colleges.[45]

Studies of curriculum and influence on students also note the distinctiveness of Christian schools, particularly evangelical schools. One study conducted by Allen Fisher included a comparative curricular study of unaffiliated, Presbyterian, and Evangelical colleges in which he looked for required courses emphasizing values. He found that 100 percent of the evangelical colleges required such courses, 73.8 percent of the Presbyterian schools, and 48.3 percent of the unaffiliated schools.[46] With regard to the actual attitudes, behaviors

Table 6.1   National Norms for the HERI Faculty Survey

National Norms for the 2004–2005 HERI Faculty Survey: Goals for Undergraduates Noted as Very Important or Essential

Goals	Universities		Colleges			
	Public	*Private*	*Public*	*Nonsectarian*	*Catholic*	*Other Religions*
Develop moral character	48.8	55.7	56.7	62.6	73.5	75.9
Help develop personal values	43.4	49.7	49.5	57.0	65.5	69.3
Instill commitment to community service	30.4	33.3	38.1	37.8	48.8	48.8
Prepare for responsible citizenship	53.1	54.7	62.2	62.9	69.5	68.7

Source: From Jennifer A. Lindholm, Katalin Szelényi, Sylvia Hurtado, and William S. Korn, *The American College Teacher: National Norms for the 2004–2005 HERI Faculty Survey* (Los Angeles, CA: Higher Education Research Institute, UCLA, 2005).

National Norms for the 1998–1999 HERI Faculty Survey: Issues Believed to be of High or Highest Priority at Institution

Goals	Universities		Colleges			
	Public	*Private*	*Public*	*Nonsectarian*	*Catholic*	*Protestant*
Help students understand values	34.5	59.7	44.6	72.3	80.7	82.3
Involvement in community service	22.9	46.6	30.5	55.6	63.9	62.1

Source: From Linda J. Sax, Alexander W. Astin, William S. Korn, and Shannon K. Gilmartin, *The American College Teacher: National Norms for the 1998–1999 HERI Faculty Survey* (Los Angeles, CA: Higher Education Research Institute, UCLA, 1999).

and character of students, George Kuh found in a study of moral development at private, liberal arts colleges and public, research universities that the institutions with the most distinctive impact on character were evangelical colleges associated with the Council for Christian Colleges and Universities (CCCU).[47] More recently, Donna Freitas, in a qualitative study of sex, spirituality, and ethics on a range of secular, Catholic, and Evangelical college campuses, found that evangelical institutions stood out from the rest, especially with regard to breaking what she perceived as a destructive "hook-up" culture on college campuses. She noted, "The only institutions at which I encountered a shared identity and common values—which I now believe are keys to a healthy college experience, especially when it comes to reining in hook-up culture—were the two evangelical schools."[48]

Previous studies of student moral reasoning using Kohlbergian developmental classifications have also found that private liberal arts colleges, most of whom were religious, demonstrated the greatest gains in moral reasoning with somewhat smaller gains made at large public universities and the smallest gains among Bible colleges.[49] While some scholars have concluded from studies of moral reasoning among Bible college or fundamentalist students that conservative religious ideology may inhibit growth in moral reasoning,[50] the results of studies that include religious liberal arts colleges indicate that subtle distinctions need to be made between fundamentalist or conservative Bible college students and evangelical Christian students. As mentioned, the majority of the liberal arts colleges in the study by McNeel (and reanalyzed by Pascarella and Terenzini) were actually Christian colleges with strong commitments to developing students' Christian faith and moral lives (e.g., Alverno College, Bethel College, Houghton College, Messiah College, Wheaton College).[51] In this case, the Christian moral tradition may have played a role in furthering moral reasoning although interestingly, Pascarella and Terenzini attribute the growth less to the Christian moral tradition and more to "a genuine focus on liberal arts education."[52]

With regard to alumni perceptions, a survey by Hardwick-Day discovered that 65 percent of alumni from church-related institutions claimed "their experience often included integration of values and ethics in classroom discussions."[53] By contrast, only 24 percent of the students at the top fifty public schools indicated that they experienced such discussions. In addition, 36 percent of alumni from church-related colleges said "their college experience helped them develop moral principles," while only 7 percent of alumni from the top fifty public schools claimed this outcome. Alumni from church-related colleges were the most likely to say that their college experiences helped them develop a sense of purpose in life.

Finally, evidence indicates religious institutions are also more like to demonstrate a particular interest in the moral education of their students. For instance, a book published by The John Templeton Foundation, *Colleges that Encourage Character Development*, lists a variety of exemplary programs as well as an honor roll of "100 colleges and universities that exhibit a strong campus-wide ethos that articulates the expectation of personal and civic responsibility in all dimensions of college life."[54] Although church-related colleges and universities make up less than one-third of the total number of institutions in higher education,[55] over seventy percent of the institutions making up Templeton's list are church- or religiously affiliated. At the religious schools in the Templeton list, educating morally committed students as defined within a specific religious tradition remains an institutional priority.

Overall, evidence indicates that liberal arts colleges and universities associated with the Christian tradition, particularly those in the Protestant evangelical tradition, give greater support for moral education and this support influences student outcomes. Chapter seven will give specific details about the nature of moral education at Christian universities. The specific problems facing religious universities regarding constrained moral agreement will be discussed in chapter eight.

Conclusion

While Anthony Kronman's work may seek to open up space for questions to be asked in academe that scholars such as Stanley Fish may otherwise dismiss, the problem is not that Kronman goes too far. In contrast, we argue that the problem is that Kronman does not go far enough. It is not enough for colleges and universities to open up space for questions to be asked concerning matters such as the meaning of life. Such questions must also be framed by some particular tradition if for no other reason than universities are not neutral spaces. Too often, colleges and universities speak of liberal democracy not because of some overt commitment but because it proves to be the only thing we may have in common. When the fabric of even such a thinly spread commitment becomes worn, colleges and universities are left with little to no justification for their particular policies or procedures. As a result, even faculty members and administrators who may yearn to offer something more for their students than Fish's aspirations for professional ethics are left with little to nothing. The response, we believe, is not to slide back and accept what Fish is proposing but to go beyond what Kronman is proposing and develop an even deeper sense of appreciation for the tradition that defines the fabric of a particular community.

Chapter Seven

Moral Education in the Christian Tradition: Contemporary Exemplars

> ...people may have different commitments behind [their] common enterprises, and thus they need to wrestle with those differences that take account of each other's distinct identity. Christians will never meet this challenge better seeking to be less specifically Christian. They will meet it better if they take it on faith that Christ is Lord over the powers, that Creation is not independent of Redemption.
>
> —John Howard Yoder, *The Priestly Kingdom*[1]

Throughout this book, we have argued that the education undertaken in most colleges and universities relies upon less than human frameworks. We should not be surprised at this development. We should not expect to find many state-sponsored universities with common moral ideals in pluralistic liberal democracies (except perhaps at military academies and other unique forms of institutions). Instead, we would offer that such common moral ideals are best cultivated within educational communities keenly aware of and well-defined by comprehensive humanistic moral traditions. Their common metanarratives springing from their comprehensive identity supply ends, virtues, practices, principles, wisdom, mentors, and models that stretch beyond restricted identity boundaries.

The previous chapters demonstrated the different ways some secular colleges and universities find more expansive forms of moral agreement that extend beyond professional identity. Significant portions of the rest of the book will involve a description, defense, and constructive critique of moral education in the Christian tradition within American higher education. We begin the description in this chapter by undertaking an empirical overview of moral education at Christian colleges and universities. First, we describe our own document survey of 156 Christian colleges and universities as well as our findings. Second, we briefly offer an overview of seven of our nine case studies of exemplary Christian universities and colleges that give particular attention to moral education. In the last section, we highlight the two remaining case study institutions and the important relationship they demonstrated between a rich theological tradition and a comprehensive approach to moral education.

The Distinctiveness of Moral Education at Christian Colleges: Methodology

To gain further insight into the institutional approaches of Christian universities and colleges to transmitting a moral tradition, we undertook our own study of 156 different Christian colleges and universities. From this sample, we chose nine colleges/universities that demonstrated significant attention to moral education according to their literature. Our study sought to discover the Christian institutions of higher education that promote particular forms of moral knowledge as true and encourage intellectual, willful, and active commitment to a particular vision of the good life. We also wanted to identify not only the important ways that Christian colleges and universities as a whole make moral education central but also the unique differences there may be among institutions that do so.

We began our study by examining course catalogs, admissions view books, and student handbooks from a group of 156 American Christian colleges and universities associated with two large partnerships, the Council for Christian Colleges and Universities (CCCU) and the Lilly Fellows Program (LFP).[2] We chose these partnerships for a couple of reasons. First, they represent the same schools at which Lindholm et al. and Sax et al. found significant faculty support for moral education and at which Kuh uncovered significant success with moral education.[3] Sixty-four of the 156 schools (41 percent) were also listed in the *Templeton Guide's Honor Roll of Colleges that Encourage Character Development* as honor role schools or as institutions having particularly outstanding character education programs.[4] Second, these partnerships provide a diverse sample of religious colleges and universities. The LFP contains schools from a wide range of Catholic and Protestant traditions. The CCCU schools are largely evangelical Protestant institutions but they also include schools from a variety of religious traditions (e.g., Wesleyan, Reformed, Nazarene, Baptist, Quaker, Mennonite, Presbyterian, etc.).

We collected academic catalogs, admissions view books, and student handbooks from each one of the 156 institutions and then examined the documents to identify whether they gave attention to ethics in the curricular and co-curricular realms. In addition to examining general trends of Christian institutions, we also wanted to identify universities and colleges that clearly demonstrated, to borrow from Robert Benne's phrase, quality with soul in moral education.[5] When looking for schools that take moral education seriously, we considered some of the following sources of evidence: (1) A clear moral mission; (2) the prevalence of appeals to moral ideals in marketing the school; (3) the integration of ethics into the curricular realm; (4) the integration of ethical ideals and language into the co-curricular realm; and (5) an integration of efforts being made in the curricular and co-curricular realms.

Based on our findings in these five areas, we chose nine schools from different types of traditions that demonstrated evidence of a comprehensive interest in moral education. The schools selected were Bethel University (MN-Baptist, General Conference), Calvin College (Christian Reformed Church), Eastern Mennonite University, George Fox University (Quaker), St. Olaf College (Lutheran—ELCA), Seattle Pacific University (Free Methodist), University of Dallas (Catholic), the University of St. Thomas (MN-Catholic, Diocesan), and Xavier University (OH-Catholic, Jesuit). We then made site visits to each one of these institutions to interview leaders who could describe and articulate the specifics of their moral education ideals in more detail. The leaders usually included the chief academic officer, the officer in charge of general education, the chief student development officer, the officer in charge of residence life, the officer in charge of student discipline, and the officer in charge of religious life. Afterward, we analyzed the interviews, field notes and other additional documents to identify ways that these schools both represented and departed from findings in the wider literature.[6]

Evidence from the Literature

Significantly, almost every one of the 156 Christian colleges we studied included a moral goal in their mission statement. In our overall study, the institutions with ethical elements in their mission statements could be divided into four types. Some of the schools simply mentioned ethical goals, usually particular virtues or values, without reference to a particular tradition or theological language derived from the Christian tradition. For instance, Morningside College articulates its mission as cultivating "a passion for life-long learning and a dedication to ethical leadership and civic responsibility."[7] Interestingly, not one of our nine case study schools demonstrated this approach which perhaps reveals that there may be a connection between secularized mission statements devoid of reference to Christianity or a particular Christian tradition and a curriculum with less focus on ethics.

A second type of mission statement made reference to the broad Christian tradition in connection with its moral mission or general Christian language. For example, Seattle Pacific University (SPU) claims, it "seeks to be a premier Christian university fully committed to engaging the culture and changing the world by graduating people of competence and character, becoming people of wisdom, and modeling grace-filled community."[8] George Fox and Bethel, representing the Radical Reformation tradition, made reference to Christ. George Fox's mission statement reads, "To demonstrate the meaning of Jesus Christ by offering a caring educational community in which each individual may achieve the highest intellectual and personal growth and by participating responsibly in our world's concerns."[9]

The third type of school would make reference to a particular Christian tradition and a moral mission. For instance, the University of Dallas stated:

> The University of Dallas is a Catholic institution that seeks to educate its students to develop the intellectual and moral virtues, to prepare themselves for life and work, and to become leaders in the community. Through intensive teaching, interactive discourse, and critical analysis, the university pursues truth, virtue, and wisdom in the liberal arts and professional studies.[10]

The fourth type would combine all of the above elements. These mission statements referred to a particular Christian tradition, Christianity as a whole, and particular theological groundings. Calvin College stated it "is a comprehensive liberal arts college in the Reformed tradition of historic Christianity. Through our learning, we seek to be agents of renewal in the academy, church, and society. We pledge fidelity to Jesus Christ, offering our hearts and lives to do God's work in God's world."[11] Similarly, Eastern Mennonite University's statement contained all of the elements identified above:

> Our Anabaptist Christian community challenges students to pursue their life calling through scholarly inquiry, artistic creation, guided practice, and life-changing cross-cultural encounters. We invite each person to experience Christ and follow His call to: witness faithfully, serve compassionately, and walk boldly in the way of nonviolence and peace.[12]

As we will note later, we found it interesting that institutions with more comprehensive mission statements with regard to each type also demonstrated more comprehensive approaches to moral education with regard to scholarly typologies.[13]

Schools in this last group also clearly resisted the trend noted by James Burtchaell in which secularizing Christian institutions usually downplay their particularity.[14] John Wright claims that such pressure comes from liberal-democratic polities or accrediting boards that "demand that institutions translate their Christian commitments into liberal democratic language."[15] We believe that other pressures, such as attempts to market the school to a wider constituency also play a role.

Interestingly, we also found little reference to other identities. For example, less than 10 percent (15) of the 156 colleges referred to educating citizens (and two of those references referred to world citizenship). Moreover, we rarely found appeals to the liberal democratic identity or tradition as a basis for moral education. Official documents, such as mission statements, always described moral goals and ideals in the context of the Christian tradition.

A school's marketing material may tell a more accurate story of what it prizes than its official mission statement. As David Kirp notes of college marketing today, "Top college applicants are treated like pampered consumers whose demands must be satisfied. The notion that these are adolescents who are supposed to be *formed* by a college education is dismissed as quaint."[16] In contrast, the vast majority of Christian schools we studied marketed their moral vision. This fact was particularly true for our case study schools. SPU's view book boasted, "At SPU you'll gain competence and character. SPU links the growth of academic competence with the formation of personal character. It's a powerful combination that enables you to choose from many different options for your life—and to make a profound difference in the world."[17] Calvin proved one of the most comprehensive in its appeal. Its view book discussed providing a "Christian liberal arts education" that would "help you shape your Christian character" and promoted the Reformed theological perspective which seeks to "aid the Spirit's work of restoration by seeking to make all things better."[18] In this case, all three types of identity referents, Reformed, Christian and the triune God, provided the moral perspective and selling point. Clearly, the schools we studied understood as one Xavier interviewee noted that the moral mission of the school is "a selling point."[19]

As discussed in chapter two, scholars tell a common story of the marginalization of moral education from the curriculum of the

American research university. Even the recent "ethics boom" heralded by some scholars has occurred primarily in the area of professional ethics.[20] In contrast, one-third of the 156 schools we studied *required* an ethics course in the general education curriculum.[21] In addition, many institutions still offered a wide range of ethics courses in professional majors including technical subjects such as engineering and computer science.[22] All of our case study schools required at least one ethics course or a first-year seminar focusing on Christian ethics in their general education curriculum. Eight of the nine schools also offered a variety of professional ethics courses in majors. For example, Xavier University offered classes such as Business Ethics, Morality and Employment Issues, Bioethics, Professional Issues and Ethics (in occupational therapy), Human Dignity in the Helping Professions (criminal justice), Legal and Ethical Issues in Sport, Current Issues and Ethics in Health Education, Ethics for Educators, Media Ethics, Law and Ethics in Mass Community, and Public Relations Ethics in Society. Clearly, a concern with ethics pervaded not just the curricular realm of these institutions.

Quality with Soul in Moral Education: Profiles from Our Case Studies

In our evaluations of our findings during our nine case study visits, we explored two particular angles. First, we evaluated the degree to which these institutions might fit within the theoretical framework offered by Colby et al. that could be used to determine whether an institution's approach to moral education was holistic. As mentioned earlier Colby et al. identify three themes of different campuses: (1) the community connections approach which focuses upon "connections with and service to particular communities"; (2) the moral and civic virtue approach which emphasizes personal virtues and values such as integrity, courage, and responsibility; and (3) the social justice or systematic social responsibility approach which typically involves teaching students how to contribute to social change and public policies that will increase address various economic, political or social injustices.[23] In general, we found these categories helpful, although leaders on our campuses also referred to what we consider an additional moral strand not covered in Colby et al.'s three types: (4) the holiness strand of ethics that emphasizes an individual's and community's relationship to God.

The second thing we examined was the unique way that the Christian identity of an institution played a role in shaping moral education. In particular we looked at the language, reasoning, and ethos that contributed to these institutions providing more extensive attention to the moral life. The section below will characterize the schools using Colby's categories while also describing what we found on the campuses regarding the relationship of the ethical language, reasoning, and ethos to the Christian identity of the institution. Although past works on this subject, such as Arthur Holmes' *Shaping Character*,[24] make an accurate assessment of the ways theological traditions will shape the moral ethos of an institution, we also found some unique surprises.

Specialists in Faithful Service

St. Olaf College. If one wants to discern the major moral strand emphasized at St. Olaf, a private liberal arts college of 3,000 students in Northfield, Minnesota, one simply has to look at their view book. On six different pages the view book mentions how students learn, as its mission states, to lead "lives of unselfish service to others."[25] Administrators also reiterated this theme. As one boasted, "We're one of the top suppliers of volunteers into the Peace Corps, the Lutheran volunteer Corps, the Jesuit volunteer Corps, Vista, [and] Teach for America. Our students are service driven. Almost sixty percent of our students are in a volunteer service program of some variety."[26]

The source of this emphasis upon service clearly stems from St. Olaf's Lutheran identity.[27] St. Olaf's opening portion of its mission statement provides this orienting perspective as well as a refutation of Fish's professional vision for the university and an affirmation of Christian humanism:

> St. Olaf, a four-year college of the Evangelical Lutheran Church in America, provides an education committed to the liberal arts, rooted in the Christian Gospel, and incorporating a global perspective. In the conviction that life is more than a livelihood, it focuses on what is ultimately worthwhile and fosters the development of the whole person in mind, body, and spirit.[28]

Nonetheless, in our study of literature and conversations we noticed less emphasis upon particular Lutheran distinctives or Christian theological beliefs than our other schools. St. Olaf's view book made little mention of its Lutheran identity and talked in general terms about its "religious heritage."[29] In addition, its moral language drew less upon theological terms and more upon having a general worldwide concern for all humanity. Its view book claimed that it would prepare a student to "do good work in the world," "be a citizen in an increasingly multicultural world," and be "responsible citizens of the world."[30] It advertised that students enjoyed conversations about the question, "What does it mean to be human?" and helped students "grow as human beings."[31] In other words, it touted its approach to ethics using language rooted in a more general Christian humanism. Likewise, in the curriculum little attention was given to exposing students to particular forms of Christian ethics. While students were required to choose courses in Christian theology and "Ethical Issues and Normative Perspectives" from a variety of options, the courses may not necessarily relate to the Lutheran theological tradition or even Christian ethics.

Although the service strand clearly predominated at St. Olaf, we also found emphasis upon the virtue and social justice strands at St. Olaf. Interestingly, some of these strands also appeared less connected to its Lutheran tradition. For instance, a statement adopted by students called the R.I.C.H. Statement (for Respect, Integrity, Celebration, and Honesty) reads

> In order to nurture and foster the spirit of the St. Olaf Community, I will strive to practice and encourage among my colleagues: Respect for the dignity of others, despite differences in our beliefs; Integrity in actions and intent; Celebration of the gift of community, by becoming engaged in it; Honesty in all aspects of life, in and out of the classroom; and recognizing that community has no boundaries, I will carry these values with me as I travel, work, study and serve.[32]

While containing a number of virtues, it reads much like an honor statement at any secular private or public university and was actually inspired, in part, by the University of South Carolina's Carolinian Creed. Thus, while we found an incredibly strong form of moral language and subsequent ethos pervasive at St. Olaf in its curricular and co-curricular realms, it was not necessarily always strongly connected to the sponsoring denomination's theological particularities or even more general Christian theology.

St. Thomas. A second institution that clearly prioritized the service strand was the University of St. Thomas. An 11,000-student university in St. Paul, Minnesota, St. Thomas seeks "to be a recognized leader in Catholic higher education that excels in effective teaching, active learning, scholarly research and responsible engagement with the local community as well as with the national and global communities in which we live."[33]

A review of the academic catalog immediately brings to light the role that this conviction plays in the life of the St. Thomas community. It requires a theology course covering the Christian tradition, a philosophical ethics course, as well as a philosophy of the human person course. In some respects, St. Thomas' general education requirements mirror the Christian humanism of St. Olaf. In addition, St. Thomas offers both a major and a minor in Justice and Peace Studies as well as Catholic Studies. In his book, *A Catholic University: Vision and Opportunities*,[34] Terrence J. Murphy, president of the University of St. Thomas from 1966 to 1991, discusses how Catholic universities are not only called to think deliberately about their Catholic identity but also to reach out to other communities. He notes that programs such as Catholic Studies were established in response to the needs of the diocese for well-educated lay leaders. The peace and justice studies, he observed, program had similar origins.

St. Thomas' commitment to serve both the ecclesial and local community is evidenced by the fact that it has appointed a special faculty member who is in charge of helping integrate service-learning into courses. It holds two workshops a year during which faculty can learn about service-learning and brainstorm about how to integrate such practices into their courses. One such project among an immigrant parish in the Twin Cities involved twelve faculty members from eight different academic departments in tracking the history of that immigration in the Parish community and what the Parish can do to serve that community. Several other service-learning programs were developed in response to the needs of the diocese and the larger world.

St. Thomas' commitment to developing a Catholic understanding of service within its students extends beyond the classroom. The campus ministry office "believes that the depth of our faith powerfully affects the way we live and what we become."[35] Seeing one effort leading to the next, the campus ministry office coordinates both opportunities for spiritual formation as well as service to the larger community. Each residence hall at St. Thomas now also has a live-in chaplain who seeks to extend such efforts to all students. Such a presence contributes to what one administrator referenced as a developing model for residential life at St. Thomas, one rooted in Catholic social teaching and the language of "community, living out your faith, and service."[36]

Specialists in Virtue

University of Dallas. Of our nine case study schools the University of Dallas most clearly focuses upon emphasizing studying, contemplating, and practicing virtue. To do so, this 2,000-student university emphasizes the neo-Thomistic synthesis of Aristotle and Christianity often associated with Catholic approaches to moral education.[37] As one administrator mentioned, "We can have all kinds of ethics courses in the classroom, and talks, but I really think it's like that St. Francis dictum that we preach the gospel [and] even if necessary use words. More of that Aristotelian perspective."[38]

What is intriguing is that although Aristotle emphasizes the importance of habituation for developing moral virtue, there was little emphasis upon service-learning at the University of Dallas. The moral virtues, they believe, will be developed both through encounters with particular texts and the narratives or lives of professors and other students. One administrator described the vision:

> So beginning from the premise rooted in both reason and faith that there is truth, and that there is such a thing as a life well lived, and therefore better and worse ways of living, we proceed in a humble way to approach the greatest minds throughout history and try to help our students engage in a conversation with them, a conversation we hope will go on all their lives and we believe the texts themselves are the best teachers....We seek to implicate certain virtues through first education and what they are, and then second, maintaining a community that applauds the exercise of those virtues and then seeks to root out vices understood again out of this Catholic [tradition].[39]

We found this vision consistent among curricular and co-curricular educators. In the curricular arena, the University of Dallas focuses upon a coherent core curriculum which includes two required theology courses (Bible and theology), three philosophy courses (including philosophy and the ethical life), and four history courses covering the Western Tradition. Its mission statement even mentions the curriculum and states that its purpose is "to invite students to disciplined inquiry into fundamental aspects of being and of our relation to God, to nature, and to fellow human beings. The curriculum as a whole seeks to enable students to achieve the knowledge of nature and the understanding of the human condition necessary for them to comprehend the fundamental character of the world in which they are called to live and work."[40] The co-curricular arena also coheres with this vision. For instance, student life professionals pointed out how their programming incorporated discussions of moral virtue, especially as related to prominent ethical issues within the Catholic Church (e.g., abortion, physician-assisted suicide, sexual ethics, etc.).

Seattle Pacific University. While discussing moral education at some schools, there might be few if any references to the institution's mission statement. This was certainly not true at SPU where presidential leadership ensured that others know SPU seeks to graduate *"people of competence and character, becoming people of wisdom and modeling grace-filled community."*[41] Biblical categories and language clearly served as the foundational support for the ethical emphasis. An SPU administrator claimed that moral education at this 3,900 student institution started with "the theological dimension" or as another administrator stated, "To work on the identity, the Christian identity of a person that then drives that outward and makes sure that it's understood that one of the key ways to love God is by loving one's neighbor and serving one's neighbor."[42]

This concern with character education informed by the Christian tradition guided the curricular realm with students taking courses in Christian Formation, Christian Scriptures, and Christian Theology their first three years. In addition, first-year students must take a course in Character and Community while juniors study Belief, Morality, and the Modern Mind. Their efforts also extended to others areas of both curricular realm and the co-curricular realm. One administrator added, "We also try to drive it across disciplines and it is in extracurricular, be it chapel, be it emphasis on service-learning, be it an emphasis on short term mission trips."[43] Thus, when it came to a specific effort to form the social conscience of students, an ethnic and racial diversity initiative, the initiative according to an administrator, "is clearly theologically driven, it's not pc [politically correct] at all. I have no interest in political practice with this issue; it has to do with the Kingdom of God being multi-colored, multi-racial."[44] Likewise, student life professionals set forth a discipline process in the same manner. The Student Handbook notes, "Seattle Pacific University seeks to follow the biblical model of discipline as described in Matthew 18:15–18 and Galatians 6:1–2. The purpose of this kind of discipline is redemptive in nature, seeking to reconcile the person to God and to his or her neighbor."[45]

Specialists in Social Justice and Service

Xavier University. Of all the institutions we studied, Jesuit institutions showed some of the most pervasive attention to ethics and Xavier proves a clear example. The mission statement for this 6,600-student university begins by claiming that "Our essential activity is the inter-action of students and faculty in an educational experience character-ized by critical thinking and articulate expression with specific attention given to ethical issues and values."[46] The moral emphasis pervades the campus in numerous ways. One student life professional even claimed, "Students could probably quote you the presidential vision statement word-for-word...'Xavier's about forming students intellectually, morally, and spiritually with rigor and compassion towards lives of solidarity and service.'"[47]

The theological language that informed this moral outlook stems from the common phrase we heard on campus, "the invitation of St. Ignatius Loyola to find God in all things...."[48] As a result of this orientation, the moral language, and reasoning at Xavier tended not to focus on theological distinctives, although Xavier clearly empha-sized its Jesuit identity in numerous ways.

Moreover, while it gave attention to the virtue strand in its commitment to ethical issues, it clearly elevated the social justice and service strands. For instance, in addition to the presidential vision statement focusing on service, its mission statement goes on to state, "Xavier shares [a] worldwide Jesuit commitment to a creative and intelligent engagement with questions of peace and justice."[49]

Xavier's core curriculum provides a clear basis for this focus. All student must take a course in philosophical ethics, theological foundations (which focuses upon "the ethical consequences for living in a world community"), and a course in moral imagination. The co-curricular realm extends Xavier's commitment to social justice and service. For instance, Xavier's view book proclaims, "Peace and justice programs gather students to plan activities, share ideas and reflect upon social action in their lives. Organizations that support peace and justice issues include Pax Christi, Amnesty International, Earthbread, Earthcare, Students for Life, Habitat for Humanity and the Muslim Student Association."[50] Moreover, while we visited, one administrator talked about celebrating Xavier's 175th anniversary by asking all students and student groups to participate in 175 hours of community service as individuals or groups. The campus ministry office also offers student liturgies and retreats which are then lived out through a variety of local and global efforts sponsored by the peace and justice programs office. Xavier students are thus challenged to serve and promote peace and justice in not only greater Cincinnati but around the world.

Virtue and Service

George Fox University describes itself as "a Christian university of the humanities, sciences and professional studies founded in 1891 by Quaker pioneers."[51] The basis of moral education at this 3,300 student institution was evident in how one administrator articulated George Fox's moral vision. In his view, "The students are on a journey and the goal is to reflect the image of Christ more and more. And within that context comes the whole idea of moral formation or spiritual formation...they're incorporating into their lives things that are more reflective of Jesus..." As a school in the Radical Reformation tradition, the moral emphasis in the mission is placed not upon general values or virtues but upon imitating Christ.

The imitation motif fed the two themes of character development and service. For instance, students are required to take a course in spiritual formation that seeks to have students acquire the Christian practices that help students cultivate the character of Christ. This emphasis also extended beyond the curricular realm to the co-curricular realm. As a result, George Fox allowed students to turn some of the nearby homes it owns into living-learning communities with particular moral and spiritual themes. In one house, students sought to practice classical spiritual and moral formation through spiritual disciplines, while another house sought to put the Sermon on the Mount into action through service and other Christ-like virtues, while still another adopted an Augustinian monastic code.

George Fox also emphasized the importance of demonstrating Christ-like service in various ways. For instance, leaders described a whole range of service activities such as Serve Day, a day when all 1,300 students as well as faculty and staff go out into the community for some kind of service, Saturday service group, the service components of their living/learning communities, non-semester service opportunities officially called Winter, Spring and May Serve. Although the emphasis upon service might be understood as merely an expression of common concern for others that any college could and should promote, administrators articulated the rationale for it in distinctively Christian ways. As one administrator noted of the Serve Day and serve trips, "That's part of who we are. What do we think Jesus would have us do?...He would have us serve."[52]

The focus on Jesus' story also led to a focus on the importance of narratives for moral formation. As a school in the tradition of the Radical Reformation, chapel focused less on symbolic forms of remembrance (e.g., the sacraments) and more on story-telling about what Christ has done in someone's life or in the life of the church. One administrator even observed about a course on church history, "I think there will be a lot of moral formation going on as they look at the history of the church and look at how they fit into this story and how they deal with the world they are going to deal with."[53]

Holiness and Virtue

Bethel University. Bethel University, a liberal arts college of 6,200 students located in St. Paul, Minnesota, is affiliated with the Baptist General Conference. Nonetheless, as one administrator noted, "We in some ways identify with the broader Evangelical world more than with a denominational title."[54] As theological traditions, both the Baptist and Evangelical traditions share much in common. They both emphasize the importance of "conversionism (an emphasis on the 'new birth' as a life-changing religious experience), [B]iblicism (a reliance on the Bible as ultimate religious authority), activism (a concern for sharing the faith), and crucicentrism (a focus on Christ's redeeming work on the cross)."[55]

At Bethel, these themes clearly predominated in ways that shaped moral education. Their first two core values state, "We are Christ-followers—orthodox, conversionist, and evangelical; rooted in the authority of Scripture," and "We are character-builders—concerned with personal and spiritual formation and therefore committed to the development of whole and holy persons."[56] Likewise, Bethel moral education clearly took place in a larger Biblical and theological context. The curriculum particularly modeled this approach. For example, one administrator noted:

> General education is organized around a fairly clear spine that is developmental, so you've got for instance, Intro to Bible, which is followed by the sophomore theology class which is followed by a junior level hermeneutics class, which is followed by a senior level course called Contemporary Christian Issues. And so there is this weaning of the explicitly Biblical studies and then into the framing tools of theology, the application of that into the hermeneutics course and then a further application that pools in all of these issues into a topics course that, the Contemporary Christian Issues courses are explicitly not associated with departments.[57]

Bethel's interest in contributing to students' ethical development beyond their professional lives finds evidence in the fact that its capstone ethics course, unlike many senior capstone ethics courses we've studied, resides outside the disciplines.

The co-curricular realm at Bethel would also be shaped by its identity. The conversionist strand of evangelicalism comes through in the ways Bethel leaders see moral education as involving the sharing of life-changing religious experiences. Consequently, they ask faculty and staff to tell their faith stories in places such as small group Bible studies or chapel. Chapel services also involved efforts to foster specific character qualities or virtues. As one administrator shared, "So, we have a responsibility in the chapel program to think about how do we teach about integrity, how do we teach about justice, how do we teach about compassion and love, how do we teach about humility and care for one another and being attentive to personal sin and those kinds of things."[58] Beyond chapel, community life at Bethel is governed by a community covenant, "Becoming Whole and Holy Persons: A Covenant of Life Together at Bethel University."[59] Biblical and theological in language, the covenant represents the expectations of "an educational community committed to integrating evangelical Christian faith with learning and life."[60] A comprehensive document, it covers a whole variety of moral ideals including matters of academic expectations, friendships, sexual relations, racial relationships, and more. For instance, under the heading "We believe that life is sacred and people have worth because they are created in God's image," it sets forth the following:

- We will value human life in all its diversity and fullness, recognizing that women and men of all races, ages, and ability levels reflect the creative genius of our Maker.
- We view racism and sexism as sinful and reflective of some of the most harmful aspects of our culture. We will abstain from discrimination based on race, ethnicity, gender, age, and disability. We will also abstain from gossip, deliberate divisiveness, and malicious humor.[61]

Clearly, in both its curricular and co-curricular realms Bethel placed an emphasis upon a Biblically informed moral ethics characteristic of the evangelical world.

The Language of Moral Education and Comprehensive Moral Education

Overall, with regard to the role of the religious tradition in nurturing moral education, we noticed an important difference between three types of schools regarding the nature of the conversation. Thus, we divided the schools using three categories. One set of schools we labeled the Christian Humanist schools (Xavier, St. Thomas, University of Dallas, and St. Olaf). The second set we labeled the General Christian Ethics schools (Bethel, George Fox, and SPU). The third set (EMU and Calvin) we called the Comprehensive Christian Identity schools. The key variations among these three types concerned the particular Christian or confessional language and identity used to support the goals and processes of moral education or formation.

At Christian humanist schools, unless interviewing someone in the chaplain's office, we infrequently heard professors or administrators using distinctly theological language. In other words, interviewees mentioned particular moral or theological traditions and sometimes referred to God but rarely made reference to specific Christian terms or theological concepts. Instead, they tended to use more general moral language. A Xavier administrator's description exemplifies the non-particularistic moral language that was used in our conversations. He noted, "We spend a lot of time thinking about what makes Xavier distinct from other institutions and what are the core values that undergird that? So that's the framework that we will probably use. What is this ethic of care and service? What is this attention on promoting justice?"[62]

By contrast, at what we refer to as the Christian Ethics schools, we found clear references to specific theological language that is rooted in the Christian tradition. For instance, an administrator at SPU addressed the difference between a vision of moral education with a theological or psychological approach in this manner:

> I want to start theologically and say, what does it mean, or what are the central stories, what is the master story that guides the Christian faith? For the question of moral and spiritual formation, what does it mean to be created in the image of God? What does it mean to be fallen? And you will get different answers. If you start with psychological theory, and it depends on what psychological theory you start with, you get different answers, but you know, you get a self of humanistic psychological answer that says, you know its Mister Rogers neighborhood; everyone is just fine and dandy....And so it does make a difference, particularly around the issue of theological anthropology...So all that to say, I hope we are theologically grounded.[63]

Clearly, this administrator sought to ground the school's perspective in particular expressions of Christian doctrine.

The last group of schools proved the most interesting. Out of all of the institutions we surveyed in terms of our document analysis and our interviews, Calvin College and Eastern Mennonite University used the most particular and comprehensive theological language in ways directly connected to their specific traditions. Interestingly, they also demonstrated the most comprehensive attention to the various moral strands outlined by Colby et al. The following descriptions demonstrate the nature of the ideals in place at these two institutions and why they prove to be significant.

Calvin College

Calvin College, a liberal arts college of 4,000 students in Grand Rapids, Michigan, demonstrated the most comprehensive ethical emphasis of any campus we studied. Interviewees often discussed their Virtues across the Curriculum Initiative, the Service-Learning Center, and the importance of social justice as representations of all three of Colby et al.'s strands. As one professor noted, Calvin's emphasis upon community action and service is "embedded within an intellectual framework that's heavily emphasizing both virtues and social justice."[64] Some of the interviewees were also some to note the absence of a holiness strand in the Colby typology that spoke of a person's moral obligations to God.

This holistic emphasis, we observed, springs from an institution that prizes particularity. For instance, a Calvin professor made this contrast, "We take Christian formation seriously, and we don't say spiritual formation because that's kind of big 'S,' big generic spiritual that could be misinterpreted.... We talk about Christian formation because it is rooted in the life and work of Jesus Christ and the Trinity here."[65] Even more importantly, the community continually stressed the significance of the Reformed tradition as a support for the comprehensive moral vision. In essence, we observed a correlation between Calvin's ability to reflect the moral commitments of all of these strands and its relationship to the Reformed tradition and the Christian Reformed Church (CRC).

One question which emerges then is what narrative arises from its particular identity that guides faculty and administrators at a place such as Calvin? The answer resides in the Reformed emphasis upon the Biblical narrative of creation, fall, and redemption. In *Engaging God's World: A Christian Vision of Faith, Learning, and Living*, Cornelius Plantinga, Jr., the former Dean of the Chapel at Calvin and now president of Calvin Theological Seminary, argues that "learning is a spiritual calling: properly done, it attaches us to God."[66] In his book designed for students enrolled in first-year seminar courses, Plantinga offers that "The point of all this learning is to prepare to add one's own contribution to the supreme reformation project, which is God's restoration of all things that have been corrupted by evil."[67] As a result of human sin, creation fell from grace. However, redemption is made possible by the sacrifice of Jesus Christ. The purpose of a Calvin education is to help students find their place in this story and then cultivate the virtues that will make it possible for them to faithfully participate in these wide-ranging redemptive efforts.

One finds this Christian narrative and Calvin's Reformed identity woven throughout Calvin's official documents. In its *Expanded Statement of Mission*, the College acknowledges that "Calvin's confessional identity arises from a specific community of faith, a particular people of God who continue to seek obedient discipleship in a confessional way."[68] Calvin's admissions view book, unlike the St. Olaf view book mentioned above, also reinforces this perspective. On the third page, students may read "The Reformed Tradition: God created *all things*, and they were good. *All things* have fallen from that original goodness. Christ, who has redeemed *all things*, eventually will restore them."[69] Prospective students are thus invited to think about themselves as participating in such efforts of renewal.

Unabashedly theological language resounds throughout Calvin's curricular documents as well. Echoing the title of Plantinga's book, the section on the core curriculum in the Calvin College Academic Catalog offers that "the core equips students for a life of informed service in contemporary society at large, for an engagement with God's world."[70] To engage the world in this manner is understood to participate as an agent of renewal. In order to do so, one will need "to cultivate dispositions such as patience, diligence, honesty, charity, and hope that make for a life well-lived—of benefit to others and pleasing to God."[71] As a result, one finds in the Calvin College catalog courses such as "CAS 352: Communication Ethics." In this course, "Christian positions are reviewed and applied" while examining "the moral dimensions of human communication."[72] However, in order to take such a course as a communications major, one must first take Biblical Foundations I, Developing a Christian Mind, and Philosophical Foundations—all courses in the core curriculum.

In the Academic Catalog, the Student Development section evidences a similar theological commitment where it acknowledges that

"Calvin encourages students to apply a Christian worldview to all areas of life, including popular culture."[73] Such an understanding is communicated in greater detail in the student handbook. Echoing the emphasis on redemption, the welcome statement acknowledges that members of the Calvin community seek "to be agents of reclamation, reconciliation, and renewal."[74] This emphasis is present in a number of places throughout the student handbook but is perhaps most notice-able in the section on "Building Community." For Calvin, community is defined by an impulse "to weld its participants together around beliefs that all people are made in God's image and that members of Christ's church need one another, such that their educational endeav-ors, interpersonal relationships, and personal actions might reflect the Lord's provisions more closely."[75] Although curricular efforts such as the core curriculum and co-curricular efforts such as resi-dence life ask students to participate in different sets of practices, at Calvin these practices are both shaped by an over theological frame-work and tradition. At these points, not only the integration of the curricular and the co-curricular realms becomes possible but such a relationship also has the possibility of providing a viable understand-ing of moral formation.

Our interviews reinforced what we found in Calvin's documents. One student life professional referred to his or her colleagues as "Thinky People."[76] In essence, they are people who take the time to think deeply about how matters of doctrine shape and form their existence. This same administrator then offered that this "thinky" disposition translates in terms of how the creation, fall, redemption, restoration" narrative is shared with students. Even more general terms that dominate the campus culture were linked to these theolog-ical terms. For example, interviewees at Calvin often talked about the emphasis on responsible freedom pervasive on campus (e.g., no par-ticular prohibition exists at Calvin concerning alcohol consumption). Without a larger narrative framework, a concept such as responsible freedom can translate into any number of moral ideas. However, behind the explanation for the concept, administrators articulated a deeper theological vision:

> In the freshman Prelude course, responsible freedom is "defined as developing a Spirit-guided life. The Holy Spirit inside you. So it's Scripture [and] it's advice from trusted friends, but it's ultimately where the Holy Spirit is vibrant in your life and it's helping you to make the right choices. And that fits with our Reformed perspective on life and learning...[77]

When a student fails to exercise his or her freedom within the Calvin community in a responsible manner, this same co-curricular administrator suggested that the student is asked to participate in any number of practices designed to facilitate restoration.

Finding a way of facilitating such efforts in a community which enrolls approximately 4,000 students is not an easy venture. A curricular administrator offered that "it's hard! We have to have campus-wide conversations."[78] Fostering an appreciation for the tradition and thus a particular narrative framework comes through deliberate efforts in a number of areas and efforts are not limited to isolated academic disciplines "but in how we teach love and caring across the curriculum."

This same curricular administrator detailed that such efforts cannot end with just the curricular realm but must also be woven into the co-curricular realm. One example of such an effort is found in the investment Calvin has made in service-learning. Service-learning at Calvin is viewed as a great aid in cultivating an engaged campus. In the end this same curricular administrator wants to know "how are we an engaged campus? Not just by sending students out and using the community but again by partnering. So we work hard on that and we read a lot of articles about that too." Such an effort leaves one with the impression that the boundaries between classroom experiences and out-of-class experiences are difficult to distinguish. In addition, the surrounding community of Grand Rapids is not simply a diminutive object in need of service but a valued partner in the larger effort of redemption.

Another area at Calvin reinforcing the notion that theory is not simply the domain of the classroom is orientation. One co-curricular administrator offered that "I spend time during orientation talking about Reformed kinds of ideas and it makes a difference in terms of the way we do our business here, our educating." For this co-curricular administrator, these Reformed ideas then translate into how student activities are initiated on the campus. "Although Calvin brings a host of films and musical artists to campus that express a wide variety of views, if Calvin students are going to learn how to serve as agents of redemption in the world, they need to learn to think through ideas and practices different from their own. Some of these ideas and practices may even offer evidence of the fallen nature of the world."[79]

To the credit of both the curricular and co-curricular administrators that serve the Calvin community, if one removed their references to particular programmatic efforts, it might prove difficult to make any distinctions between these two segments of Calvin administration. Facilitating such a common voice is a well-cultivated appreciation for the Reformed tradition and its narrative of creation, fall, and redemption. Regardless of whether one reads their printed materials, is in the classroom, or in the residence hall, this framework provides a theological foundation for the moral idea embodied by the Calvin College community.

Eastern Mennonite University

Reflective of a very different theological tradition than the one which animates the Calvin College community, Eastern Mennonite University seeks to form students in relation to the Mennonite and larger Anabaptist tradition. Perhaps one way to best summarize the difference between the two is that whereas adherents to the Reformed tradition begin with critical reflection and then seek to put it into practice, adherents of the Anabaptist tradition begin with practice and then seek to reflect upon what such efforts have taught them. As a result, few traditions have as rich a legacy as the Anabaptist tradition in terms of encouraging its members to commit their lives to efforts of service and reconciliation.

Perhaps the one of the best contemporary expressions of the Mennonite tradition is offered by Donald C. Kraybill in *The Upside-Down Kingdom*. Kraybill, Distinguished College Professor and Senior Fellow in the Young Center for Anabaptist and Pietist Studies at Elizabethtown University, is the former Provost of Messiah College and also once served as the chair of the board for his alma mater, Eastern Mennonite University. In *The Upside-Down Kingdom*, Kraybill offers that the heart of the example set by Jesus Christ as detailed in the New Testament is one where the power structures of the Roman World were inverted. Authoritarian power is met with service. Opulence is met with simplicity and force is met with a spirit of reconciliation and peacemaking. However, Christ did not come to simply invert the power structures of the Roman world. He commissioned the Church to continue Christ's efforts in its communal life. Kraybill goes so far as to contend that "Kingdom values challenge patterns of social life taken for granted in modern culture. Kingdom habits don't mesh smoothly with dominant cultural trends. They may, in fact, even look foolish."[80] Such an understanding of the world defines the kingdom of God that the Church is called to share. As a result of its commitment to the Mennonite tradition, EMU believes it is called to prepare students to foster such an understanding of the kingdom of God wherever this is needed.

Stepping foot on to the Eastern Mennonite University campus one can clearly observe the results of this ethical outlook. Flyers on billboards promote discussions about programs to help the inner-city poor, America's involvement in Iraq, and other social concerns. As one administrator noted, "You pick it up on this campus, we are clearly a denominational school and if you come here and you are not a Mennonite you're going to know this is a Mennonite school before you've been here very long, and the values that that brings with it."[81] In fact, what we found at Eastern Mennonite is the only one of the Radical Reformation schools where the denominational narrative and tradition still dominates the larger evangelical tradition and thus guides the vision and practice shaping moral education.

The ethical components of their vision and mission statements also reflect the Anabaptist heritage. The vision proclaims, echoing Micah 6:8, "We commit ourselves to do justice, love mercy, and walk humbly with God" while the Mission Statement reads "We invite each person to experience Christ and follow his call to witness faithfully, serve compassionately, and walk boldly in the way of nonviolence and peace."[82] Additional evidence of this commitment is present in the materials EMU generates. For example, in the admissions view book prospective students are invited to "to get involved and make a difference."[83] In terms of academics, "Ethics, values, and faith are integrated into every course."[84] In addition, EMU claims to be one of the few schools in the country to offer a major in Justice, Peace, and Conflict Studies. Beyond the classroom, the EMU view book also indicates that students are challenged to volunteer for any number of community service efforts. Some of these efforts are adjacent to the campus in the Shenandoah Valley while others are beyond the borders of the United States.

As indicated by the admissions view book, these community service and cross-cultural experiences are preceded by host of curricular and co-curricular experiences on campus. At the heart of the curricular realm at EMU is what is called the Global Village Curriculum. This form of general education is rooted in the conviction that "Preparing students for an independent world requires an understanding of our cultural and religious heritage, the development of personal faith, and the achievement of cross-cultural understandings which enable a responsible contribution in the global village."[85] As detailed in the academic catalog, the Global Village Curriculum is woven into all four years of study at EMU. Eleven credit hours are required in religion or theology. Twenty credit hours are required in an area referred to as "In the Village." Finally, nine credit hours are required in an area referred to as "In the World." In essence, "EMU's cross-cultural requirement fosters students' sense of global awareness in an experiential program of listening, observation, and reflection in a different culture."[86] Locations that host students seeking to fulfill this requirement include the Middle East, Europe, Central America and Mexico, and a site in Washington, DC. In addition, students have the option of going in the summer to a host of sites coordinated in conjunction with the Mennonite World Conference. In the past, such sites have included Zimbabwe, China, and the Navajo Nation.

Perhaps the course which typifies how EMU prepares its students for these cross-cultural experiences is CHST 311/2: Faith and Praxis. Placed within the sequence of religion or theology courses all students are required to take as part of the Global Village Curriculum, Faith and Praxis builds upon courses such as a course in the Bible and CHST 211/2: Faith and Christian Heritage. While Faith and Christian Heritage introduces students to Anabaptist theology and the historical context from which it emerged in the 1500s, Faith and Praxis looks toward how the lessons and ideals of this heritage apply to the myriad of problems facing the Church and the global society today. In particular, the Faith and Praxis course:

> ...more sharply focuses the nature of the Christian life through a biblically-based analysis of social institutions, economic institutions, economic systems, professional structures and issues of power and gender. The role of the church in shaping personal identity and values is of particular concern. The quest for alternative corporate structures of faith that provide sustained presence in today's marketplace is pursued within the context of the Anabaptist tradition.[87]

With these theoretical ideals in place (as well as the ideals from other courses leading up to this one), EMU students are then challenged to go forth from the campus and participate in a cross-cultural experience that will demonstrate the viability of such concepts.

Like Calvin, EMU's commitment to sharing such a narrative embodies both curricular and co-curricular realms to the point that these two segments of EMU's life converge. The most obvious points for this convergence are the community service and study abroad opportunities which EMU offers. This narrative and the ideals it seeks to foster are also embedded in the very qualities EMU students are asked to uphold. For example, students pledge to exercise:

> Social responsibility in my standard of living and use of economic resources. Realizing the destructive character of an unforgiving spirit

and harmful discrimination based on prejudice, I will seek to demonstrate unselfish love in my actions, attitudes and relationships. I will be honest and show respect for the rights and property of others."[88]

These principles are highlighted in the programs offered by units such as residence life, religious life, and student activities. However, the most pointed example may be found in how EMU seeks to administer student discipline. In this capacity:

> EMU believes that personal maturity and growth are encouraged most when the entire university community shares in responsibility for one another. Matthew 18:12–17 outlines the principles of this approach to behavior and relationships. Thus, growth is not entirely an individual process but involves the entire Christian community as we seek to share our own concerns and at the same time respect the convictions of other Christians.[89]

Although self-discipline is espoused as being the foundation of the student experience at EMU, redemption and restoration are also perceived as being communal endeavors. Students have the responsibility to approach one another in love just as faculty and staff members are also encouraged to do so. While the bureaucratic responsibility for such efforts resides with the president and the vice president for student life, the responsibility for caring for the fabric of the community is something in which all community members share.

EMU's commitment to the Anabaptist tradition as told by the narrative of service, simplicity, and peacemaking is also expressed in the responses offered by a number of faculty members and administrators. Like Calvin, these narrative ideals are not simply found in printed materials but also in how these individuals seek to lead and shape the EMU community. One administrator offered that "the values that we [EMU] believe are just throughout the curriculum, we have no apologies about that. We don't indoctrinate. Mennonites are less strong on doctrine and stronger on doing than many other denominations."[90] Talking explicitly about peacemaking, this same administrator went on to offer that "Mennonites centrally believe that we should try to follow in the way of Jesus and what Jesus was trying to tell us. We read the whole Bible but we model ourselves after Jesus and that's why we have the peace stand that we do and so we think Jesus' message was to us you can find throughout our curriculum." A faculty member also offered that "the tradition of the church is very real in our lives and how that's handed down, how that's manifested, in classes are our social structures here at the university." He went on to offer that he not only serves on the faculty but also works with a group referred to as University Accord. This group "deals with conflict on campus at all levels but with the purpose of creating and building on our culture of peace as we understand it from being part of the historic peace church." Another administrator noted how even the symbols on campus communicate the campus's primary identity allegiance:

> We don't have a flag on campus....When we have an NCAA game here on Saturday night, we will do it...there is a flag set up in the gym for the brief moments while we sing the Star Spangled Banner...but the flag is not part of the tradition of the eastern churches of the Mennonite church."[91]

This same administrator explained that peacemaking is a central focus of the residence life program in terms of how they are seeking to teach students to live with one another. In particular, this administrator offered that they were working with their community advisors (CAs/Resident Assistants or RAs at most schools) "to see how they can intervene in conflict situations in ways that they can be peacemakers and help people resolve differences, interpersonal differences and issues and that sort of thing." This same administrator acknowledged that peacemaking is certainly something that gets talked about a lot at EMU in theory. However, part of what sets EMU apart from other colleges and universities is the way, according to this administrator, it gets modeled for students by not only faculty and staff members but also by their peers.

Comprehensive Christian Identity and Moral Education

Clearly, there exists a variety of Christian approaches to shaping comprehensive communities of character. All of the institutions we studied prioritized moral education, but they did so in different ways. For instance, various schools often specialized in and exemplified how to cultivate one or two ethical strands. In fact, each of these institutions, one can argue, provides an example of how to approach at least one particular strand of moral education. As a result, both secular and Christian institutions could learn from St. Olaf about how to cultivate service.

The question we found ourselves asking is whether a Christian institution should be expected to encourage the development of all the strands. While we will not engage in a normative defense of this proposition here, we would argue that the Biblical narrative places an emphasis upon the need for all four strands to receive emphasis in any Christian approach to moral education: (1) holiness before God; (2) Christian virtue; (3) social justice; and (4) active service. In this case, Calvin and EMU demonstrated the most balanced and holistic approaches to each of the strands. What we also found intriguing is that these are the same schools that demonstrated the most obvious connections between their Christian and particular theological identity and their moral education. While the relationship we note between comprehensiveness of moral education and theological identity is noteworthy, more research would need to be done, however, to determine if the emphasis upon theological particularity found at comprehensive schools perhaps accounts for the more equitable focus upon all the strands.

Still, we believe such research is vitally important for another reason. Old and New Testament teaching reveals that ethical thinking in the Jewish and Christian traditions proceeds from an understanding of one's identity and place in the larger story of God's redemptive activity. Certainly, Christian ethics in the New Testament is fundamentally based upon an understanding of God's work in the world through Christ and a person or people's identity in relationship to God.

Conclusion

At the high point of the Enlightenment, morality was thought to be a science fostered by neutrality and objective observation. Such convictions, however, have waned and we now find ourselves returning to the qualities fostered by particular traditions. These traditions, traditions such as the Reformed and the Mennonite, have something unique to say about what it means to be Christian and to live out that faith in a complex and pluralistic society. While no one tradition is able to capture the full significance of a faith such as Christianity, such traditions do prove to be means which temper and form moral thought and action. All institutions share in some tradition regardless of whether such a relationship is conscious or not. As a result, the question is not how a particular institution minimizes its respective tradition but how it invites its students, faculty, and staff to appreciate it. Perhaps too many colleges and universities fail to value the traditions which not only brought them into being but also brought them to this point in history. For the sake of the students they serve, the best way to think about moral formation may be to create a hospitable climate in which students come to appreciate the particulars of a given place.

Chapter Eight

Moral Identity, Moral Autonomy, and Critical Thinking

> But what if most colleges and universities do not advocate any particular value system, even a humanistic one, in practice? What if most colleges and universities, like their students are afraid to 'impose' any values at all on their community members? Some may see this is a plus. As a longtime professor and teacher,...I have watched too many students floundering and faltering without any sense of direction, or any idea where to go to get any, to regard this hands off approach as advantageous any longer.
>
> —Donna Freitas, *Sex & the Soul*[1]

Any approach to moral education must face the potential criticism that it reduces student freedom or perhaps may fail to foster critical thinking. While approaches to moral education rooted in Christian humanism often face this complaint, we must recognize that even less than human approaches face this danger. To help illustrate our point, in the first part of this chapter we will consider one of the most basic forms of moral socialization that universities use to preserve the most basic moral tradition in the university—the honor code. Even at this most basic level of the life of a university, the tension between social-ization into a particular identity tradition and the preservation of autonomy and critical thinking will exist.

The difficulty that more particularistic human approaches face involves the fact that they set forth a broader range of moral ideals across a whole variety of human identities. Certainly, this factor poses an additional challenge. Nonetheless, we contend these institutions can also aid the development of critical thinking in ways that institutions which refrain from setting forth specific visions of human flourishing cannot. The second part of this chapter presents that argument.

Freedom, Moral Orientation, and Moral Development

Every college demands that those who enter the institution submit to the academy's basic moral tradition. They set forth ideals about what it means to be good student as well as the basic moral rules, principles and virtues that relate to those ideals. They expect students to comply with those requirements. They mandate that students choose a course of study and then engage in educating the student to be a good historian, teacher, accountant, et cetera according to traditions of formation. Merely because universities expect a person to meet certain minimal moral standards related to being a good student and dismiss the student if they do not meet the criteria does not mean the student's autonomy is somehow being violated. The individual is free to choose or reject the intellectual and moral ideals associated with being a good student and the intellectual and moral tradition of the academy.

Similarly, an institution that sees its mission as helping students become something more than a good student (e.g., a good citizen or Christian) is quite similar. Institutions such as the service academies may even be quite heavy-handed in how they achieve that mission, but merely adding an additional layer of identity to be formed does not mean that the students' autonomy is undermined. Students can still choose to abandon the institution and its approach. Borrowing from the classic song by the Eagles, there are no "Hotel California" institutions of higher learning. One way or another, they will all allow a student to leave.

Students do face limits upon their autonomy in two other important ways. First, the major threat to student freedom would be for the government or an accrediting agency to prohibit colleges or universities that adhere to particular understandings of moral development with specific visions of human flourishing. For instance, all noncommunists of any identity faced this sort of restriction in the former Soviet Union. Fortunately, today there are now numerous private universities from which students can choose that reflect various sorts of identities and moral orientations.[2] However, not every country, even among liberal democracies, allows for such a wide range of higher educational institutions like those in the United States. Furthermore, even in the United States pressures from various levels of federal or state governments and accrediting agencies may produce pressure to conform to a particular pattern that ends up limiting the range of institutions from which students can choose.

The second major threat to student autonomy occurs when universities fail to be explicit about their moral orientation and developmental paradigm or they fail to be honest about the plurality of understandings of moral development. We find such a situation takes place when certain educational institutions operating from secular moral frameworks claim to be neutral. Our book has attempted to demonstrate that secularity does not equal neutrality.[3] In essence, no morally neutral universities exist. Thus, universities should contribute to a young person's autonomy by being honest about their campus' moral orientation and the way they prioritize moral identities. For instance, when it comes to the curricular realm, private institutions need to be quite clear that they often prize certain kinds of moral formation linked to professional or civic goals more than more humanistic approaches to moral formation. State institutions should also be clear about the moral tradition guiding any behavioral expectations that go beyond the mere enforcement of the law. What becomes problematic is when universities implement speech codes or other sorts of community codes that really are trying to transmit a particularistic moral tradition stemming from a controversial ideology or identity tradition.[4] Our agreement with Fish's argument described earlier is that higher education institutions are not very clear about their moral commitments and how those commitments orient the institution.

Institutional Commitment and Individual Rational Autonomy

Another major concern raised in the context of moral education involves the issue of indoctrination.[5] Despite the fact that one hears the concern of indoctrination bantered about in discussions of moral education, educational philosophers remain quite confused about what the term actually means or involves. Does it involve a certain attitude of the teacher, a particular approach to educational content or methods, the consequences of education, or all of the above?[6] Philosophers do not agree. Yet, Elmer Thiessen observes, "Despite all this disagreement, people go on making the charge of indoctrination against religious schools as though the meaning of the term were perfectly clear to them."[7] We would suggest that an educational institution may be in danger of stunting a person's intellectual growth if they fail to do the following:

1. Enrich students' understanding of their own moral tradition;
2. Help students understand the basic views of other dominant moral traditions with which they may be unfamiliar; and
3. Equip them with the cognitive abilities that allow them to take their own or even a foreign moral tradition and analyze it with the paradigm of another tradition.

As we will see below, some definitions of indoctrination focus on points two and three and forget the first. Yet, any institution's attempt to transmit moral ideals will face the danger of socializing students into a moral culture with its narrative, ends, virtues, principles, models, and moral wisdom without helping them in any of the three areas. In fact, students from Christian institutions may be quite capable at understanding foreign paradigms of thought while they are perfectly unfamiliar with their own tradition.[8] This problem also holds true when dealing with the socialization of college coeds into the lowest level academic expectation associated with being a good student.

Case Study: Honor Codes

Honor codes serve as some of the most basic and all-encompassing sets of moral principles governing universities or colleges. Adhering to them does not guarantee that a student will reach high academic or moral ideals associated with being a good student. Adherence only allows the individual entrance into the academy. Thus, honor codes provide a helpful example of a limited approach to moral education employed in a variety of ways at institutions with various levels of moral commitment. They also may or may not be employed in a way that fosters critical thinking. This last fact may be true at institutions with various types of moral orientations.

As with any moral principle and practice, the moral tradition from which honor codes sprang proves important to understanding its current use. Honor codes largely emerged from a particular type of Southern culture that prized a more general social honor code. The Southern honor code, as Robert Pace observes "consisted of a set of rules that advanced the *appearance* of duty, pride, power, and self-esteem; and conformity to these rules was required if an individual were to be considered an honorable member of society."[9]

The honor codes that developed in Southern universities, however, were slightly different than the one which existed in the wider Southern society, although such codes drew upon the language. One of the first known honor codes was created by a professor at the University of Virginia in 1842 after the shooting death of another professor engaged in settling a disturbance. The professor offered the resolution: "resolved, that in all future examinations...each candidate shall attach to the written answers...a certificate of the following words: I, A.B., do hereby certify on my honor that I have derived no assistance during the time of this examination from any source whatsoever."[10] Initially, the code was meant to govern only academic work, however, the students ended up extending it beyond academics, adopting it, and governing it themselves. Many other Southern universities and some in the mid-Atlantic region of the country would follow with their own honor codes.

Since honor codes do not reinforce the highest academic ideals of being a good student, the existence of the honor codes merely gives evidence to their role in preserving basic scholarly expectations. They did not and still do not always succeed in changing the academic culture of an institution. For example, Helen Horowtiz quotes one prominent University of Virginia student from the mid-1800s who noted that it was "bad form to do reading for the course above and beyond the assignment and to let that be known."[11] Moral models, moral coaches and the moral practices in which such coaches encourage one to engage are much more likely to help form such moral ideals (e.g., what does it mean to be a good student or scholar).

Likewise, other elements in a university's moral culture, such as the overall ethos, the nature, and severity of punishment and peer attitudes will play a role in establishing a culture of academic integrity at an honor code school.[12] For example, honor codes worked in the South for various reasons, but certainly one of them related to the fact that they integrated successfully with the Southern man's concept of himself. As Pace notes, "Challenging students' honor was tantamount to challenging their self-concept, and that challenge need not be serious for it to be taken seriously."[13] In fact, the concept of being honorable extended to one's whole life, since "it provided the basic rules of engagement in all parts of their social and intellectual interaction."[14] Thus, original honor codes, as is still true at institutions such as Hampden Sydney and Washington and Lee University, applied not merely to academic issues but to the whole life of students. Students in earlier days may be tried for cheating at cards, insulting ladies, or someone's manhood or failing to pay a debt. Honor was not merely the basic virtue of good students but also of good human beings.

Since the virtue of honor was primarily cultivated in Southern culture, it is not surprising that honor codes are largely a regional phenomenon found in the South as well as parts of Maryland, Pennsylvania, and New Jersey. In fact, today only 24 percent of 110 nationally ranked liberal arts college catalogs even contain some type of honor code or code of conduct and a large number of these institutions are in the south or states close to the South.[15]

Certainly, not all students are aware of the fact that they are going to an honor code institution when they apply, and we also doubt that students seriously consider leaving an institution when they are informed about the honor code tradition at the school or faced with signing an honor code. The codes, while not forced upon students, are not always moral options chosen in a morally neutral setting or environment. Colleges and universities pass along honor codes as venerable moral traditions to which the institutions are committed. In some cases they are moral consciousness raising instruments and bearers of both Southern and academic tradition.

Far from merely being external instruments of socialization, studies indicate the codes make a difference when established as part of an institution's moral order. They appear effective at reducing the self-reported incidences of cheating.[16] Faculty at colleges with honor codes are more likely to report cheating than at non-honor code schools and students are less likely to engage in serious test cheating or other forms of serious cheating.[17] Moreover, they may have a long-term influence on the behavior and attitudes of students beyond college.[18]

As in the case with any officially promulgated moral principle or rule, however, they may be ineffective[19] or they may not be used as teaching tools to help students think critically about moral rules, principles or even the moral ideals associated with being a good student.[20] The fact that only a little more than half (56%) of honor codes in handbooks contained additional justification for honor may serve as part of the problem.[21] Certainly, honor codes can be promulgated in ways that may not promote critical thinking about academic integrity.

Most universities, however, would likely argue that they neither want unreflective commitment nor critical thinking without commitment. Instead, they want students to make a critical commitment to particular moral ideals pertaining to academic honesty and honor. Nonetheless, the institution attempts to produce this critical commitment within a school that is already committed to these ideals. Thus, these singular academic honor codes may be supported in a whole variety of ways that are similar to schools that require students to ascribe to moral standards based in a religious tradition. Vanderbilt University, for example, requires students to indicate a personal commitment to the Vanderbilt code, a practice similar to some religious colleges, but it does so by asking students to sign a class banner that then hangs in a prominent place in the student center. The University of Maryland at College Park has held pep rallies for academic integrity that seem to share some similarities, sociologically speaking, to worship services.[22]

To appeal to students' rationality, many institutions with honor codes do offer justifications with most of these being based on the normal student development mantra of individual growth and development. The rationale offered at Rhodes College provides a classic example. Its student handbook reads:

> Within the Honor System, Rhodes students have found a moral ideal by which to guide their actions. This ideal is absolute honesty to oneself and to others in all aspects of life. It is not only a guide for college life; it is also a principle which Rhodes students believe to be fundamental in ethical life, both during and after college. The objective of the Honor System is the spiritual, moral, and intellectual development of the individual student.[23]

The actual source of this ethical principle is not addressed. Moreover, unlike the Southern academic culture in which they originated, the vast majority of universities apply honor codes solely to the curricular realm. These schools do not attempt to enforce the code on other areas of a students' life. If a student lies about underage drinking, the honor code would not apply. In these instances, the campus is using the honor code solely to uphold moral ideals associated with the profession of being a good student. Stanley Fish would likely approve of this use of the honor code.

Justifications for honor codes also reflect the range of moral orientations we have discussed in this book. On a few campuses the concept of honor extends beyond academic identity to ideals associated with citizenship or gender. Schools such as the Hampden-Sydney College and Virginia Military Institute (VMI) embody these ideals. Thus, one finds honor codes in places such as schools serving male students as well as at military academies. Finally, on a few other campuses the concept relates to respect for broader human rights and relationships.[24] For these campuses, the honor code draws upon its justification based upon a broad form of humanism or a particular religious tradition. Wheaton College's (MA) honor code provides a helpful example of the former:

> As members of the Wheaton community, we commit ourselves to act honestly, responsibly, and above all, with honor and integrity in all areas of campus life. We are accountable for all that we say and write. We are responsible for the academic integrity of our work. We pledge that we will not misrepresent our work nor give or receive unauthorized aid. We commit ourselves to behave in a manner which demonstrates concern for the personal dignity, rights and freedoms of all members of the community. We are respectful of college property and the property of others. We will not tolerate a lack of respect for these values.[25]

Interestingly, in the survey mentioned only one college offered a religious reason for adhering to an honor code (Wheaton College, IL—a different Wheaton college than the one quoted above).[26]

Although there have been studies of honor code schools and how the use of honor codes can curb cheating, we do not know of a study that has distinguished between the extent to which honor codes effectively curb cheating at colleges or universities and the justifications offered (if they are offered). In fact, what is striking about the research on academic integrity is the absence of any attention to the larger moral traditions that an institution may connect to the honor code. The research reflects an old scientific approach that overlooks the particularistic traditions of institutions. Our own hypothesis would be that upholding honor, merely because it is part of a school tradition or for the mere sake of it being a good internal to the professional practice of being a student, will be less convincing to students than reasons linked to students' broader humanity. Moreover, since many students do not share the values of academic integrity,[27] they will likely need more human reasons to convince them.

Certainly, the larger narrative in which an honor code exists proves particularly important for whether students find the code morally compelling. For instance, in the South the broader honor code of the gentleman sometimes even undermined the concept of honor associated with academic integrity. Pace writes, "It seems incongruous to discuss cheating as a method of preserving honor, but for many, that was exactly what it represented. When faced with the possibility of humiliation, the Southern code recognized that saving face was more important than conforming to moral or ethical rules of behavior."[28] As this example indicates and as mentioned earlier by Pace, the Southern culture of honor tended to place much more emphasis upon the appearance of honor than what is commonly thought of as academic integrity, a type of consistency between outward public actions and private convictions and actions.[29] If institutions wanted to overcome a competing narrative undermining the concept of academic integrity, they would need to offer different reasons rooted in a moral orientation that provides a richer moral tradition.

A Different Kind of Freedom and Honor: Hillsdale College

Perhaps there is no better example of a college with a unique narrative regarding freedom and honor than Hillsdale College (1,300 students).

Located in Southern Michigan in a town bearing the same name, Hillsdale remains one of only a few colleges that refuses to take any federal funding. Receipt of such support is viewed by Hillsdale as a form of entanglement that would diminish the school's commitment to independence. Such a commitment is not seen as an expression of dissent from the liberal-democratic tradition. On the contrary, Hillsdale administrators believe that a commitment to such an understanding of independence is essential to the fabric of democracy.

Established in 1844 by Freewill Baptists, Hillsdale understands its educational mission as resting upon two principles, "institutional independence and educational excellence."[30] Hillsdale's commitment to independence does not mean it has ignored matters of social justice. In contrast, it "was the first American college to prohibit in its charter any discrimination based on race, religion, or sex, and became an early force for the abolition of slavery. It was also only the second college in the nation to grant four-year liberal arts degrees to women."[31]

Hillsdale's longstanding battle with the federal government over institutional independence defines the modern dimensions of its story. Although Hillsdale was the first college to prohibit discrimination based upon race, it also resisted federal pressure to count and record students based upon race. This refusal, conjoined with the possibility that Hillsdale students received federal aid, led to almost a decade of litigation. Initially, the Hillsdale Board of Trustees offered two responses, "One, the College would continue its policy of non-discrimination. Two, 'with the help of God,' it would 'resist, by all legal means, any encroachments on its independence.'"[32] When the United States Supreme Court ruled against Hillsdale in 1984, the College announced it would no longer receive federal funding.

Hillsdale's spirit of independence, however, does not extend to its vision for forming students both intellectually and morally. It requires seven courses of all students and requires all first-year students to live in a residence hall. Another fascinating element of the fabric of Hillsdale's co-curricular realm is the fact that the College is not obligated to abide by the Family Educational Rights Protection Act. By virtue of its commitment to independence and its subsequent unwillingness to receive federal aid, Hillsdale officials may freely communicate with the parents of its students. While not eager or desirous in any way to make such calls, one Hillsdale administrator offered:

> There are times when, and I'm not going to exaggerate, I think lives have been saved here, I can name people [whose] lives have been saved

because we were able to pick up the phone, call mom and dad, and say she's been skipping classes, her grades are tanking.

I think there is a real episode, psychological episode, depressant episode; you need to get up here.[33]

As a result, *en loco parentis* never disappeared from the fabric of the Hillsdale community. While this same administrator remarked that the institution's overall goal is to wean students into adulthood, the College reserves the right to step into the lives of students when it thinks such action is in the best interest of the students.

In an attempt to contribute to Hillsdale's ability to wean students into adulthood, the College recently worked to develop and incorporate an honor code. One administrator remarked that "It took us five years to draft an honor code. It's on my wall here as you walk out the door. We send it to the freshmen in the summer and they have to sign it. It's not a set of things you can't do; it's designed to raise their sights."[34] This orientation sets Hillsdale's code apart from many other codes. Although an honor code is a defining part of a system of student discipline, this same administrator viewed the honor code more as a means to encourage students to rise to self-governance and to higher academic ideals. As a result, Hillsdale's honor code offers that "A Hillsdale College student is honorable in conduct, honest in word and deed, dutiful in study and service and respectful of the rights of others. Through education the student rises to self-government."[35] In this sense, an honor code becomes part of Hillsdale's commitment to not only institutional independence but also independence for each student—an independence rooted in high ideals and not base-line standards.

Critical Moral Thinking within More Human Institutions

We have discussed honor codes as a basic form of moral education that takes place within morally committed institutions. The presence of such commitments by the institution does not necessarily impinge upon critical thinking although the possibility exists. Nonetheless, the presence of a moral commitment, such as adherence to an honor code, can actually serve to foster critical conversations about moral subjects while at the same time fostering moral commitment to high ideals within a particular identity.

Universities that make additional moral commitments will face the same challenges and possibilities on a greater range of issues. For example, Arthur Holmes worried that "the Christian college environment, with its often unreflective acceptance of conventional Christian views and with its behavioral rules, plainly minimizes dissonance...."[36] Certainly, there are Christian schools with norms, such as those regarding sexual behavior, that fail to foster critical thinking about such standards.[37] Yet, the lack of institutional commitment or even the presence of religious diversity by itself does not necessarily help critical thinking about a subject. In fact, lack of institutional commitment, when coupled with an unreflective commitment to diversity, may merely create silence about a subject. Donna Freitas, in her book *Sex & the Soul*, made this observation about her qualitative research on the book's subject at secular campuses:

> In theory, religious diversity should enhance student dialogue and exchange about faith. But if a college doesn't intentionally cultivate and invite personal, religious expression, students end up navigating a campus atmosphere that makes faith-talk awkward, and even unwelcome, the so-called benefit of this diversity lost in students' real experiences.[38]

She went on to observe:

> Regardless of its origin, students at nonreligious institutions experience a separation of church and college, an expulsion of religion from the public square that is so extreme that many of them are rendered mute on the subject. This is an odd reality even for a so-called secular school, given that institutions of higher education typically advertise themselves as places where students can openly pursue any kind of question or topic.[39]

In this regard, the strength of an institution in relation to critical thinking involves more than the presence or lack of diversity, but an institution's ability to provide a framework or frameworks for critical thinking about a subject.

The Orientation of Critical Thinking

The problem for some theorists, when it comes to institutions committed to certain moral traditions, is that they believe the frameworks in which students are encouraged to think will be limited. For example, Amy Gutmann describes indoctrination as efforts to "restrict rational deliberation of competing conceptions of the good life and the good society."[40] We find such a definition hopelessly vague. After all, every teacher restricts rational deliberation to some selected conceptions of ethics, morals, or the good life. In essence, the neutrality of a given teacher is just as implausible as institutional neutrality. Moreover, we doubt that students in committed higher educational institutions find professors who say, "We don't talk about the X version of the good life, because we are a Y institution." We imagine the more likely probability is that faculty at such an institution will encourage students to think about the X version in light of the Y identity and narrative. In other words, the concern pertains to institutional attempts to encourage students to think according to one particular form of moral identity.

A good example of this concern is found in Harvard's *Report of the Task Force of General Education*. Not surprisingly, the authors of the report want to suggest an alternative to professional training provided by professional schools which "*de*liberalize students: they train them to think as professionals."[41] Interestingly, liberal education, according to this committee, is not learning how to think and critique professional ways of thinking from an individual's other identities. Instead, it involves faculty helping "to unsettle presumptions, to defamiliarize the familiar, to reveal what is going on beneath and behind appearances, to disorient young people and to help them find ways to re-orient themselves."[42] David Brooks notes, "This approach is deeply consistent with the individualism of modern culture, with this emphasis on personal inquiry, personal self-discovery and personal happiness."[43] While we agree with Brooks, the claim that the university is going to help re-orient students sounds as if the university does recognize its role in providing intellectual and moral orientation. The committee, however, never clearly states the ways it will help re-orient students.

This understanding of liberal education faces a couple of limitations. First, it reflects a largely cognitive understanding of education that divorces these activities from the holistic nature of human commitments. Both Gutmann and the Harvard committee are concerned with ways of thinking. We agree with Thiessen who observes:

> The whole Western liberal and rational tradition has tended to focus on the human being as a learner, as mind. But a person is more than a rational animal. There is a need for a more holistic view of human nature which recognizes that our rational nature is intimately bound up with the emotional, physical, moral and spiritual dimensions of our being.[44]

Second, the Harvard approach shares the common liberal failing of pretending to be neutral, encouraging the liberation of students from their parochial pasts, while still claiming to provide help orienting students without specifying the nature of this orientation. True liberal education would recognize that students require more sophisticated understandings of their current identity commitments as well as the liberation that comes from being able to understand, take, and evaluate perspectives from different identities and commitments.[45]

The difference between the liberal-cognitive approach from nowhere and critical thinking within a moral tradition is that the second approach is more honest about its own moral orientation and the necessity of taking into consideration the moral orientations of students. This point can perhaps be illuminated by an analogy that takes into account the holistic nature of moral development, especially since it would include the role of behavior, affections, and the community for moral education.

Most cognitive-liberal approaches to the development of students treat competing conceptions of the good life or good society in a similar fashion as prospective dates or romantic relationships. In fact, we suspect that one of the reasons for the hook-up culture in higher education is that it reflects the way that colleges and universities approach answers to life's most important questions. They encourage students to try them out intellectually for a night or week without commitment. Critical thinking in the liberal-cognitive dating model takes place from the standpoint of the uncommitted student who is currently exploring all the options.

In contrast, we believe it would be more helpful to use a marriage analogy. In college, most students are approaching the world of ideas and identity commitment with a whole range of prior commitments and even marriages. For some students, their life commitments are like arranged marriages. They have largely adopted the commitments their parents arranged for them or perhaps the commitments they have inherited. Student attitudes toward their identity as American citizens often functions in this manner as well. Case in point, how much time do we spend explaining to kindergarteners why they are saying the pledge of allegiance versus just assuming they will do so. This line of thinking in relation to the liberal-democratic state may begin in kindergarten but it can continue through the life of one's education.

For others, however, they have already given their identity loyalties some degree of thought and they have engaged with a certain level of commitment. They may even have adopted these commitments with a degree of critical reflection. We find young students usually more reflective and thoughtful about their religious identities than they are about their civic identities. Of course, even commitments made with a great deal of thought at one stage of life may need to be reconsidered at other stages. Just as some enter marriage with a great deal of thought, they will constantly be reevaluating their marriage commitment in light of new knowledge and experiences. In this respect, Perry's cognitive model of intellectual and moral development may provide some descriptive assistance. Perhaps, students made their commitments within a dualistic framework instead of within a framework offering a multiplicity of options.

We believe our marriage analogy takes into account the seriousness of these decisions as well as the presumption of critical faithfulness that students often face. Decisions about the good life, like marriage, involve one's fundamental identity. They may involve name changes, transferring one's family or national loyalties, a whole new set of virtues, principles, practices, and models, additional lifestyle changes and more. They are not merely cognitive commitments, although cognitive thinking at various stages of development should play an important role. Critical thinking under the marriage model would recognize the crucial role of prior commitments and engagement in a tradition to students. It would also recognize that critical thinking can be considered within a marriage. After all, married people do it all the time regarding their spouses. In fact, often it is only by living within that commitment that one is best able to experience the joys and costs of such commitment.

Only with this analogy in mind can we begin talking about what it means to avoid indoctrination, as well as to engage in critical thinking about various views of the good life and the good society. Critical thinking in this context is different. For students with previous commitments it involves consideration of divorce and faithfulness and not merely playing with arguments. In this respect, the prospect takes upon a seriousness not found in the dating approach where an assumption is made that a person only has begun the dating process.

A second weakness of the critical approach from nowhere is one outlined by MacIntyre. The professor can give additional attention to how to think critically within a tradition (e.g., how might we think about this issue within the pacifist tradition of the Mennonite Church). Moreover, the professor could actually model a form of sophisticated critical thinking within this particular tradition. As MacIntyre argued, to move thinking forward within a moral tradition, an institution may need to focus on cognitive dissonance within that tradition.[46] In fact, if one considers Perry's model of intellectual and moral development and applies it to institutions, colleges and universities, one would consider such institutional commitment necessary for intellectual growth. After all, those institutions demonstrating the most growth are those who are not stuck in a stage of relativism (correlate, competing or diffuse) but that make commitments with a knowledge of relativism (or what we would call pluralism). Such institutions are models of intellectual and moral development. Just as we would not say that individuals who have made moral commitments cannot help a student develop morally, so the same should be said of institutions. The mere fact that an institution has made a complex form of moral commitment does not mean it cannot lead students through the path of moral development. Professors at state universities cannot model critical commitment within identity traditions in the classroom. In contrast, Christian institutions can be places where professors, and even the institution itself, model critical thinking within complex commitment. In fact, in our examination of the literature from various Christian institutions along with the interviews, we were often struck by the ways schools drew upon various identities or forms of language when faced with moral controversy.

Critical Thinking and the Christian Tradition

The way that Christian institutions draw upon their moral identities and particular moral language depends upon the type of Christian institutions. In chapter seven, we described three types of Christian schools: (1) Christian Humanist; (2) General Christian, and (3) Comprehensive Christian. In the case of what we have been calling humanist schools, a focus on ethical humanism predominated. For example, St. Olaf clearly prioritized service to others perhaps even above nourishing a particular theological orientation. Two issues mentioned during our visits certainly pertained to this question. In one case, the school decided to install condom machines in the residence halls, one might argue, as a service to students. One student life professional noted, "When the condom thing happened [some] students had a tough time reacting because in their eyes we did something that the church would never have agreed with and so it threw them."⁴⁷ Although there may have been a robust theological dialogue about the issue, we did not find mention of it in our interviews or the school newspaper. In other words, it was not clear that dialogue about the condom machines among the community took place with priority given to either the larger Lutheran theological tradition or a broad Christian context in ways that might have provided contours and meaning to an ethic of service. Instead, the rationales for bringing the machines to campus we heard involved an attempt to serve both the local community and the larger American community. As one student life professional mentioned, "It's a humungous health care cost issue in America, STDs and unwanted pregnancies and what not."⁴⁸

A similar, second example involved allowing a mosque on campus. In the name of service to their Muslim neighbor students they set up a mosque on campus, because the closest mosque was down in Rochester, and their small group of Muslim students was having trouble getting to the required Friday prayers. Interestingly, resistance to the idea from some quarters was seen as concern that "St. Olaf is sort of losing its Norwegian identity." One administrator noted that what the college is actually affirming its roots since, "It was founded by people whose parents didn't speak English, who were at the margins in society who were often discriminated against."⁴⁹ Of course, it also raised questions about the Christian identity of the institution. As one administrator admitted, "It's an identity issue for St. Olaf right now, we're a Christian college, we're a college of the church, we take that seriously, but here we've got some other people who practice their faith quite differently than ours." As one administrator noted, at St. Olaf the calling to service is what triumphs, "That's sort of a story that helps understand this idea of what mission and faith and moral education—how that actually plays out in college corporate life. Bunch of kids who want to pray, we're going to go and find a mosque for them."⁵⁰

In contrast to this ethical approach that placed less emphasis upon theological particularity, the comprehensive and theological nature of Calvin's moral education allowed it to respond to what could be controversial campus conversations in a way that integrated their Christian Reformed tradition and identity, the faculty, the curriculum and the co-curricular. One faculty member described an example of an approach to one of their controversial issues:

We showed the movie Fahrenheit 9/11. Why do we do that? This is a partisan movie, this is Michael Moore, and he's whatever.... We think it's important to expose students to these things and we talk about, well that's being driven by our vision of Reformed worldview.... We had reviews printed from opposing positions, one more affirming of the direction Michael Moore took, one less so. So we wanted them to be reading those, and we made them available for them to read before. And then we had two professors who just did a marvelous job afterwards, from different points of view in fact, but they both picked this piece of art, called Fahrenheit 9/11 and they just started pulling it apart and shining lights on different corners of it and saying this is a good thing that was being said, here's a bad way it was being told, this truth, this untruth whatever. So I think students walked out of there having evidence in front of them with these two professors, you just can't walk out and simply say, "That was good or that was bad." It was both. It was good and bad. You know what, that's the way it is with music and poetry and visual art and church sermons and hymns. There's good and bad because there's sin woven through and there's grace woven through, so you've got to do the hard work of tearing it apart.[51]

It is interesting to compare this response to what we heard at St. Olaf about condom distribution. Instead of having faculty at St. Olaf committed to the tradition, perhaps with some difference of views, explore and discuss the issue with students in a theological context, these incidents were not necessarily seen as learning opportunities to be addressed within the theological framework of the institution. Instead of approaching each incident with the understanding, "There's good and bad because there's sin woven through and there's grace woven through, so you've got to do the hard work of tearing it apart," it was not clear St. Olaf exposed the idea of placing condom distribution machines in the residence halls to a rigorous theological examination.

It is also interesting to compare how one of the Mere Christian Ethics schools approached controversy to the other two types of schools mentioned above. In this example, George Fox University leaders drew upon theological particularity without necessarily making it a determining guide to the outcome. They discussed how the pacifist and social activist dimensions of its Quaker tradition sometimes created conflict with some evangelicals who are not pacifists.

Our Quaker ethos gives us a strong sense of social justice.... The war in Iraq is a classic example, we had quite a discussion on our campus because several of our faculty and students were opposed to the war in

Iraq because of the Quaker ethos and peacemaking and stuff. We also had a number of faculty/staff and students who were in favor of wanting to support the troops and we had a special chapel where it was really a time of prayer for the whole situation and we had a person from the Christian peacemaking team share, we also had a former armed forces vet share, and we had an international student share from an international perspective and then we gave students the opportunity to write cards either to Iraqi families and children that would be delivered through Christian peacemaking teams or to write letters to the troops and/or to do both if they so desired....It wasn't as though there was this great division, I think it was great conversation both ways.[52]

Interestingly, dissonance, at least in certain areas, may be productively produced at Mere Christian Ethics schools between the moral tradition of an original sponsoring denomination or group (e.g., Quakers) and a wider Christian tradition (e.g., evangelical Protestantism). Certainly, in these examples cited, theological particularity did not produce moral indoctrination but instead added a critical theological perspective to moral discussions within a particular Christian tradition.

Conclusion

Universities with a whole range of moral orientations do not need to abandon their identities to ensure autonomy and critical thinking with regard to moral education. Instead, such identities should help students come to terms with the nature of the moral commitments linked to their own and the universities identity and critically evaluate both of them. This exercise would help students realize the complexity of the moral order created by humans, and it would also help students understand the nature and costs of identity commitments. For example, students contemplating commitment to the Air Force Academy must understand the intellectual, emotional, and behavioral aspects of being an officer in the U.S. Air Force. Only then can they truly understand what a commitment would require. Merely sitting in classes to learn about that commitment would distort the nature of it. Similarly, one should expect Christian colleges and universities to engage in a similar form of moral formation. Christian commitment does not involve merely cognitive assent but entry into a way of living.

In the final two chapters, we will move beyond describing and defending the necessity of approaches to moral education rooted in comprehensive identity traditions to setting forth ways to strengthen such approaches within one particular identity tradition. Again, we will not presume to be able to speak to everyone about this matter, and as a result, we will be speaking primarily to the community of Christian colleges and universities. Nonetheless we hope others will find our suggestions engaging and provocative.

Part III

Strengthening the Moral Tradition of Christian Humanism

Chapter Nine

Christian Humanism and Christ-Centered Education: The Redemptive Development of Humans and Human Creations

...the old education...may be summed up by stating that the center of gravity is outside the child. It is in the teacher, the textbook, anywhere and everywhere you please except in the immediate instincts and activities of the child himself...Now the change which is coming into our education is the shifting of the center of gravity. It is a change, a revolution, not unlike that introduced by Copernicus when the astronomical center shifted from the earth to the sun. In this case the child becomes the sun about which the appliances of education revolve; he is the center about which they are organized.

—John Dewey[1]

To speak of Christ-*centered* liberal arts education is to make the claim that Jesus is the centerpiece of all human knowledge, the reference point for all our experience. It directs our attention to the only One who can serve as the centerpiece of an entire curriculum, the One to whom we must relate everything and without whom no fact, no theory, no subject matter can be fully appreciated.

—Duane Litfin[2]

Among Protestant colleges and universities, especially those associated with the evangelical movement, much as been written about the integration of faith and learning.[3] In fact, integration language and the implied task have become the hallmark of serious Christian institutions. For instance, David Dockery writes, "The integration of faith and learning is the distinctive characteristic of Christian higher education."[4] Despite the important contributions of the project, however, we believe the *language* of "integration of faith and learning" does not prove helpful when considering the overall purpose of Christian higher education or the moral development of Christian students. Our conclusion stems not from past or recent critiques of the integration *model.*[5] In fact, we think the recent criticisms largely miss the mark and at times misrepresent the diversity of those approaches which adopt the language. Instead, we are more concerned with the habits of thinking that such language may foster when considering the overall purpose of Christian higher education and Christian moral education than with the general integration model (which we will largely defend). Thus, in this chapter, we propose an alternative language that we believe provides a more helpful way to articulate the moral purposes of Christian higher education. We then go on to discuss what this language might mean for the development of Christian identity in students.

Rethinking the Integration of Faith and Learning

Various definitions of what the "integration of faith and learning" involves have been offered. William Hasker provides one such definition:

> Faith-learning integration may be briefly described as a scholarly project whose goal is to develop integral relationships which exist between the Christian faith and human knowledge, particularly as expressed in the various academic disciplines. Here the terms faith and knowledge are taken quite broadly; in speaking of "the Christian faith" we are focusing on the cognitive content of faith.... Integration is concerned with integral relationships between faith and knowledge, the relationships which inherently exist between the content of the faith and the subject matter of this or that discipline.[6]

The project Hasker describes has spawned vast literature base which "has as its primary objective the integration of Christian faith and learning on both the intra- and inter-disciplinary levels."[7] In addition, the language has been adopted by institutes or centers at universities such as Baylor,[8] Pepperdine,[9] and Whitworth.[10]

What we find striking about the phrase "integration of faith and learning" is the absence of what John Dewey, in the quote cited above, believes should be central. The learner is missing. The current language focuses upon integration as something performed with knowledge in disciplines and not something that needs to be incorporated into the overall lives of students (as well as faculty). Although we agree with Duane Litfin that Christian universities should retain their "Christ-centered approach" and reject placing the center of educational gravity in the student, we believe Christian universities may still have something to learn from Dewey in this regard. For example, faith-learning integration, as Hasker describes the task, focuses upon scholarly results and not necessarily upon the lives of students. As an academic project taking place at colleges and universities and in journals such as *Christian Scholar's Review* and *Intégrité: A Faith Learning Journal*, we find this emphasis understandable. Nonetheless, we find an odd absence of reference to students in some discussions about Christian colleges and universities that we believe needs to be addressed.[11]

To address our concern, Christian colleges and universities could talk about the integration of faith, learning, and the learner. However, we want to suggest an alternative language that we believe captures the important theological mission of Christian universities, directly addresses the moral mission of Christian institutions with regard to their students, and consequently broadens the task of Christian educators to include the development of students. Education within the Christian metanarrative, we suggest, should seek to provide a broader and more unifying goal. Instead of talking about integrating faith and learning, we submit that the Christian academic vocation should be placed within the larger purpose of the Church which involves the *redemptive development of humans and human creations.*

We use the terms "human and human creations" because we believe other options may reduce the mission of schools. For example, Christian colleges and universities could specify their mission as the redemptive development of students and scholarship. The problem with this approach is that it reduces the aims of the college to a narrow aspect of human identity (e.g., student) and a narrow professional practice (producing learning). In contrast, we believe the aims of and language within Christian higher education must always resist becoming too narrow and should always be considered in light of the larger mission of a particular Christian tradition as embodied by the worshipping community of the Church.

We choose the words "redemptive development" for a number of reasons. First, we believe human development needs to be understood within the Christian story and not as some sort of objective view from nowhere. According to this view of development, both nature and culture can be good expressions of God's developing creation. Consider the biblical understanding of creation described by Al Wolters:

> Creation is not something that, once made, remains a static quantity. There is, as it were, a growing up (though not in a biological sense), an unfolding of creation. This takes place through the task that people

have been given of bringing to fruition the possibilities of development implicit in the work of God's hands. The given reality of the created order is such that it is possible to have schools and industry, printing, rocketry, needlepoint and chess.... We are called to engage in the ongoing creational work of God, to be God's helper in executing to the end the blueprint for his masterpiece.[12]

In this respect, the Christian interest in the development of students, knowledge and institutions shares parallels with the developmental interests of others in the larger academy. The academy is fundamentally built upon the idea that there can be progress or growth in humans, human knowledge, and human society that can be aided by the educational process.

We add the word "redemptive" because as we discussed in chapter one, development always occurs within the context of a larger metanarrative about the world that contains ideals about how we measure progress in any developmental metanarrative. Redemptive development makes clear that something happened to the original condition of humanity that resulted in problems with development (i.e., the fallenness of humanity and the world corrupts the developmental process). In this respect, something must occur to restore the developmental process to its original direction.

Due to the fall of the whole world, the redemption of development must take place (i.e., freeing God's creation as well as human creations from the bondage of the fall). Christ accomplished this redemption by restoring God's reign (the Kingdom of God). We are also asked to join in that work. As Al Wolters writes, "Humankind, which has botched its original mandate and the whole creation with it, is given another chance in Christ; we are reinstated as God's managers on earth. The original good creation is to be restored."[13] This restoration or redemption involves not only humans. Wolters notes:

> Scripturally, the kingdom is about God's reign over the entire creation; the kingdom stresses the all-encompassing nature of the salvation Jesus embodied, announced and accomplished. The gospel is the power of God through which the exalted Christ, on the basis of his death and resurrection, restores *all of life* by his Spirit to be subject to his authority and word.[14]

For example, when it comes to the human creation of scholarship, the redemption of scholarship entails freeing it from the effects of sin since our learning faculties and created products are fallen. Such redemption must take place not only at the personal or cognitive level—"the renewing of our minds" to which Rom. 12:2 refers and to which some Christian scholars focus the task of higher education[15]— but it also involves seeking to renew or redeem fallen scholarly products, theories, et cetera.

The major advantage of rearticulating Christian higher education's task as the redemptive development of humans and human creations is that this language communicates the Christian scholar's highest calling to imitate the model and actions of the Triune God. Theologically speaking, we do not believe God goes about integrating faith and learning. Our need to integrate faith and learning stems not from our imitation of God's actions in the world, but from our human limitations—our lack of omniscience and our fallenness. Biblically speaking, however, God continually engages in the business of developing and also redeeming his fallen creation. By understanding our task as the redemptive development of humans and human creations, Christian academics will undertake a sacred task—one of imitating and joining in on the actions embodied by the Triune God. It is then that those in Christian in higher education truly become image bearers of God in their vocation. The rest of this chapter and the final chapter unpack what we believe this purpose would involve for various dimensions of university life.[16]

Redemptive Development and the Cultivation of Christian Identity in Students

Focusing upon the redemptive development of humans and human creations would require a shift in the current conversation regarding Christian higher education. Most scholarship in the field of Christian higher education over the past decade addresses the task of preserving and fostering the Christian identity of Christian colleges.[17] Few talk directly about the role of enriching a student's Christian identity, particularly with regard to moral education.

One of the few books that discusses the overall cultivation of moral identity in students is Arthur Holmes' *Shaping Character*.[18] The topic of moral identity is the last one Holmes addresses, and in only four brief pages he outlines the relationship of moral identity to moral character, a general Christian understanding of identity, and some general suggestions for forming students' moral identity. For instance, he suggests that the study of literature fosters reflection upon the moral identity and that the modeling of teachers and the act of worship all help order one's loves and give coherence to one's identity.

We contend that the formation of Christian identity should be the first consideration and not the last when thinking about moral education in Christian colleges. Our rationale stems from the example of how Biblical writers approached the topic. Ethical instruction in the New Testament epistles is largely left to the latter half of a letter that first lays out a theological perspective regarding Christian identity and belief.[19] These writers understood that one's fundamental identity and the larger metanarrative in which an individual's or community's identity is understood influences how one conceives of ethical ends, principles, virtues, practices, and the reasons one may find for adopting them.

Understandings of Identity and Identity Formation

In Holmes' description of the relationship between identity and moral character, he notes that there are two basic schools of philosophical thought about how best to understand identity. The first, with roots in the work of John Locke, understands personal identity as dependent upon one's experience and memory. The second, with roots in the work of G.W.F. Hegel, stresses the social nature of personal identity. This second approach emphasizes that one can only understand one's identity in relationship to others. In other words, a person understands who he or she is through his or her role as a child, a parent, a spouse, a sibling, an employee, a citizen and so on. Willem Wardekker and Siebren Miedema present an understanding of identity that incorporates both streams while seeing the latter approach as the dominant one:

> On this view, identity is the way we explain, in the form of a life story (autobiography), the choices we make in our commitments, and their consistency, to others and to ourselves. The advantage of this model over others is that it does not posit the individual as the sole creator of its [sic] own self-concept. Individual stories are created through the use of story schemata, genres, motives, metaphors, examples, and other elements that are found in culture. (It is exactly the use of such cultural elements that makes an individual's story comprehensible to others and to the self.) Moreover, other people play a role in the construction process: as audience, as people to relate the story to, as co-constructors.[20]

As Wardekker and Miedema make clear, according to this view one cannot even make or retell individual memories without reference to the social relationships and schema that culture provides and others understand.

Beyond the two philosophical schools of thought described by Holmes, we would also add a third approach to this group. Well-known studies addressing higher education and identity use elements of these first two approaches, but they also draw heavily from psychological theories that emphasize the affective realm.[21] These popular psychological views of identity draw upon Erik Erikson's work. According to Erikson, people go through eight different types of psychosocial development in which they attempt to achieve stable ways of feeling about themselves in various affective and cognitive categories. As a result, the primary task of adolescents and young adults involves the stabilization of identity.[22]

An example of an approach that draws primarily upon Erikson's work, as well as the other strands, is Arthur Chickering's well-known view of identity. He understands developing identity as achieving resolution about the following issues:

(1) comfort with body and appearance; (2) comfort with gender and sexual orientation; (3) sense of self in social, historical, and cultural context; (4) clarification of self-concept through roles and life-style; (5) sense of self in response to feedback from valued others; (6) self-acceptance and self-esteem; and (7) personal stability and integration.[23]

As can be seen from the above list, most of the categories deal with affective states such as "comfort," although some facets, such as one's "sense of self in social, historical, and cultural context" clearly draw from the second philosophical approach previously mentioned. Moreover, how or whether one finds comfort with certain aspects of one's identity or understands one's self-esteem will involve the metanarratives we tell about ourselves.

A Christian View of Identity

Holmes argues that a Christian view of identity would favor the second, more relational account. We would concur, although we also believe it would incorporate some elements of all these approaches. Descriptively, we agree with Wardekker and Miedema's basic point that individuals primarily understand their individual and collective identities in the form of narratives. While one's individual or communal identity may involve one in certain practices (e.g., being a Texan and eating Beef Brisket or being a Hoosier and eating Pork Tenderloin), there is much more to one's identity. In other words, whether it is one's personal name (e.g., John), family name (e.g., Doe), one's ethnic identity (German-Norwegian, African-American), national identity (e.g., American, Canadian), gender (e.g., male or female), religious identity (e.g., Christian, Jew), professional identity (e.g., doctor, bricklayer, landscaper), family identity (e.g., child, parent, sibling), or another form of identity, all of these aspects of identity have stories attached to them. One of the predominant ways we understand what it means to be an American, for example, concerns not only learning the ideas in the United States Constitution or participating in certain practices (e.g., voting for a president), but also engaging in conversations and disagreements about what those ideas mean in practice. Through learning and creating narratives about these struggles we understand the core of our identity.[24]

We also would agree with Chickering that one's personal struggle both to understand these identities and order any ethical demands associated with them will entail affective struggle. Yet, even when people encounter tensions or discomfort regarding some portion of their identity, they often relate how they resolved these tensions in the form of a personal or communal narrative.[25]

Regarding this basic understanding, there is little that is distinctively Christian about our approach. What makes a Christian understanding of identity unique, we believe, is that it posits a normative ideal for how one should understand and order one's identities. In other words, we believe Christians should disagree with Wardekker and Miedema's conclusion that "there is no such thing as the 'right' outcome"[26] with regard to identity formation. By contrast, we argue that an essential claim of the Christian tradition is that one's Christian identity is one's most important and fundamental identity over and above other identities (e.g., national, ethnic, familial, vocational, etc.). In fact, one can only properly understand oneself and these other identities in light of one's Christian identity and the Christian story that gives meaning to that identity. This story posits that humans are made in the image of God and therefore only find their proper end or telos in proper relationship to God. Although humans became alienated from God, they may now recover what it means to live as image bearers of God through Jesus Christ. In fact, one aspect of conversion basically involves placing one's individual life narrative within the context of God's story and the stories told by God's people.[27] It is through these stories that one learns about the character of the Triune God and God's redemptive action in the world.

Augustine provides a significant example, not only of a Christian whose conversion story involves the adoption of God's story, but also of a Christian thinker who understood the connection of his personal identity stories to the moral life. Augustine noted that an essential feature of the moral life involves ordering one's loves.[28] One of the primary ways that a person orders his or her loves is by understanding his or her various identities and then ordering them according to their importance. For Christians, discovering one's true identity, as a human made in the image of God, allows us to discover what should be of ultimate importance to us and what should possibly be of penultimate importance. For example, Christians are to love God first and then, in turn, love God's creation second.

Moreover, understanding oneself as made in the image of God has other important moral implications. Particular virtues become important to acquire because they help order one's desires and one's identities toward these ends. One can only properly bear the image of God when one imitates the character qualities of the Triune God in whose image we are made (love, holiness, justice, patience). When we acquire God's virtues, we bear God's image. In other words, if one believes humans are made in God's image, one needs to acquire the qualities that fulfill his or her originally created capacities to complete the Imago Dei and become fully human.

Cultivating Humanity in the Christian College or University: The Great Identities

In light of this approach to identity, Christian colleges and universities interested in cultivating the redemptive development of humans make the bold claim that, when it comes to their primary meta-identity, they know who students are and that they have a rather extensive responsibility for nurturing their humanity in light of this identity.

In this regard our student-centered approach diverges significantly from Dewey's child-centered approach in which the child's interests played a formative role in determining the course of study. Robert Maynard Hutchins' words reflect our own sentiment regarding Dewey's approach:

> The child-centered school may be attractive to the child, and no doubt is useful as a place in which the little ones may release their inhibitions and hence behave better at home. But educators cannot permit

the students to dictate the course of study unless they are prepared to confess that they are nothing but chaperons, supervising an aimless, trial-and-error process which is chiefly valuable because it keeps young people from doing something worse.[29]

Hutchins believed that a general education curriculum focused on great texts would be the best approach. More recent proposals, such as the one mentioned earlier by Kronman, also take this view. While we believe there are strengths to approaches such as the Great Texts, we actually think it would be more helpful to focus on the student instead of a particular curriculum or "great texts." However, instead of focusing upon student interests, which Dewey and other Progressives did, we suggest the redemptive development of humanity requires focusing on the "great normative identities" of young people with Christianity serving as the meta-identity. Richard Foster's quote below reflects this kind of focus:

> As apprentices of Jesus we are learning, always learning how to live well; love God well; love our spouse well; raise our children well; love our friends and neighbors—and even our enemies—well, study well; face adversity well; run our businesses and financial institutions well; form community life well; reach out to those on the margins well; and die well—*ars moiendi*.[30]

Foster observes that we are engaged in figuring out how to perfect our various identities and the moral obligations that are attached to those identities. In all of these areas there are different normative ideals associated with competing narratives, ends, virtues, principles, wisdom, models, et cetera. We would suggest that a more human education will focus upon the following two sets of human identities:

- Christian identity: Loving our Creator and Redeemer
  - Salvation history, Worship and Theology
  - Embodying the love: Worship and Church history
- Creational identities: Loving God's creation:
  - Student
  - Friends, Neighbors, and Enemies
  - Family
  - Citizenship
  - Race, class, and gender
  - Stewardship (money, the nonhuman world, and one's own body)

We believe there are a number of advantages to this approach. First, the categories make it quite clear how the Christian university will both order its loves and thus, in turn, cultivate humanity. Christian universities acknowledge that they are trying to form good human beings and that this task should be approached from a particular moral tradition. Moreover, it involves unpacking what it means to be a good student, friend, citizen, man, or woman, and steward of natural and created resources in light of a particular metanarrative. Second, this approach builds bridges between theory and practice in ways that integrate faith with the identities of students. Third, it provides a way to both order and integrate the curricular and co-curricular dimensions of the university. Fourth, it draws upon identities that are common to all humans everywhere. In fact, the basics of this idea find commonalities with the secular humanism discussed by Kronman in that it identifies one of the tasks of general education as being "to identity the elements of our common human nature and to help us understand the consequences that flow from them."[31] The humans entering universities will all be students, friends, neighbors, members of families, citizens, members of a gender, racial, and ethnic group, stewards of money, the nonhuman world and their own bodies. Finally, it recognizes the university's responsibility to help students think about their future commitments more deeply and in more complex ways. One of the problems with William Perry's theory is that it talks about commitment in general and fails to differentiate among the different types of commitment that students inevitably must make in relation to their different identities. It refers to the intellectual development of students as proceeding toward a general form of commitment that lumps many different forms of commitment together. We need to differentiate between the different types of commitments that students will be making and then help students explore the normative conversations and obligation related to those commitments in less dualistic and more complex ways

Loving Our Creator and Redeemer

Worship in the Christian Story

One of the fundamental premises of Christian higher education revolves around the reality articulated by Philip Kenneson, "Every human life is an embodied argument about what things are worth doing, who or what is worthy of attention, who or what is worthy of allegiance and sacrifice, and what projects or endeavors are worthy of human energies. In short, every human life is 'bent' toward something. Every human life is an act of worship."[32] Augustine's confession to God that "you have made us for yourself, and our heart is restless until it rests in you" articulates the foundation of Christian identity.[33] Christian universities understand humans as created for the worship and love of God. In this respect, worship plays an instrumental role in helping us find our true selves. Kenneson expands upon this point:

> In gathering to worship, the *ekklesia* opens itself up to receive the proper orientation to all that is, in order that it might live in that world in ways consonant with the reign of the triune God. In gathering to pay attention to the right things, to speak the truth, and to adopt the proper posture toward God and the world, the *ekklesia* opens itself up to being formed into the kind of people who can glorify and enjoy God forever.[34]

Numerous elements of worship, such as gathering to meet God and one another, re-encountering the Christian story, and participating in its embodiment and re-enactment through ordinances or sacraments such as baptism and the communion, play roles in this process.[35] For instance, Jim Foder identifies one way that listening to the Christian story in the context of a worship service serves to form the moral order of a people and institution:

> It is in the liturgy...that Christians are schooled and exercised in the scriptural logic of their faith; here desires are cleansed, realigned, and given concentrated focus. Indeed, the repetition and regularity with which the faithful gather to listen to God's Word serves to collect, arrange, position, and coordinate the entire spectrum of practices and habits that comprise Christian life.[36]

In this manner, worship in the academy plays the central and definitive role in shaping the identities and schooling the desires of both faculty and students.

It can also foster redemptive development in ways the Church may currently neglect. First, worship can and should make room for doubt. Unfortunately, contemporary worship as practiced by most Christian faiths and the formative worship discussed by Christian ethicists[37] neglects this Biblical aspect of worship. If the Psalms are a model of corporate worship which can also be ethically formative, which most Christians would agree they are, one finds that a fifth of the Psalms are what are known as laments. They are, in large measure, petitions to God about injustice. Worship, especially for college age students, needs to make room for the doubt and frustration with God that they may experience. The result of such expression is the foundation for growth in terms of one's Christian identity. Second, part of Christian worship in an academic community involves exposing students to the variety of practices that Christians observe in the worship of God within the Christian tradition, although this diversity will vary and may also be defined by the denominational tradition of the college.

As revealed from our interviews at some campuses, particularly St. Olaf, and our own experiences of teaching higher education courses related to student services, one of the central questions that faces Christian colleges and universities that also admit non-Christians involves how to work with non-Christians and non-Christian forms of worship on campus. We believe this question goes to the heart of the identity of an institution. Since a Christian university is not a liberal democracy that seeks to profess no particular religious identity, models of religious liberty suited for the nation-state should not be applied to a college campus. Instead, Christian campuses need to develop a theological response to non-Christian religions rooted in language different from the liberal-democratic tradition.

The best guidelines from the Christian tradition stem from the Biblical concept of hospitality toward the stranger. Hosts have serious moral responsibilities. David Smith and Barbara Carville provide a helpful description of these responsibilities when someone different visits one's home space:

> Simply throwing one's home open without serving as host is not enough. Giving notice that the house is vacant and available to anyone who cares to use it is not hospitality. Neither is it particularly hospitable to pretend one's home is perfect and to ignore the presence of disrepair that could harm our guest....As hosts, we are called to lament and grieve what is inhuman, unjust, broken, and destructive in our society. We also must acknowledge both our own participation in the wrongs around us. Listening to the guest's perspective may make us want to change some aspects of our home that, until then, had seemed normal to us. This, too, is part of what it means to have a hospitable home. We are to both accept and take responsibility for who we are.[38]

Clearly, Christian colleges and universities, by virtue of their very identity, bear the responsibility of being hospitable to those who do not profess that identity.

The question of whether a guest's requests to set up worship spaces in one's home, however, raises significant concerns. We believe that this also is why the home metaphor is more appropriate for the university than the public square metaphor. When guests start to believe that the Christian university should be treated the same way as the public square, the Christian university begins to lose its distinct purpose and identity. In homes as in universities, especially around meals, education, dialog, and mutual understanding take place. Nonetheless, there is a clear understanding that one should not demand that this home become like one's own home or place. As a result, hiring policies in places such as Calvin College make sense in that the institution requires all of the members of its community to attend a Reformed Church and enroll their respective children in Reformed schools. Such moves, while deemed restrictive by some, are ways that the Calvin community seeks to foster an appreciation for its unique understanding of the Christian story.

The Curriculum—God, God's Story and God's People

Scholars who study the shape of the curriculum now acknowledge that matters of identity enhancement or understanding have always served as a major educational purpose and thus should be a major component of the curriculum. As Frederick Rudolph observed, curriculum "has been one of those places where we have told ourselves who we are."[39] For example, early in their history, public schools began to inculcate a sense of national identity. As William Reid notes, curriculum did not attempt to provide universal, objective knowledge. Instead, "Curriculum became a place where people would tell themselves what it meant to be American, to be English, to be German, and so on."[40] Thus, public schools not only teach about their nation's constitution, but they also require courses about national history, including the significant turning points that shaped the nation's identity. Likewise, it is largely for this reason that most colleges or universities see it as perfectly reasonable to teach American Constitutional Law in ways that preclude challenges to the Constitution and focus instead on the various traditions of constitutional interpretation. These courses cultivate American identity by orienting academic conversations.

We contend that within a Christian college or university that the curriculum should not only enhance students' understanding of their various identities, especially their Christian identity, but it should also model a way to order one's loves in relation to these identities. To affirm a college's or university's Christian identity, as Stanley Hauerwas notes, "is nothing other than the claim that certain past and present conversation partners are crucial for this community to know what is its good. To say that an institution is Christian is to say that certain matters cannot be left out of the conversation if we are to know better what it means to be Christian. Thus, it might be expected that the curriculum of a college that claims Christian identity would look different than those that do not."[41] One of the most obvious ways the curriculum should differ is that a Christian college or university should acknowledge that the Christian identity will be more fundamental than American or professional identities when ordering and arranging the curriculum. Such an understanding and ordering entails helping students live and think about their own stories, first and foremost, in light of Christianity's story and the community that embodies it, the Church.

Interestingly, few scholars in Christian higher education address this issue. Holmes makes only a short reference to curricular matters, such as how historical and literary characters can aid one in thinking about moral identity.[42] We suspect that when it comes to thinking through the matter of Christian identity and moral formation at the curricular level, more work needs to be done. As Stanley Hauerwas once noted, "When asked what makes [a college] Christian, administrators appeal to campus atmosphere or the convictions of those teaching. But what is not clear is how those convictions, which no doubt are often quite real and genuine, make a difference for the shape of the curriculum and/or the actual content of the courses."[43]

In light of our understanding of identity and the fact that the curriculum necessarily communicates an understanding about particular identities and how those various identities should be valued, we believe Christian colleges and universities should help students enhance and order their identities in at least two ways. First, they should employ one of their most common methods of helping students enhance the understanding of a particular identity—teaching the stories and facilitating the practices associated with that form of identity. Thus, one should expect Christian colleges and universities to teach, not only basic doctrine and practices, but also the stories of God's work in the world and the stories associated with the Christian Church.

Second, we believe that they should model to students what it would mean to order their identities by valuing knowledge of Christian identity stories above all other identity stories. After all, contemporary colleges and universities recognize that to offer a course with attention to a particular ethnic group's history (e.g., women, African-Americans, Latinos) is to demonstrate a value judgment toward that group's story and identity. Christian colleges and universities should be no different. These institutions should teach students to understand themselves first and foremost as Christians. As a result, students need to know the stories of the Christian Church first and foremost—even more than the story of their particular nation (e.g., U.S. history), the particular story of an ethnic group (e.g., the story of Dutch Americans, German Americans or African Americans), or even the general story of humanity (e.g., world history). The most obvious way this might occur would be to require that all students study Biblical narratives (a rather common approach that unfortunately, in our opinion, too often uses "scientific" methods), but also narratives about the Church (a less common approach).

Theology

The theology faculty would prove particularly important in this work. We use the term theology faculty for a specific reason. Religion departments are a symptom of the identity confusion at colleges and universities. In other disciplines, it is quite clear what sort of identity formation is taking place. History classes attempt to form historians, psychology classes introduce students to the practice of psychology, and in biology classes students are taught to be biologists. Religion classes, however, do not try to teach students to be religious. As C. John Sommerville notes, teaching religion "is rather like learning Language without learning any particular language."[44]

In fact, the measure of where a Protestant university or college is on its path toward secularization is often best discerned by looking at the name of the department that deals with "God stuff." You will find a variety of names such as "Bible," "Christian Studies," 'Religion," and "Religious Studies." Perhaps the "Christian Studies Department" would be an appropriate title. "Studies" reveals only the subject and tells you nothing about the methods used, although "studies" departments usually fall into the ideological advocacy of the causes associated with a particular identity (think African American studies, feminist studies, or queer studies).

While Christian Studies departments may seek to enrich one's Christian identity, by what method do they do so? Teaching someone to be a Christian involves acknowledgement of a previous commitment to Christianity and engagement in the life of the Church and in spiritual disciplines such as worship and prayer. This difficulty reflects the problem with religion departments at Christian universities, and all universities, for that matter. They are built on the assumption that religion can be studied without involving a commitment to become a particular type of person who engages in particular practices. Instead, they merely ask the student to commit to the methods of some other discipline. In this respect, religion departments are adverse to that form of commitment.

We would suggest that Christian universities should be committed to the teaching and practice of theology as the language of the Church. The Oxford English Dictionary calls a theologian "One who is versed in theology," which is the study of "God, His nature and attributes, and His relations with man and the universe."[45] The theologian makes a fundamental commitment to study God and God's relationship to us. Such study, by its very nature, requires avoiding the methodological atheism or agnosticism that is theoretically associated with "scientific" methods in other disciplines. In contrast, religion scholars in religion departments, while perhaps including God as an object of study, usually take their methods from other disciplines and the methods usually require some sort of methodological atheism or agnosticism. Not surprisingly, the methodological atheism or agnosticism of these methods does not mix well with the study of God. Certainly, serious Christian universities should rename their religion departments and educate students to be theologians. At the very least, students taking courses from the theology department would know what the professors are trying to make of them as people.

Church History

We also believe every Christian university and college should require church history since it merely extends the Christian identity story. Of course, some questions can and should be raised about this recommendation. Whose Christian history will be taught—Catholic, Protestant, or Orthodox? Moreover, various Christian colleges and universities are part of specific traditions with specific stories both at the larger level (e.g., Catholic, Protestant, and Orthodox) and at the denominational level (Baptist, Methodist, Quaker, Dutch Reformed, etc.). They will all tell the story differently and wish to emphasize their particular identity. How should these stories be told?

Granted, we recognize that any telling of the story of the Church, like any identity story, will be a contentious one told by particular actors in a particular time. Depending upon which individual or community is telling the story, the teller or tellers may leave certain groups and elements out of the story while also emphasizing certain other elements. What we merely want to argue is that making the conversation about the telling of the Christian identity story the most important identity conversation is an important curricular commitment of a Christian college or university.[46] In fact, the identity stories and conversations that a particular college or university requires or offers indicate how the institution seeks to form its students.

If an institution merely allows students to choose what stories they would like to learn, it also reflects a particular view of identity more closely akin to Enlightenment liberalism. In such a situation, the administration allows students to construct their own identities by individual choice. When and if Christian identity is considered in light of the curriculum, it becomes another identity choice. For example, some Catholic institutions have developed Catholic studies departments similar to the way universities developed women's or ethnic studies departments.[47] While these departments provide help for a self-selected group of students who wish to enhance their Catholic identity, they also communicate that the Christian identity is merely one of a number of identities that the college or university values and wants a student to explore. By contrast, we contend that a Christian university should order its curriculum so that the priority of the Christian identity is communicated to all students.

Case Study: The Story of the Church in the Curriculum

In order to see how our theoretical recommendations regarding church history might square with reality, we decided to discover what types of religion, history, and other interdisciplinary classes the 156 Christian colleges and universities we studied in chapter seven require of all students. We chose religion, history, and interdisciplinary classes because we wanted to discern the degree to which Christian colleges and universities seek to expose students to historically based identity narratives. We also wanted to test a hypothesis. We suspected that Christian colleges and universities are probably more likely to require students to gain knowledge of the American or Western story than the post-biblical Christian story. In this way, they may be more apt to reinforce and inform their students' American or Western identity than their Christian identity.[48]

In our study of 156 Christian colleges and universities, we found that 44 schools (28 percent) required students to take a course to help them understand the story of Western civilization and thus their Western identity, and 30 schools (19 percent) required students to learn about the American story to understand their American identity. Amazingly, only 20 (13 percent) required students to learn post-biblical stories of the Christian Church.

In light of our findings, we recommend that Christian universities and colleges should teach the Christian story in a way that includes post-biblical church history. Faculty who may be frustrated that students tend to think of themselves as United States citizens or Westerners first and Christians second should recognize that education at most institutions reinforces this tendency. As a result, their general requirements are more effective at teaching the American or Western story and identity than the larger Christian story and identity. Yet, as John Howard Yoder writes:

> ...the ultimate meaning of history will not be found in the course of earthly empires or the development of proud cultures, but in the calling together of the 'chosen race, royal priesthood, holy nation,' which is the church of Christ.... The meaning of history—and therefore the significance of the state—lies in the creation and the work of the church.[49]

If Christians want to affirm Yoder's claim, it is critical that Christian students understand the story of both their particular tradition and its place in the larger Christian tradition more than the American or Western story.

Ideally, we believe that if Christian schools have any history requirement, they should require a course in church history. Such a course would be similar to that offered by Eastern Mennonite University which seeks "to form a biblically-based prophetic, theological, and ethical perspective of the Christian heritage and identity." It would seek to foster both an understanding and appreciation of the broad Christian community's various stories and the story of the particular tradition.[50]

Conclusion

We suggest that the transmission of the Christian tradition must take place in a more transformative manner than most Christian colleges and universities recognize and practice. It should involve the redemptive development of humans and human creations. One aspect of redemptive development for the Christian college would involve the development of approaches that would "try to offer to its students opportunities and help in the process of learning to construct and maintain an identity story."[51] The final goal of transformation is not only for students to learn the Christian story, but also to practice the story of the Christian Church as their primary communal and individual identity. The Christian college or university should model what it means to order the importance of one's identities and thus order one's loves by integrating as much as possible the ideals offered in the curricular arena with the ideals of the co-curricular arena. Even if the transmission of the Christian story does take place in classes, colleges and universities ask too little of students out-of-class. Very few have any requirements beyond simply living on campus and abstaining from certain behaviors. However, how might things look if the policies and practices in residence life mirror the expectations students receive in their Church history courses? For example, given the Anabaptist tradition's strong emphasis on reconciliation, what would it look like if policies related to roommate conflict or judicial hearing mirrored these ideals? At some schools, such as Eastern Mennonite, this possibility approaches reality. At too many other schools, a great disjunction exists between the ideals of the curricular and the co-curricular.

A Christian or Christ-centered moral education, we argue, requires that this vision for developing human beings involves the ordering and informing of one's loves with regard to one's various human identities. This chapter focused upon how Christian colleges and universities can cultivate the foundational ordering love and identity. Chapter ten then addresses how Christian colleges and universities can help students explore the whole range of human identities in light of the Christian identity.

Chapter Ten

A More Human Christian Education: Cultivating and Ordering the Great Identities

When I was a child, I talked like a child, I thought like a child, I reasoned like a child. When I became a man, I put childish things behind me. Now we see but a poor reflection as in a mirror, then we shall see face to face. Now I know in part, then I shall know fully, even as I am fully known. And now these three remain: faith, hope and love. But the greatest of these is love.

—I Corinthians 13:11–12

We suggested in the last chapter that Christian colleges and universities should seek the redemptive development of humans and human creations. This vision of Christian humanism would mean that an institution's moral purpose would extend beyond shaping good professionals or citizens, but it would not neglect these identities. Instead, it would understand these identities as minor loves that should be shaped in light of love for God. This chapter engages in an exercise of moral imagination about how Christian colleges and universities could further a redemptive form of human development that encompasses these identities.

Identity in the Christian Story and University

Colleges or universities may influence the identities of students in four ways. First, they (hopefully) educate students about the identities students either inherit or choose. In other words, they supply students with an understanding of what it means to be a student, a scholar, an American/Canadian, a Texan/Hoosier, a Christian/Jew, a man/woman, a Democrat/Republican, an African American/German American, et cetera. Second, they help students to think critically about these identities and how such identities inform a host of practices in their lives. Third, they bestow and enrich new identities (e.g., through placing students in particular curricular and co-curricular contexts). Finally, they also help one ask critical questions about these identities and how one should prioritize or understand them.

We have argued that every university, through the way it orders its ideally integrated curricular and co-curricular efforts, sets before students a particular way of understanding and ordering their identities. In essence, every institution offers a particular moral order and model. At times administrators or faculty members may also talk about creating autonomous critical thinkers and choosers, but the reality is that we must always think or choose in the context of a set of identities we have inherited or selected. After critically thinking about these other identities, we may alter our understanding of them, choose to relinquish some of them, adopt new ones, or form old ones. However, we always think and act within their context unless new identities take their place in some capacity. The same holds true for institutions.

For Christian colleges, human identity as a whole, as well as particular aspects of human identity, receive meaning and ordering in light of the Christian metanarrative. Humans are made in the image of the Triune God, and the vast majority of additional identities humans inherit or choose comprise part of God's good creation. These include our family name, race, gender, vocation or our designations of ourselves as a wife/husband, friend, or neighbor are social roles. To create professional organizations or to adopt a particular vocation as a doctor, an engineer, or teacher also perpetuates a good part of the social world.

Nonetheless, living in a fallen world means our loves are disordered and our relationships fractured. All of these identities and their functions have become corrupted and filled with the injustices, alienation, and other characteristics of fallen relationships. Humanity and all of humanity's creations, including the identities and roles we have inherited and created, need redemption.

Ultimately, Christ offers Christians the primary hope of redemption, but Christian colleges and universities, as extensions of the Church or Body of Christ, can play a unique, redemptive role. Education within the Christian/biblical narrative takes on a unique significance and purpose. As Nicholas Wolterstorff writes, "The graduate who prays and struggles for the incursion of justice and shalom into our glorious but fallen world, celebrating its presence and mourning its absence—that is the graduate the Christian college must seek to produce."[1] The graduate seeking right relationships, including justice, reconciliation and peace along with other virtues and characteristics of rightly ordered relationships, will need an education that develops the whole range of practices, habits, and virtues needed for that redemptive development.

The Curricular Arena in Right Relationship: Defining a More Human General Education

If Christian educators seek to join with God in the redemptive development of humans and nature (God's creation) and culture (human creations), they must foster rightly ordered relationships and loves between the Triune God, humanity and creation. Education's primary focus should not merely be helping the student master a particular academic discipline or even the relationship between faith and knowledge in a particular academic discipline. It should consider enriching the full humanity of the student.

As mentioned in the last chapter, we would suggest that general education in a Christian college or university should focus on what we call the lasting identities (e.g., student/scholar, friend/neighbor, family, citizen, race, class, gender, steward). We chose these identities, because college students already inhabit them in some fashion, but they need to think about each of these identities in more complex ways. In particular, they need to think about the different normative ideals associated with competing narratives, ends, virtues, principles, wisdom, models, et cetera associated with these identities.

There would be numerous advantages to forming a general education program around these student identities. First, these courses would focus not upon texts but upon the identities common to humans everywhere. In fact, this idea finds commonalities with the secular humanism discussed by Kronman in that it identifies one of the tasks of general education as being "to identify the elements of our common human nature and to help us understand the consequences that flow from them."[2] The people entering colleges and universities are all students, all people seeking friends, members of families, neighbors, single or married, citizens, members of a gender, racial and ethnic group, and stewards of the natural world (including one's own body) and human culture.

Second, courses of this nature would be concerned with building bridges between theory and practice in ways that intersect with the identities of students. Various scholars have begun to note the absence of attention to this matter in general education. For example, Colby, Beaumont, Ehrlich, and Corngold observe in their book, *Educating for Democracy* that "The focus that has dominated political science for the past half-century, however, is the objective, often mathematically driven study of political institutions and behavior rather than more normative goals or applied work of educating for citizenship."[3] In this respect, the current approach to general education carries with it the remnants of the encyclopedic mode of inquiry described by MacIntyre. Colleges still behave "as if there is some overall coherence to and some underlying agreement about the academic project" similar to that envisioned by the writers of early encyclopedias.[4] Thus, they encourage students to learn bits of the encyclopedia without understanding what kind of relationship unites them as a whole.

Harvard's recent general education curriculum attempts to overcome this issue by taking a broader, less disciplinary defined, view of different subject areas. Students take courses in aesthetic and interpretive understanding, culture and belief, empirical reasoning, ethical reasoning, science of living systems, science of the physical universe, societies of the world, and the United States in the World.[5] The courses still demonstrate a concern with the introduction of students to various types of disciplinary professions or callings ("acquiring broader interests and preparing for a career") and the acquisition of various skills (e.g., learning to communicate and think).[6] Yet, as Nicholas Wolterstorff writes, "Throwing some abstract political science at the student along with some abstract economics and sociology will not do the trick. The goal is not to understand the world but to change it."[7] We would add that changing the world starts by enriching one's understanding of one's identities and loves in relationship to the world and then transforming them according to the Christian vision. Our approach would require directly addressing our normative moral ideals about what it means to be a good student, citizen, woman/man, neighbor, et cetera.

Third, these courses would overcome the problems that occur by allowing general education to be dictated by subject matter boundaries. Christian colleges and universities must structure their curricula differently so that it coheres with their particular aims. Again, we find Nicholas Wolterstorff's comments instructive:

> When our concern is simply to appropriate the stream of culture, then the relevant packages are available and familiar: physics, literary criticism, music theory, economics and so on. But when our concern is

to equip our students to reform society, then we walk in uncharted territory.[8]

What Wolterstorff labels reforming society, we would broaden to the redemptive development of humans, nature, and culture. In our approach, faculty would not merely use general education to take a bird's eye view of disciplines or courses as training grounds for future professionals/scholars. Instead, the courses would contribute to the redemptive development of students as human beings. In this regard, our approach helps balance the university's focus on the learner as well as learning.

Fourth, this approach would require students to think about their future moral commitments more deeply and in more complex ways. As mentioned earlier, William Perry's theory produced the unfortunate tendency of talking about student commitments in college in ways that fail to differentiate between the different types of commitment that students inevitably must make.[9] Even the empirical examples he uses lump many different forms of commitment, such as vocational and worldview commitments, together. We believe it would be better to differentiate the types of commitments that students will be making and then require courses that will explore the normative commitments that students will make or the relationship between who they already are (e.g., members of a family or nation) and the commitments with which they will be face. Students with dualistic views of their moral outlooks in these areas will certainly understand what it would mean to talk about being a good friend, family member, or citizen. The course would then expose students to the multiplicity of understandings regarding these normative commitments, but it would always recognize that students must eventually make complex commitments in these areas.

Finally, ordering general education around the great identities instead of the great texts would recognize the need for curricular flexibility. A class addressing what it means to be a good citizen at a Christian college or university in India will be quite different from a comparable class in America. In an even greater sense, a class addressing what it means to be a good citizen at a Baptist university would be quite different than a comparable class at a Wesleyan university. The necessary knowledge and moral virtues, as well as possible practices, moral wisdom, and models, would need to be shaped accordingly.

Critics may raise the concern that such courses would be biased or involve indoctrination. Of course, any decision about how to structure the curriculum involves preference for one identity or another. The curriculum always represents an ordering of moral identities. In addition, general education courses exploring various ways of understanding what it means to be a good friend or good citizen, in our case with particular emphasis upon Christian approaches, would not necessarily be indoctrinating or limited. After all, a diversity of answers to these issues exists both inside and outside the Christian tradition. The beauty of this approach is that Christians could then argue about these differences by using the commonalities within the tradition. In fact, the advantage of a college or university with a clear sense of identity is that it can approach these tasks with a way of ordering, informing, and unifying them (e.g., preparing Christian citizens, or preparing a student for a vocation or calling and not merely a career).

We recognize that some faculty may express deep resistance to such courses even at Christian colleges and universities. For example, one of us participated in a survey project of religious universities that, among other things, sought to uncover faculty support or resistance to moral or civic education courses that moved beyond exposing students to cognitive traditions of thought and actually sought to shape students in some manner. While a majority of faculty members supported such courses, a small minority of professors indicated concerns about having normative moral or civic ends for courses.[10] Below are some of the qualitative responses from these dissenters.

- Students can't learn morals in the classroom.
- Sounds positive but I doubt that a truly "academic" course could have such a goal.
- I don't believe an academic course is appropriate, but some other method may be.
- We are not a church.
- The university is not responsible for teaching or requiring "Morals 101."
- This is more of a church practice than a university's.
- In my experience courses rarely have any significant impact upon students' behavior. If virtue is to be taught (as it should be) it must be taught much earlier, and by example much more than by formal instruction.
- Nice idea, but I don't think courses do this.
- Beyond the reach of a course as such.
- Role modeling in and out of class. Needed attitudes caught more than taught.
- I'm not sure how these courses could be designed.
- Virtuous living does not come from a course, but from a willingness to be guided by the Holy Spirit in word and action.

- Virtue can't be taught.
- I'd like to see the syllabus for this class. Comical question.
- Courses do not help people live virtuous lives.

- It is naive to think that a required course will achieve this.
- I have no idea how a "course" could do this.
- Courses don't inculcate virtue.

More qualitative analysis would need to be undertaken to determine the reason why these professors do not believe virtue can be taught in a class. Perhaps some faculty members accept the dichotomy between objective knowledge and subjective values. In other words, perhaps they affirm that moral and civic education remains impossible because morality is about values and is not objective knowledge. Yet, some professors indicated sympathy with a Classical (e.g., Aristotle) or Christian approach to virtue that emphasizes that moral virtue must be acquired by training, habituation, and modeling and suppose that, thus, moral education or moral formation does not require courses to help one think about the formation process. For members of this faculty group, morals are "caught and not taught." Again, more qualitative research is needed to ascertain the fundamental reasons for this sort of objection. While we would agree that courses can only play a limited ethical role, we believe these professors underestimate how purpose, content, and shape of a course play a morally formative role.

Space will not allow us to address what each of these courses might look like in great detail. In addition, these courses will vary to a great extent depending upon the tradition of the particular college or university. Nonetheless, we want to offer a brief explanation of each course. After these brief explanations, we will outline a couple of extended examples regarding the classes on citizenship and the class pertaining to the general professional identity of students.

The Courses

Friends, Neighbors, and Enemies. All of our students will be friends, neighbors, and enemies in their lives. These normative, relational categories take on added significance at residential colleges where new friendships, neighbors and enemies form. One of the most obvious signs of less than human approaches to education concerns the fact that faculty leave discussions of such matters solely to the co-curricular arena of college life. In fact, the paucity of scholarly material in the modern era upon friendship reflects an incredible lack of attention to these sorts of practical relational matters. A more human education would help students reflect upon the characteristics and normative ideals associated with these identities. Students would explore their own conceptions of these categories in light of other moral traditions and how they approach these matters. Of course, in a Christian college, special attention would be given to the way Christian Scripture uses these categories when challenging notions about ethics. In the Gospel of John, Jesus serves as a model friend. He expands our notion of a neighbor that crosses over ethnic and gender lines and commands us to love our enemies.

Family, Singleness, and Marriage. The redemptive development of humans always involves developing those areas that every student will face—family relationships as well as the possibility that they will or will not choose to marry and create a family. A more human education would provide students with opportunities to think expansively and critically about their family relationships, the diversity of norms as well as those considered conducive to healthy family lives. Obviously, how these matters have been explored within the Christian tradition would be included in such a course.

Race, Class, Gender, and Sexuality. Race, ethnicity, gender, and sexuality are currently consuming topics on any college campus because they involve identities in which everyone is invested. Moreover, they involve identities that have been the source of legal and other forms of discrimination in America's past. Usually, these identities are understood as the province of special interests groups in the co-curricular arena of the university or they are left to certain interdisciplinary "studies" departments on campus. While such "studies" departments can be important, a more human education would recognize that every student needs to spend time reflecting about both the descriptive and normative issues associated with these identities. In essence, they need to think critically about how these forms of identity influence their view of the world and how a particular understanding of the Christian story may challenge, alter, and even deepen their appreciation of what it means, for example, to be female.

Stewardship I: Culture. The question of how Christians should interact with culture, which we will define simply as human creations, has been one of the perennial ethical questions.[11] We will merely mention one area of culture. One of most revealing evidences of our loves concerns our use of money. Most personal finance courses discuss how we can earn money. Yet, an equally important class involves exploring the question of how we should we spend it. The secular university, as John Sommerville has pointed out, fails to offer answers to this question:

> The way I put it to my students is to ask where in the university they would go to learn how to *spend* their money. We have lots of programs that tell you how to make money and be useful to the economy. But where would you learn how to spend your money intelligently? That is, where does one learn what is valuable in and of itself? What is the point of money? It is not self-evident, although we increasingly treat it as such.[12]

A Christian university could explore this question within a particular moral context in ways that further the redemptive development of students.

Stewardship II: The Natural World. While not everyone will be a professional scientist, all humans will have some relationship to the rest of the natural world. In fact, how humans should interact with the rest of the natural world is another of the most important questions facing humans. What should be our relationship to the rest of nature? While science classes and vocations can expose students to the wonder of nature, not all of them will broach this essential, normative question. As a result, it is one thing to understand various processes which occur in the natural order; it is another thing to understand oneself as a steward of that order.

Stewardship III: The Embodied Human Self. What does it mean to love oneself in a way that leads to one's own bodily flourishing? This course, while drawing upon the subject matter of the disciplines of theology, philosophy, psychology, biology, and physical education, would examine answers and engage in practices related to the normative question of how one should best care for one's own self to promote one's own flourishing. What ends should one pursue, what virtues should one acquire, or what practices should one develop in order to contribute to one's bodily flourishing? All of these questions are life-long normative questions about which students should not only be taught to think critically but also make commitments that they put into practice. This kind of class would prove especially helpful as a context for discussions about sexuality and spirituality that Freitas claims need to take place at evangelical colleges.[13]

Good Citizens—Moral Orientation and Critical Thinking

In our contemporary world every person must be a citizen. One cannot escape to the desert as the early Church Fathers did. By offering a general education on citizenship, a university would face the fact that every student must think about being a good citizens. In every course, an instructor must prioritize the intellectual traditions to which it exposes students and this course would be no different. Since most universities are government-funded in some capacity, it should be no surprise that they prioritize some form of the American liberal-democratic story and identity. Of course, other identities can orient the approach to citizenship. We noted earlier that Stanley Fish argued:

> No doubt, the practices of responsible citizenship and moral behavior should be encouraged in our young adults, but it's not the business of the university to do so, except when the morality in question is the morality that penalizes cheating, plagiarizing and shoddy teaching, and the desired citizenship is defined not by the demands of democracy, but by the demands of the academy.[14]

For Fish, one's professional identity and community should be the primary guide to citizenship in the academy. Obviously, a Christian university will take a different approach. We agree with John Wright who claims, "An orthodox Christian faith requires commitments to fellow adherents that transcend the narrow confines of a particular modern nation-state."[15]

Of course, a variety of Christian understandings about what it means to be a good citizen exist, so it would be a mistake to believe that prioritizing Christian approaches would somehow make it narrow or subject to one particular political ideology or philosophy. Throughout history, Christians have defended different forms of government and suggested different ideals of good citizenship. As Adrian Thatcher writes:

> a Christian theology of education has no alternative but to be self-critical, not because it is compelled to import Cartesian methods of inquiry into itself or to assume radical empiricism as the fount of all earthly wisdom, but because its understanding of Christ's death is a "No" to the adequacy or self-sufficiency of any human endeavor before God.[16]

Thus, the course would be liberal in how it exposes students to the strengths and limits of different traditions of citizenships.

It should also be liberal in that it should it looks at the practice of citizenship in a wholistic fashion. It should recognize the importance of the narrative or worldview shaping one's conception of citizenship and its ends. It should explore the whole range of virtues and vices associated with citizenship (and not merely procedural forms of justice, for example, or courage in the context of one national or political story). It should expose students to range of practices, models, and wisdom associated with being a good citizenship. Yet, this course would also reflect institutional commitments in that it would help students engage in certain Christian practices (e.g., prayer for leaders, service, political dissent, engaging political life, and leaders regarding moral issues, learning from models, particularly of Christian social activists such as William Wilberforce and Martin Luther King, and culling wisdom from those presently engaged in social activism from a Christian perspective). Moreover, it would critically examine such practices (e.g., Rick Warren choosing to pray at Barrack Obama's inauguration or Barrack Obama choosing Rick Warren to pray at his inauguration) through the lens of being a Christian citizen.

We also envision the class addressing Fish's concern, by recognizing that Christians need to understand the multiple contexts in which Christian citizenship takes place. Therefore, a general education class on citizenship in a Christian university should be liberal in that it would expose students to questions and issues related to being a Christian citizen in other political contexts and countries besides that of liberal democracies. In this respect, such a class could be more liberal than some of the classes related to citizenship that Colby et al. cite that focus largely on citizenship within the context of American liberal democracy.[17]

Certainly, a class such as one on citizenship would involve discussing the various ways being a good citizen has traditionally been understood and practiced by Christians and others, but it would also involve discussing what might be distinctive about being a Christian citizen and perhaps thinking about practices that help achieve this end. For instance, they may engage in different sorts of practices (e.g., praying for their leaders or for justice, not voting[18]) or undertaking similar sorts of activities (e.g., nonviolent protests) for different reasons and different motivations (e.g., a faith in God's final judgment and ultimate justice and not the pragmatic results of a nonviolent strategy). Finally, it would require that professors not only explore these practices but even conceive of themselves as models to help them teach the class. In essence, professors would have to recapture some under-standing of what it means to be public intellectuals in order to serve as teachers in such a context. After all, the goal of such classes would not be merely to expose students to a variety of intellectual traditions but to set before students a model of a critically committed Christian citizen that engages in certain practices, demonstrates certain virtues, and can dispense the wisdom gained by practice.

We believe that there are numerous advantages to discussing the moral life in this context which will contribute to the task of promot-ing a more fully human moral education. In an immensely practical chapter on cultivating humility, Scott Waalkes discusses how he uses various pedagogical strategies in his international studies course to cultivate humility grounded in the Imago Dei. He teaches:

> When other nations get angry at the United States for its unilateralism, maybe we need to see it from their point of view. They too are God's creatures. Students need to understand why American foreign policy is resented and take a humble look at their own country. Getting stu-dents to think critically in this way is the main point of the course, and obviously it requires the cultivation of humility. One way I seek to pro-mote humility in our UN simulation is by requiring that no student be allowed to represent the United States and by requiring that students stay in character in representing another country.[19]

We certainly find much to commend in this approach. What we would merely note is that this exercise involves helping students understand their disordered identity loves. A course focused on the ordering of loves with regard to one's citizenship would provide a helpful context for such exercises, and it would help students think through the prac-tice of their citizenship.

The Good Student—An Argument

In this section, we want to set forth an argument that would illustrate a Christian perspective offered in a course about what it means to be a good student. A more human university would not assume that stu-dents have thought deeply about the ends, virtues, principles, prac-tices, models, and moral wisdom associated with being a good student. In fact, many universities offer such courses but they usually do so outside of a normative context that encompasses a larger purpose. Consequently, the course goals focus merely on academic skills (e.g., how to study/write better, how to manage your time, etc.). Such courses have now found their way into the curriculum at many colleges and universities under the guise of what we call first-year seminars. We believe that this course should include both a theoretical element that educates students about motivation and a section that introduces students to particular practices associated with being a good student (e.g., writing skills, research methods, etc.). The following argument would be one presented within the course regarding the metanarrative connected to being a good student.

Universities largely leave it to students to provide their own motivation for their studies. For most students, their prior shaping of their student identity, including the metanarrative guiding it, occurred within secondary public school systems. Students in these settings are usually taught to think about education within a narrative that sees being a good student as a means to a career or even as a means to making money and becoming financially secure. Neil Postman in his book, *The End of Education,* labels this story as the narrative of Economic Utility, "The story tells us that we are first and foremost economic creatures and that our sense of worth and purpose is to be found in our capacity to secure material benefits."[20]

At a Christian college or university, students should encounter a different moral vision of what it means to be a good student. We would argue that the good student should engage in the creation and redemption of learning. We believe this language improves upon the traditional language of the integration of faith and learning described in the last chapter for four reasons.

First, the danger of integration language itself is that it emphasizes a synthesizing of ideas, theories, et cetera, with a student's faith but fails to capture the theological narrative in which this task must take place. In essence, integration can, at times, leave students with the impression that faith and whatever discipline in question are co-equal in nature and simply need to be drawn into some constructive relationship.

Second, the approach we are proposing counters narrow conceptions of the Christian scholar's task as well as the Christian student's calling. When scholars "integrate faith and learning" they have already admitted that the original learning created failed to demonstrate "faith" and therefore the faith must now be integrated. Certainly, this sometimes is the case. Yet, it leaves out the responsibility of Christians to also be involved in creating scholarship. In contrast, rearticulating the Christian scholar's and student's task as the creation and redemption of learning emphasizes the broad, positive theological work of Christian academics and students. Scientists who teach students to delve into the mysteries of nature as well as other scientists who help students redeem creation from our own fallen abuse of it are involved in the creation and redemption of learners and learning. The historian who creates a masterful biography of a particular figure and the one who teaches a student to correct an unjust critique of a figure that was poisoned by a heavy dose of some other form of identity (e.g., nationalism) are also involved in the creation and redemption of learners and learning.

A third advantage of rearticulating the Christian scholar's task in this manner is that it may help reshape views about the limited relationship between Christianity and disciplines not always seen as amenable to integration (e.g., science, music, and engineering). For instance, Douglas Jacobsen and Rhonda Hustedt Jacobsen claim: "The integration paradigm often flounders...when applied either to disciplines that are more neutrally descriptive or pragmatic in orientation or to disciplines in which issues of human meaning rarely enter the mix."[21] They cite engineering and music as two examples. Asking how one integrates faith into jazz music or engineering may sound like a difficult question. In contrast, if one thinks about the creation and redemption of music and engineering as parts of the divine task as Christian students and scholars; it is easy to think about the productive discussions and directions such conversations might take. The musical composer and performer would then understand his or her vocation in a theological context and may ask questions such as the following: As an image bearer of God, what does it mean to create excellent music? When is music fallen? What would it mean to redeem music? What exactly is a fallen musical performance or a redemptive musical performance? Likewise, the engineer understands the creation of human structures and tools as a unique way of bearing God's image. Of course, it is quite easy to imagine what a fallen structure looks like, but it may also be productive to think about what it would mean to allow our structures to foster redemptive forms of community and life.

Fourth, if we talk about the redemption of scholarship, we realize that part of our redemption, or the reversal of the fall, involves gaining increased understanding into God's creation as a means of reversing the effects of the fall. Scientists who help discover cures for disease or gain greater insight into how to reverse human damage to the environment engage in this project. Of course, new insights into God's creation that create technology also create new opportunities for corruption (e.g., Internet pornography and extortion schemes). Thus, the Christian scholar, following the example of the Triune God, must create new ways to reverse the sinful effects of our own creations (e.g., critiquing unjust laws that create oppressive economic or political systems, researching institutions or corporate structures and revealing possible ways they may dehumanize others, discovering ways to restore an environment damaged by human abuse, etc.).

Redemptive Development in the Co-curricular Arena

Christian humanism cannot be perpetuated solely within the curricular arena. In reality, courses prove to be rather limited forms of education that deal primarily with the cognitive dimension of students' lives. Instead, a college or university attempting to promote a redemptive form of humanism must set forth more holistic ways to support such a vision. Unfortunately, even places with specific visions of human flourishing, such as Christian colleges and universities, face challenges with the way higher education tends to be structured. V. James Mannoia points out that one of the great tragedies of Christian liberal arts colleges is "that at many, there is a 'divide' between those responsible for curricular arena and those responsible for co-curricular arena. One staff is responsible for social development, another for faith development, another for cognitive development, another for physical development, and who knows, who cares for moral development?"[22] We do not believe that division of labor at colleges or universities is necessarily a bad thing, however as Mannoia indicates, this division may leave some areas neglected, fragmented or secondary. The truth of the matter is that the strength of any campus, Christian or otherwise, to imprint upon the students it serves with a particular identity is directly linked to the level of integration shared by the curricular and co-curricular realms. In ideal terms, students would not even notice the difference between the two in terms of the narratives being shared, just a difference in their locale on campus.

At most universities, they achieve coherence by using the language of student life or psychosocial development. For instance, George Kuh has noted the following characteristics of high-quality co-curricular efforts: (1) intentionally designed with specific developmental outcomes in mind; (2) aligned with the mission of the campus; (3) involve collaboration and coordination between the curricular and the co-curricular realm; (4) they are overseen and guided by social service staff and faculty; and (5) they are assessed in terms of their level of impact upon students.[23] As already noted, underneath many developmental theories exists a belief that we all agree that development is a good to be pursued and that we can find out through empirical research what development might look like for everyone. We have contended that such presuppositions prove deeply problematic when it comes to the areas of both student identity and moral development.

If there is no such thing as a neutral, universal ideal of identity formation and moral development that we can observe anywhere, we must be conscious of the way larger metanarratives form developmental theories. As Stanley Hauerwas observes, "[T]he language of spiritual growth, holiness, and perfection directs attention to the moral self in a manner quite different from the contemporary concern with moral development."[24] This fact must be taken into consideration when thinking through recommendations about what colleges or universities should do in relation to moral education in the co-curricular realm.

If co-curricular practices should be linked to specific developmental outcomes and the vision of development must be linked to the moral tradition and mission of the campus, more attention must be paid to the specific outcomes associated with what we have been calling redemptive development. The vision we have sketched would help address this issue. Those in charge of redemptive student life, we argue, should seek to foster students' relationship with God (cultivating theological reflection and engagement), as well as particular virtues, principles, rules, practices, wisdom and models linked to the Christian moral tradition as these relate to aspects of students' identities. In other words, those in charge of the co-curricular realm would need to further students' development with regard to Christian ideals of being a friend or neighbor and dealing with enemies, being a good citizen, fostering reconciliation between different races, classes, and genders, being a good steward, and caring for one's self.

These identities and moral ideals provide for coherent links with the curricular realm of the university, since the mission of the schools, the general education curriculum and co-curricular programs would share similar aims in specific areas of human identity. Moreover, the role of those overseeing student life outside the classroom becomes especially important in helping students live out redemptive development in all of these areas during college. While fully articulating the vision we have in mind would require another book, we will merely provide some examples of how this vision could help bring theology into both student life and administrative structures that relate to student life.

Much of what already takes place on a college campus would fit naturally into the framework we have developed. The language and categories we have proposed regarding redemptive humanism, we believe, would merely provide a way for schools to think in theological categories regarding the practices in which such programs are already engaged.

For example, worship involves the practice of reminding us who we are and helping us order our loves. One of the central questions facing students in the transition to college involves identity and continuity. What gives students continuity beyond their own stories which are now being disrupted? All students are made in the image of God. As a result, their worth hinges not upon their old identities, such as being a high school athlete, valedictorian, choir member, cheerleader, or even the new ones they may adopt (e.g., premed major and possible future alumni/donor). In the midst of this transition, they can find continuity in their personal identity based on their relationship to God. Worship, thus becomes the central way that students continue to order their conception of their selves.

Numerous others examples exist. For example, a new recycling initiative would be communicated as an expression of stewardship. Larger co-curricular efforts such as residence life, student activities, student leadership programs, and support services for underrepresented students would arise not merely out of a political framework or pressure but out of a vision for Christian humanism. This vision of Christian humanism would be introduced in the curricular realm and then practices in the co-curricular realm. For example, an interviewee from Seattle Pacific University discussed their ethnic and racial diversity initiative by claiming that:

> What we are working on is clearly theologically driven...I have no interest in political practice with this issue; it has to do with the kingdom of God being multi-colored, multi-racial. And we have to do that. That is an "ought." I have been working and any time I talk about it to really ground it particularly out of 2 Corinthians 5. You have been reconciled to God. You now are ambassadors of the ministry of reconciliation...it is centered around who we are as Christians.[25]

Therefore, efforts in the co-curricular realm will build upon theories being introduced in the curricular realm and thus provide ways for students to grow in all facets of their lives. They will provide avenues for students to put into action their developing ideas about what it means to be a good student, neighbor, friend, citizen, steward, et cetera.

Who Are We? The Institution and Identity in the Christian Story

One of the identities we have not considered extensively concerns that of the institution itself. If other identities should be transformed in light of the Christian story, what might it mean for an institution to understand its own identity in light of the Christian story? We think Christian institutions should be different in this regard.

One way this might be embodied would be for Christian institutions at some point to move beyond marketing when introducing students to the institution. There is probably no better method for developing cynicism than to read through the marketing brochures of 156 Christian colleges and universities over the course of a week and then witness the disconnect in place on some of these campuses. In essence, it is quite amazing the claims that each college makes for itself. If all these claims are true, every college has well-educated faculty members that care about their students, will be a place of deep friendships, can lead you to fulfill all your dreams, et cetera. We suppose that like the dating process, one cannot and should not expect the hopeful suitor to start by revealing his or her imperfections. When pursuing or being pursued, we always put on the best face. Admissions efforts in the age of student consumerism are no different.

Nonetheless, students attending an institution that seeks to live out the Christian story must know that the institution's story is not always perfect. Perhaps an institution failed to admit African American students during a previous era in time, experienced a major athletic scandal, or tolerated sub-par academic standards on the part of its faculty for far too long. What makes these dilemmas even more difficult to accept is that they may have emerged from a corrupted understanding of the theological narrative that should have propelled it in other directions. For example, too many Christian colleges and universities have shied away from the pursuit of high academic standards out of fear that such standards may diminish the religious fabric of the institution. One of the advantages, we believe, of Christian institutions that make confession part of the worship service is that it habituates students in one of the fundamental practices of Christian community.[26] Since the practice of confession reflects a reality of life, that we live in a fallen and broken world, we would argue, it should inform all of university life. In this case, we believe, some universities perhaps need to add a practice that might help them embody this part of the Christian story in their own corporate lives.

There must be a time for corporate confession where the university models the nature of its spiritual commitments. We evaluate our institution and our own lives in light of Christian ideals. We want our institution to always be seeking to be Christian. Christian colleges and universities interested in pursuing ways of living out the ideals embedded in their particular narratives will also be ones that say to their students, "We need your help and you too can offer critique of this university that helps us come closer to living out our ideals." Too often, colleges and universities that are associated with a particular Christian tradition are also associated with being more authoritarian or centrally governed. In contrast, we think it is possible that such institutions are not necessarily Christian in their commitments or practices, just in a parochial culture they are seeking to perpetuate. By virtue of their commitment to a particular understanding of the Christian tradition, Christian colleges and universities are places where freedom abounds as a result of their efforts to practice Christian confession. They know they are not perfect but with God's grace they are able to more closely live out their identity as a people created in God's own image.

Conclusion

While we do not want to pretend that what we have offered is an exhaustive understanding of how a particular Christian tradition can inform the life of campus, we are hopeful we have offered a framework for further reflection. Part of the dilemma is that no two campuses should look exactly alike. Visitors to a Baptist campus should know in quick fashion that something is different about it, something derived from its past that determines its aspirations for the future. The same should be said for Anabaptist campuses, Reformed campuses, and Wesleyan campuses, not to mention Jesuit Catholic campuses and Franciscan Catholic campuses. Even if two schools share a particular tradition, their differing histories will facilitate some variation in terms of how those traditions define particular curricular and co-curricular practices. Regardless, in the end, what should look the same is the common commitment that these institutions have to the creation and redemption of humans and the seamless integration of this purpose with curricular and co-curricular realms. While faculty may introduce certain theories in the classroom, the laboratory, the recital hall, or the studio, student life professionals then work to put these theories into practice in areas such as residence life, student activities, student leadership programs, and support services for underrepresented students. Failure to do so only allows the fragmented nature of our lives to find new forms of expression. If nothing else, the call to the Christian life, regardless of the Christian tradition, is the surrender of all of our existence to a new way of life—a life that seeks to go beyond the fall but, in grace, to live out the promise of redemption and reconciliation. As a servant of the Church, the Christian college is called to be nothing more. At the same time, it is called to be nothing less.

Conclusion

Transforming Human Animals into Saints

Tom Wolfe begins his provocative portrait of postmodern college life in *I Am Charlotte Simmons* with a brief story about an unusual experiment with cats.[1] In the story scientists remove a portion of the cats' brains that controls emotions in higher mammals. As a result, the cats "veer helplessly from one inappropriate affect to another."[2] Their sexual urges, in particular, spin out of control. All this activity did not surprise the researchers. Instead, something else did. The normal cats watching this behavior suddenly changed. Wolfe writes, "Over a period of weeks they had become so thoroughly steeped in an environment of hypermanic sexual obsession that behavior induced surgically in the...cats had been induced in the controls without any intervention whatever."[3] According to Wolfe, scientists had discovered that "a strong social or 'cultural' atmosphere, even as abnormal as this one, could in time overwhelm the genetically determined responses of perfectly normal, healthy animals."[4]

This odd opening for a fictional book about a young girl's college experience, of course, invites an obvious real life comparison going back to our opening about *Animal House*. Just as perverse and sexualized animals may influence other more "normal" developing animals, so may the perverse and sexualized college student and the moral culture of an institution influence a more innocent human such as Charlotte Simmons. Perhaps appropriately, *I Am Charlotte Simmons'* depiction of college life sometimes reminds one of National Lampoon's *Animal House*. Yet, in contrast to *Animal House*, where the hedonism occurring at that 1962 college campus primarily takes place in one fraternity and is meant to be a source of humor, *I Am Charlotte Simmons* offers a window to an institution where the whole ethos and culture of the twenty-first century university has turned into one big animal house. The results portrayed by Wolfe though are not quite as funny as those offered by John Landis in his film. As one reviewer observed, "even the partying scenes are joyless."[5]

The central character of the book, Charlotte Simmons, carries to the university different moral ideals than the one she encounters. In the midst of the postmodern animal house of DuPont University she finds few resources by which to battle the pressing moral order of hedonism. Her most illuminating insight appears to come from a neuroscience professor who reduces her identity to nothing more than physicality. Consequently, she finds nothing left by which to battle against the animalistic instincts of the student-led hedonistic liturgies of university culture except her naked self. Since the fictional DuPont University, similar to many postmodern universities, offers little moral orientation for the self she can only repeat to herself the one remaining moral identity she brought to the university, *I Am Charlotte Simmons*.

The book, although fiction, represents current-day academia quite accurately in this respect. As Donna Freitas observed in her study regarding secular schools, "The closest any school seemed to get to an operative mission statement was 'the sky's the limit.' This may seem attractive because it offers students freedom. But the 'sky's the limit' approach leaves most students with, at best, a vague sort of moral code either to adopt or to resist...unless they arrived with a formidable one to begin with."[6] In Charlotte Simmons' case, it only left her with personal identity as a moral guide, a quite limited source of moral sustenance.

Fortunately, as this book sought to demonstrate, there are schools that seek to add a moral vision to students' selves that does not merely attempt to strip away students' humanity, but actually seeks to offer students the opportunity to enrich and even strengthen portions of it. Colleges and universities with robust visions for cultivating various parts of human identity, beyond one's professional self, still exist. We contend that many Christian colleges and universities, in particular, demonstrate an encompassing humanistic vision and this book sought to uncover the nature of their visions and offer suggestions for strengthening them.

Despite the more human visions of education that are in place at many Christian universities, we wish to close with one final observation about what we did not find at Christian colleges and universities—even the case study schools that demonstrated quality with soul when it comes to moral education. We did not find talk about forming saints. This finding is surprising since after all the

Church's' aim is to form disciples of Christ who are also becoming saints. As Stanley Hauerwas writes

> Christian ethics involves learning to imitate another before it involves acting on principles (although principles are not excluded).... For the Christian, morality is not chosen and then confirmed by the example of others; instead, we learn what the moral life entails by imitating others. This is intrinsic to the nature of Christian convictions, for the Christian life requires a transformation of the self that can be accomplished only through direction from a master.[7]

Moreover, the specific Christian vision of human flourishing is ultimately that of the saint. It made us wonder if Christian colleges and universities with more human visions for moral education still aim too low. The quest to make students more human, full bearers of their divinely made image, ultimately leads one to a particular end of the story where those fully human take upon themselves a new name and identity.

Notes

Introduction   The Turn to Less than Human Moral Education: The Moral Reservations of Contemporary Universities

1. Desiderius Erasmus, "De Pueris Statim Ac Liberaliter Instituendis Liberllus" [That children should straightaway from their earliest years be trained in virtue and sound learning], in W. H. Woodward, *Desiderius Erasmus Concerning the Aim and Method of Education* (New York: Teachers College Press, 1964/1529), 187.
2. Andrew Abbott, "The Aims of Education Address," *University of Chicago Record* 37 (2002): 8.
3. Rainer Schwinges, "Student Education, Student Life," in *A History of the University in Europe, Vol. I,* ed. H.D. Ridder-Symeons (New York: Cambridge University Press, 1992), 223.
4. Helen Lefkowitz Horowitz, *Campus Life: Undergraduate Cultures from the End of the Eighteenth Century to the Present* (New York: Alfred A. Knopf, 1987), 39.
5. Julie Reuben, *The Making of the Modern University: Intellectual Transformation and the Marginalization of Morality* (Chicago: University of Chicago Press, 1996), 211–29.
6. David Brooks, "The Organizational Kid," *Atlantic Monthly* (April 2001): 53.
7. Harry Lewis, *Excellence without a Soul: How a Great University Forgot Education* (New York: Public Affairs, 2006), 159–160. Of course, there also exists great disagreement about whether students have souls.
8. Referring to Jared Diamond's *Guns, Germs and Steel: The Fates of Human Societies* (New York: W. W. Norton, 1997).
9. Christian Smith, *What Is a Person? Rethinking Humanity, Social Life, and the Moral Good from the Person Up* (Chicago: University of Chicago Press, forthcoming).
10. Erasmus, "De Pueris Statim Ac Liberaliter Instituendis Liberllus," 187.

One   Love in the University: Moral Development and Moral Orientation

1. Derek Bok, *Our Underachieving Colleges: A Candid Look at How Much Students Learn and Why They Should Be Learning More* (Princeton: Princeton University Press, 2006), 171.

2. John Rawls, *Political Liberalism* (New York: Columbia University Press, 1996).
3. Various traditions will use different terms when talking about moral education. For clarity's sake, we delineate our understanding of related terms below:

- Ethics Education—What we refer to as ethics education is usually what takes place in many contemporary ethics classes (although these efforts often extend to the co-curricular dimension). It attempts to expose students to different ethical traditions or general schools of ethical thought (e.g., Utilitarianism, Kantianism, Christian ethics, Jewish ethics, Aristotelianism, etc.), a particular ethical tradition (e.g., Christian ethics), or a particular field of professional ethics (e.g., journalism and ethics).

- Character Education—This phrase refers to educators' attempt to instill in students particular virtues or character qualities (e.g., honor, honesty, respect, etc.) prized by a particular profession or moral tradition. We will distinguish this approach from what we will call moral formation. Practices linked to character education often include formal classroom instruction and thus assume that good character is rational in nature, but they also take the form of common practices such as honor codes. They may also involve efforts by student life to emphasize virtues such as respect, tolerance, service, etc. Sometimes these efforts are undertaken in the clear context of a particular moral tradition but at other times universities and colleges undertake character education with the assumption that the virtues can be divorced from and cultivated independent of a moral tradition. When this occurs one may find the complaint that institutions are promoting a "bag of virtues" with no larger rationale.

- Moral Formation—We will refer to moral formation as educators' attempt not only to instill certain virtues or character qualities in students but also to direct those virtues toward particular ends or to order them in particular ways. In other words, not only might college leaders seek to instill the virtue of honor or justice, but they might also set forth reasons and structure school practices so that one's affections are directed according to a certain way (e.g., a love for God, fellow humans, country, etc. or some other ordering). Thus, any college that requires certain behavioral standards regarding the sexual conduct of their students in any fashion will be involved in moral formation. As a result, the practices which define moral education not only include formal classroom instruction but also a host of co-curricular practices designed to form the moral nature of the students. We believe the moral formation of students, particularly as it pertains to the various identities and associated narratives of students, is one of the most understudied and underexamined aspects of university life. It is also the primary approach to moral education of moral traditions.

- Moral Education—We will use the term moral education when referring to more than one of the approaches described above. In other words, we will use it to be a broader and more descriptive phrase that may involve all of the different things described above. With regard to moral education in a college or university, we describe it as the way that an institution, especially its leaders and faculty, seeks to educate students about the good, form their love for the good, and encourage them to do the good. In other words, it involves not only providing students with cognitive knowledge about various ethical theories or traditions (which is one part of moral education), but may also include the promotion of particular forms of moral knowledge as true and encouraging intellectual, willful and active commitment to a particular element of moral knowledge or behavior as true or good, as well as a particular vision of the good life as good or true.

4. William Perry, *Forms of Ethical Development in the College Years: A Scheme* (San Francisco, CA: Jossey-Bass, 1999); Lawrence Kohlberg, *The Philosophy of Moral Development: Moral Stages and the Idea of Justice*, vol. 1(San Francisco, CA: Harper & Row, 1981); Carol Gilligan, *In a Different Voice: Psychological Theory and Women's Development* (Cambridge, MA: Harvard University Press, 1982); James Rest, Darcia Narvaez, Muriel J. Bebeau, and Stephen J. Thoma, *Post-Conventional Moral Thinking: A Neo-Kohlbergian Approach* (Mahwah, NJ: L. Erlbaum Associates, 1999).
5. James Hunter, *The Death of Character: Moral Education in an Age Without Good or Evil* (New York: Basic Books, 2000).
6. Kohlberg, *The Philosophy of Moral Development*, 104.
7. Ibid., 105.
8. Bok, *Our Underachieving Colleges*, 64.
9. We find it noteworthy that in their study of moral exemplars Anne Colby and William Damon found that the exemplars did not score differently than the general population in their moral reasoning levels. See *Some Do Care: Lives of Contemporary Moral Commitment* (New York: Free Press, 1992).
10. Robert Coles, *The Moral Life of Children* (Boston: Atlantic Monthly Press, 1986), 23.
11. Ibid., 26.
12. Ibid., 33–34.
13. Ibid., 34.
14. Hunter, *The Death of Character*, 23.
15. For another example see Alasdair MacIntyre, *Dependent Rational Animals: Why Human Beings Need the Virtues* (Chicago: Open Court, 1999).
16. Christian Smith, *Moral, Believing Animals: Human Personhood and Culture* (New York: Oxford University Press, 2003).
17. Ibid., 7.

18. Ibid., 8.
19. Ibid.
20. Don S. Browning, *Christian Ethics and the Moral Psychologies* (Grand Rapids, MI: Eerdmans, 2006), 51.
21. James K.A. Smith, *Desiring the Kingdom: Worship, Worldview and Cultural Formation* (Grand Rapids, MI: Baker, 2009), 330.
22. Philip Kenneson, "Worship, Imagination and Formation," in *The Blackwell Companion to Christian Ethics*, eds. Stanley Hauerwas and Samuel Wells (Malden, MA: Blackwell, 2004), 55.
23. Smith, *Moral, Believing Animals*, 8.
24. Ibid., 22.
25. Ibid.
26. Charles Taylor, *Sources of the Self: The Making of the Modern Identity* (Cambridge, MA: Harvard University Press, 1989).
27. Ibid., 3.
28. Ibid., 28.
29. See Anne Colby, Thomas Ehrlich, Jason Beaumont, and Jason Stephens, *Educating Citizens: Preparing America's Undergraduates for Lives of Moral Responsibility* (San Francisco, CA: Jossey-Bass, 2003); Kaye V. Cook, Daniel C. Larson, and Monique D. Boivin, "Moral Voices of Women and Men in the Christian Liberal Arts College: Links between Views of Self and Views of God," *Journal of Moral Education* 32.1 (2003): 77–89; and Roger Bergman, "Why Be Moral? A Conceptual Model from Developmental Psychology," *Human Development* 45.2 (2002): 104–124.
30. Colby et al., *Educating Citizens*, 116–17.
31. Alasdair MacIntyre, *After Virtue* (South Bend, IN: Notre Dame, 1984), 57.
32. Ibid., 59.
33. Isaac L. Kandel, *The Dilemma of Democracy* (Cambridge, MA: Harvard University Press, 1934), 71–72.
34. David Brooks, "The Organizational Kid," *Atlantic Monthly* (April 2001): 53.
35. John W. Wright, "How Many Masters? From the Church-Related to an Ecclesially Based University," *Conflicting Allegiances: The Church-Based University in a Liberal Democratic Society*, eds. Michael L Budde and John Wright (Grand Rapids, MI: Brazos Press, 2004), 14.
36. Colby et al., *Educating Citizens*, 49–95.
37. Ibid., 52.
38. Ibid., 56, 61, 65.
39. Bok, *Our Underachieving Colleges*.
40. Perry L. Glanzer, *The Quest for Russia's Soul: Evangelicals and Moral Education in Post-Communist Russia* (Waco, TX: Baylor University Press, 2002), 15.
41. Benjamin Rush, "On the Mode of Education Proper in a Republic," *Readings in American Educational Thought: From Puritanism to*

Progressivism, eds. Andrew J. Milson, Chara Haussler Bohan, Perry L. Glanzer, and J. Wesley Null (Greenwich, CT: Information Age, 2004), 84.

42. James Smith, *Desiring the Kingdom*, 169.
43. Neil Postman, *The End of Education: Redefining the Value School* (New York: Vintage Books, 1995); Jean-Francois Lyotard, *The Postmodern Condition: A Report on Knowledge* (Minneapolis: University of Minnesota Press, 1984).
44. James W. McClendon, *Ethics* (Nashville, TX: Abingdon Press, 1986), 143.
45. MacIntyre, *After Virtue*, 221.
46. Taylor, *Sources of the Self*, 30.
47. American Association of University Professors, "1940 AAUP Statement of Principles on Academic Freedom and Tenure," http://www.aaup.org/AAUP/pubsres/policydocs/contents/1940statement.htm (accessed March 11, 2009).
48. MacIntyre, *After Virtue*.
49. Glanzer, *The Quest for Russia's Soul*.
50. Perry L. Glanzer and Andrew J. Milson, "Legislating the Good: A Survey and Evaluation of Contemporary Character Education Legislation," *Educational Policy 20*, 3 (2006): 525–50. From 1993 to 2004, almost half of the states (23) either passed new laws requiring public schools to teach kids virtues or modified old laws. Add in the three states that had such laws already and more than half the states in the nation now want public schools to teach children particular virtues to make them good students. There is little agreement among the lists which include 64 character qualities. Arizona requires public schools to teach students "sincerity." Alabama, Georgia, and South Carolina now require children to be taught "cleanliness" and "cheerfulness." Five states have mandated that children learn "punctuality" (AL, GA, SC, TX, and VA). Three states believe children must learn "attentiveness" (AZ, FL, and KY).
51. Tim Stafford, "Johnny Be Good: Can 'Character Education' Save the Public Schools?" *Christianity Today* (1995, September 11): 35–39.
52. John F. Goodman and Howard Lesnick, *The Moral Stake in Education* (New York: Longman, 2001), 143.
53. Kohlberg, *The Philosophy of Moral Development*, 11.
54. We understand practice as Alasdair MacIntyre defined the term:

> Any coherent and complex form of socially established cooperative human activity through which goods internal to that form of activity are realized in the course of trying to achieve those standards of excellence which are appropriate to, and partially definitive of, that form of activity, which the result that human powers to achieve excellence, and human conceptions of the ends and goods involved, are systematically extended. MacIntyre, *After Virtue*, 175.

55. Stanley Hauerwas and Samuel Wells, eds., *The Blackwell Companion to Christian Ethics* (Malden, MA: Blackwell, 2004).

Two   Searching for a Common, Tradition-Free Approach to Moral Education: The Failed Quest

1. John Howard Yoder, *The Priestly Kingdom* (South Bend, IN: Notre Dame Press, 1984), 40.

2. Daniel Coit Gilman, "Inaugural Address of Daniel Coit Gilman as First President of The Johns Hopkins University," http://www/jhu.edu/125th/links/gilman.html (accessed March 11, 2009).

3. Ibid.

4. John Mearsheimer, "The Aims of Education Address," *The University of Chicago Record* 32 (1997): 5–8.

5. Wayne C. Booth, "Introducing Professor Mearsheimer to His Own University," *Philosophy and Literature* 22.1 (1998): 174–178.

6. John Mearsheimer, "Mearsheimer's Response: Teaching Morality at the Margins," *Philosophy and Literature* 22.1 (1998): 193.

7. Ibid., 198.

8. Cotton Mather, *Diary of Cotton Mather* (New York: Ungar , 1957), 357.

9. Anthony Kronman, *Education's End: Why Our Colleges and Universities Have Given Up on the Meaning of Life* (New Haven, CT: Yale University Press, 2007), 49.

10. "Laws of Harvard College," in *A Documentary History of Religion in America*, ed. Edwin Gaustand (Grand Rapids: Eerdmans, 1982), 201.

11. Norman Fiering, *Moral Philosophy at Seventeenth Century Harvard: A Discipline in Transition* (Chapel Hill: University of North Carolina, 1981), 21–22.

12. Thomas Aquinas, *Summa Theologica: A Concise Translation*, ed. Timothy McDermott (Westminister, MD: Christian Classics, 1989).

13. Martin Luther, *Three Treatsies,* trans. Charles M. Jacobs (Philadelphia: Fortress Press, 1970), 93.

14. Fiering, *Moral Philosophy at Seventeenth Century Harvard*, 14.

15. Ibid., 23–24.

16. Ibid., 24.

17. Samuel Morison, *The Founding of Harvard College* (Cambridge, MA: Harvard University Press, 1935), 263.

18. Fiering, *Moral Philosophy at Seventeenth Century Harvard*, 29.

19. Ibid., 36–39; Morison, *The Founding of Harvard College*, 260–263.

20. As quoted in Fiering, *Moral Philosophy at Seventeenth Century Harvard*, 40.

21. Ibid., 41.

22. In addition to Fiering, this section relies upon George Marsden, *The Soul of the American University: From Protestant Establishment to*

Established Nonbelief (New York: Oxford University Press, 1994 and Julie Reuben, *The Making of the Modern University: Intellectual Transformation and the Marginalization of Morality* (Chicago: University of Chicago Press, 1996).

23. Reuben, *The Making of the Modern University*, 20.

24. Ibid., 19–23.

25. Richard Hofstadter and Wilson Smith, eds., *American Higher Education: A Documentary History* (Chicago: University of Chicago Press, 1961), 97–108, 232–242.

26. Marsden, *The Soul of the American University*, 50.

27. Frederick Rudolf, *Curriculum: A History of the American Undergraduate Course of Study Since 1636* (San Francisco: Jossey-Bass, 1977), 42.

28. Douglas Sloan, "The Teaching of Ethics in the American Undergraduate Curriculum, 1876–1976," in *Ethics Teaching in Higher Education*, eds. Daniel Callahan and Sissela Bok (New York: Plenum Press, 1980), 1–57.

29. D.H. Meyer, *The Instructed Conscience: The Shaping of the American National Ethic* (Philadelphia: University of Pennsylvania Press, 1972), 4.

30. Francis Wayland, *Thoughts on the Present Collegiate System in the United States* (Boston: Gould, Kendall & Lincoln, 1842), 115.

31. Francis Wayland, *The Elements of Moral Science* (Cambridge, MA: Belknap Press of Harvard University Press, 1963).

32. Fiering, *Moral Philosophy at Seventeenth Century Harvard*, 62.

33. Meyer, *The Instructed Conscience*, 161.

34. Sloan, "The Teaching of Ethics in the American Undergraduate Curriculum, 1876–1976," 7.

35. Noah Webster, "On the Education of Youth in America," in *Readings in American Educational Thought: From Puritanism to Progressivism*, eds. Andrew J. Milson, Chara Haeussler Bohan, Perry L. Glanzer, and J. Wesley Null (Greenwich, CT: Information Age, 2004), 106.

36. Ibid., 93.

37. Benjamin Rush, "Selected Writings of Benjamin Rush," in Ibid., 84.

38. Meyer, *The Instructed Conscience*; Sloan, "The Teaching of Ethics in the American Undergraduate Curriculum, 1876–1976."

39. Jeffrey Morrison, *John Witherspoon and the Founding of the American Republic*, (Notre Dame, IN: University of Notre Dame Press, 2005).

40. William Smith, *Professors and Public Ethics: Studies of Northern Moral Philosophers before the Civil War* (Ithaca, NY: Cornell University Press, 1956).

41. Morrison, *John Witherspoon and the Founding of the American Republic*, 16–17.

42. Smith, *Professors and Public Ethics*, 30.

43. Reuben, *The Making of the Modern University*; Sloan, "The Teaching of Ethics in the American Undergraduate Curriculum, 1876–1976"; Smith, *Professors and Public Ethics*.

44. Reuben, *The Making of the Modern University*, 3.
45. Helen Horowitz, *Campus Life: Undergraduate Cultures from the End of the Eighteenth Century to the Present*, (New York: Alfred A. Knopp, 1987).
46. Meyer, *The Instructed Conscience*, 30.
47. Sloan, "The Teaching of Ethics in the American Undergraduate Curriculum, 1876–1976"; Smith, *Professors and Public Ethics*.
48. Sloan, "The Teaching of Ethics in the American Undergraduate Curriculum, 1876–1976."
49. Ibid., 6.
50. Reuben, *The Making of the Modern University*; See also Sloan, *The Teaching of Ethics in the American Undergraduate Curriculum, 1876–1976*.
51. D. Tweksbury, *The Founding of American Colleges and Universities Before the Civil War* (New York: Teachers College, Columbia University, 1932).
52. Horowitz, *Campus Life*, 52.
53. Ibid., 53.
54. Reuben, *The Making of the Modern University*; Sloan, "The Teaching of Ethics in the American Undergraduate Curriculum, 1876–1976."
55. Roger Geiger, *To Advance Knowledge: The Growth of the American Research Universities, 1900–1940* (New York: Oxford University Press, 1986).
56. Sloan, "The Teaching of Ethics in the American Undergraduate Curriculum, 1876–1976."
57. Michael Davis, *Ethics and the University* (New York: Routledge, 1999), 8–9.
58. Sloan, "The Teaching of Ethics in the American Undergraduate Curriculum, 1876–1976."
59. Reuben, *The Making of the Modern University*, 77.
60. Ibid.
61. Reuben, *The Making of the Modern University*; Marsden, *The Soul of the American University*.
62. Reuben, *The Making of the Modern University*, 118.
63. Ibid., 125.
64. Ibid., 5.
65. Ibid., 136.
66. Ibid., 139.
67. Edward Bellamy, *Looking Backward* (Boston and New York: Houghton Mifflin, 1926).
68. Reuben, *The Making of the Modern University*.
69. Ibid.
70. John Dewey and James Tufts, *Ethics* (New York: Holt, Rinehart, and Winston, 1908).
71. Reuben, *The Making of the Modern University*, 186–187.

72. Anne Colby, Thomas Ehrlich, Elizabeth Beaumont, and Jason Stephens, *Educating Citizens: Preparing America's Undergraduates for Lives of Moral Responsibility* (San Francisco, CA: Jossey-Bass, 2003); Reuben, *The Making of the Modern University*; Bok, *Beyond the Ivory Tower*; Sloan, *The Teaching of Ethics in the American Undergraduate Curriculum, 1876–1976*;Hastings Center, *Ethics Teaching in Higher Education* (New York: Plenum Press, 1980).

73. Ibid., 210.

74. Kronman, *Education's End*, 74.

75. Douglas Sloan, "The Teaching of Ethics in the American Undergraduate Curriculum, 1876–1976," 43.

76. Kronman, *Education's End*, 86–87.

77. Ibid., 176–177.

78. Reuben, *The Making of the Modern University*, 225.

79. Ibid., 44.

80. Ibid.

81. Ibid., 45.

82. *The Higher Learning in America* (New Brunswick, NJ: Transaction, 1995/1936), 66.

83. Ibid., 66.

84. Ibid., 229.

85. Sloan, "The Teaching of Ethics in the American Undergraduate Curriculum, 1876–1976," 27–51.

86. Reuben, *The Making of the Modern University*, 244.

87. Ibid., 244.

88. *Report on Some Problems of Personnel in the Faculty of Arts and Sciences* (Cambridge, MA: Harvard University Press, 1939), 77.

89. Reuben, *The Making of the Modern University*; Sloan, "The Teaching of Ethics in the American Undergraduate Curriculum, 1876–1976."

90. Ibid.

91. Reuben, *The Making of the Modern University*, 254.

92. Ibid., 263.

93. *Annual Report of the President of Stanford University*, 1920–21, 34–35.

94. Reuben, *The Making of the Modern University*, 258.

95. Ibid., 255.

96. American Council on Education, and E. G. Williamson, *The Student Personnel Point of View*, (1946).

97. Ibid.

98. Ibid., 2.

99. Ibid., 3.

100. Ibid.

101. Ibid.

102. Ibid.

103. Diane Ravitch, *The Troubled Crusade* (New York: Basic Books, 1983), 183.

Three   The Rise of Less than Human
Moral Education

1. Harvard University, Faculty of Arts and Sciences, *Report on the Task Force on General Education* (Cambridge, MA: Harvard University, 2007).
2. Douglas Sloan, "The Teaching of Ethics in the American Undergraduate Curriculum, 1876–1976," in *Ethics Teaching in Higher Education*, eds. Daniel Callahan and Sissela Bok (New York: Plenum Press, 1980). 41.
3. Ibid., 38.
4. Ibid., 41. The study Sloan cites is George Henry Moulds, "The Decline and Fall of Philosophy," *Liberal Education* 50 (1964): 360–61.
5. See Helen Horowtiz, *Campus Life: Undergraduate Cultures From the End of the Eighteenth Century to the Present*, (New York: Alfred A. Knopp, 1987).
6. David Barber, *A Hard Rain Fell: SDS and Why It Failed* (Jackson: University Press of Mississippi, 2008): 223.
7. Ibid.
8. Jacques Barzun, *The American University: How It Runs, Where It Is Going* (Chicago: University of Chicago Press, 1968/1993), 240.
9. Ibid., 257.
10. Ibid., 246.
11. Ibid., 269.
12. Ibid., 264.
13. Clark Kerr, *The Uses of the University* (Chicago: University of Chicago Press, 1995), 70.
14. Ibid., 24.
15. Ibid., 1.
16. Ibid., 14.
17. Ibid.
18. Ibid., 16.
19. Ibid., 31.
20. Ibid., 32.
21. Ibid.
22. Horowitz, *Campus Life*, 231.
23. Diane Ravitch, *The Troubled Crusade* (New York: Basic Books, 1983), 194.
24. The Committee on the Student in Higher Education, *The Student in Higher Education* (New Haven, CT: Haven Foundation, 1968), 9.
25. Ibid., 58.
26. Ibid., 65.
27. William G. Perry, Jr., *Forms of Intellectual and Ethical Development in the College Years: A Scheme* (San Francisco, CA: Jossey-Bass, 1999/1968).
28. Ibid., 49.

29. Ibid., 227.
30. Ibid., 238.
31. Ibid., 238.
32. Ibid., 136.
33. Ibid., 206.
34. Michael Novak, "God in the Colleges: The Dehumanization of the University," *The New Student Left*, eds. Mitchell Cohen and Dennis Hale (Boston: Beacon Press, 1967), 259.
35. *The Student in Higher Education*, 14.
36. Mary Belenky, Blythe McVicker Clinchy, Nancy Rule Goldberger, and Jill Mattuck Tarule, *Women's Ways of Knowing: the Development of Self, Voice, and Mind* (New York: Basic Books, 1997), 9.
37. Ibid.
38. The six stages of moral reasoning are: (1) The punishment and obedience orientation; (2) The instrumental relativist orientation; (3) The interpersonal concordance or "good boy—nice girl" orientation; (4). Society maintaining orientation; (5) Social contract orientation; (6) The universal ethical principle orientation. Lawrence Kohlberg, *The Philosophy of Moral Development: Moral Stages and the Idea of Justice, Essays on Moral Development, Vol. 1* (San Francisco, CA: Harper and Row, 1981), 17–18. Part of Kohlberg's reason for developing his scheme was his disillusionment with what he called the "bag of virtues" approach to moral education (p. 9). What Kohlberg did not appear to recognize is that virtues only appear to be randomly selected if one attempts to scrape away a wider moral tradition from one's vision for the ideal human. Why a person should choose to acquire a particular virtue only makes sense in light of such the rationale offered for a tradition (See Alasdair MacIntyre, *After Virtue* [South Bend, IN: Notre Dame, 1984]).
39. Lawrence Kohlberg and Mayer, R., "Development as the Aim of Education," *Harvard Educational Review* 42 (1972): 449–96.
40. Ibid., 464.
41. Ibid., 472. These ethical postulates were taken mainly from Immanuel Kant and John Rawls.
42. Ibid., 473.
43. Carol Gilligan, *In a Different Voice: Psychological Theory and Women's Development* (Boston, MA: Harvard University Press, 1982).
44. R.A. Shweder, "Liberalism as Destiny," *Contemporary Psychology 20* (1982): 421–24.
45. Don S. Browning, *Christian Ethics and the Moral Psychologies* (Grand Rapids, MI: Eerdmans, 2006), 52–53.
46. Stanley Hauerwas, *A Community of Character: Toward a Constructive Christian Social Ethic* (South Bend, IN: Notre Dame, 1981).
47. Michael Davis, *Ethics and the University* (New York: Routledge, 1999).
48. Ibid.

49. Ibid. See also Derek Bok, *Beyond the Ivory Tower: Social Responsibilities of the Modern University* (Cambridge, MA: Harvard University Press, 1982).

50. Hastings Center, *The Teaching of Ethics in Higher Education* (New York: Hastings Center, 1980), 13.

51. Hastings Center Staff, "The Teaching of Ethics in American Higher Education," in *Ethics Teaching in Higher Education*, ed. Daniel Callahan and Sissela Bok (New York: Hastings Center, 1980), 159.

52. Ibid.

53. Bok, *Beyond the Ivory Tower*.

54. Davis, *Ethics and the University*.

55. Ibid., 18.

56. Thomas L. Beauchamp and James F. Childress, *Principles of Biomedical Ethics* (New York: Oxford University Press, 1979).

57. Derek Bok, *Our Underachieving Colleges: A Candid Look at How Much Students Learn and Why They Should Be Learning More* (Princeton: Princeton University Press, 2006), 146–148.

58. Bruce Wilshire, *The Moral Collapse of the University: Professionalism, Purity and Alienation* (Albany: State University of New York Press, 1990), 277.

59. The authors of the Hastings Center survey found that two-fifths of ethics courses were still broad ethics courses Hastings Center Staff, "The Teaching of Ethics in American Higher Education," in *Ethics Teaching in Higher Education*, 153–70.

60. "Hastings Center Project on the Teaching of Ethics: Summary Recommendations," in ibid., 300.

61. Bill Readings, *A University in Ruins* (Cambridge, MA: Harvard University Press, 1996).

62. "Hastings Center Project on the Teaching of Ethics: Summary Recommendations,", 9.

63. Ibid., 11.

64. Ibid.

65. Anthony Kronman, *Education's End: Why Our Colleges and Universities Have Given Up on the Meaning of Life* (New Haven, CT: Yale University Press, 2007), 135.

66. Ibid., 194.

67. Ibid., 195.

68. Jean M. Twenge, *Generation Me: Why Today's Young Americans Are More Confident, More Assertive, Entitled—and More Miserable Than Ever before* (New York: Free Press, 2006.

69. Laura Sessions Stepp, *Unhooked: How Young Women Pursue Sex, Delay Love and Lose at Both* (New York: Riverhead Books, 2006).

70. Donna Freitas, *Sex & the Soul: Juggling Sexuality, Spirituality, Romance, and Religion on America's College Campuses* (New York: Oxford University Press, 2008), 68.

Four The Quandary Facing Contemporary Higher Education: Moral Education in Postmodern Universities

1. Yale University, "Yale Reaccreditation Web Site," http://www.yale.edu/accred/standards/s1.html (accessed March 4, 2009).
2. Stanley Fish, *Save the World on Your Own Time* (New York: Oxford University Press, 2008), 18.
3. Julie Reuben, *The Making of the Modern University: Intellectual Transformation and the Marginalization of Morality* (Chicago, IL: University of Chicago Press, 1996).
4. Ibid., 268.
5. Ibid., 269.
6. Christian Smith, *Moral, Believing Animals: Human Personhood and Culture* (New York: Oxford University Press, 2003), 46.
7. Jean-François Lyotard, *The Postmodern Condition: A Report on Knowledge* (Minneapolis: University of Minnesota Press, 1984), xxiv.
8. Stanley Fish, "Save the World on Your Own Time," *The Chronicle of Higher Education*, 23 January 2003, http://chronicle.com/jobs/news/2003/01/2003012301c/careers.html (accessed September 15, 2008).
9. Fish, *Save the World on Your Own Time*, 18.
10. Stanley Fish, "The Case for Academic Autonomy," *The Chronicle of Higher Education*, 23 July 2004, 1.
11. Fish, *Save the World on Your Own Time*, 67.
12. Ibid., 18–19.
13. Ibid.
14. Ibid., 20.
15. Michael Davis, *Ethics and the University* (New York: Routledge, 1999).
16. Ibid., 27.
17. Derek Bok, *Our Underachieving Colleges: A Candid Look at How Much Students Learn and Why They Should Be Learning More* (Princeton: Princeton University Press, 2006), 65.
18. Bok writes, "Institutional efforts to build character or change behavior should include only goals with which no reasonable person is likely to disagree." Ibid., 64.
19. Ibid., 147.
20. Ibid.
21. See, e.g., James Davison Hunter, *The Death of Character* (New York: Basic Books, 2000).
22. Bok, *Our Underachieving Colleges*, 153.
23. Ibid.
24. Fish, *Save the World on Your Own Time*, 27.

25. Ibid., 60.
26. Ibid.
27. Charles Taylor, *The Sources of the Self: The Making of Modern Identity* (Cambridge, MA: Harvard University Press, 1989), 27.
28. Fish, *Save the World on Your Own Time*, 14.
29. Fish, "Aim Low: Confusing Democratic Values with Academic Ones Can Easily Damage the Quality of Education," *The Chronicle of Higher Education*, 16 May 2003, Career Network, 5; For some reason Fish makes a caveat about religious universities and states, "Indoctrination in a certain direction is quite properly their business." Yet, it remains unclear why Fish would not say the same about democratic universities funded by the state. Fish, *Save the World on Your Own Time*, 68.
30. Fish, *Save the World on Your Own Time*, 14.
31. Ibid., 18.
32. Mark Edwards, *Religion on Our Campuses*; Roy Clouser, *The Myth of Religious Neutrality: An Essay on the Hidden Role of Religious Belief in Theories* (Notre Dame, IN: University of Notre Dame Press, 2005); David Myers and Malcolm Jeeves, *Psychology: Through the Eyes of Faith* (New York: Harper San Francisco, CA, 2003); George Marsden, *The Outrageous Idea of Christian Scholarship* (New York: Oxford University Press, 1997); Nicholas Wolterstorff, *Reason within the Bounds of Religion*, Rev Ed. (Grand Rapids, MI: W.B. Eerdmans, 1999).
33. Myers and Jeeves, *Psychology*, 13.
34. Marsden, *The Outrageous Idea of Christian Scholarship*, 73–74.
35. Myers and Jeeves, *Psychology*, 14.
36. Ibid., 13.
37. A. Nemtsova, "In Russia, Corruption Plagues the Higher-Education System," *The Chronicle of Higher Education* 54.24 (22 February 2008): 1.
38. While Fish wants professors to save the world on their own time, he also wants to save the university. Apparently, either Fish believes the university is not part of the world or one should only save a part of the world over which one has a professional obligation. Since Fish supports what we call the professional moral tradition, it is quite clearly the latter.
39. Mark Schwehn, *Exiles from Eden: Religion and the Academic Vocation in America* (New York: Oxford University Press, 1993).
40. Ibid., 41.
41. Personal interview with Ukrainian Catholic University administrator by Perry L. Glanzer, Ukrainian Catholic University, Lviv, Ukraine June 5, 2008.
42. Olena Dzhedzhora, comments at Conference on Catholic Higher Education in Eastern Europe in Lviv, Ukraine June 5, 2008.
43. Conversation with President Borys Guziak, June 5, 2008.
44. Alan Wolfe, "The Potential for Pluralism," *Religion, Scholarship and Higher Education,* ed. Andrea Sterk (Notre Dame, IN: University of Notre Dame Press, 2002), 23–39.
45. Hunter, *The Death of Character*, 155.

46. Ibid.
47. Ibid., 276.
48. George Kuh, "Do Environments Matter? A Comparative Analysis of the Impress of Different Types of Colleges and Universities on Character," *Journal of College and Character* 2 (2002), http://www.collegevalues. org/articles.cfm?id=570&a=1; John Templeton Foundation, ed., *Colleges that Encourage Character Development* (Radnor, PA: Templeton Foundation Press, 1999).
49. Christopher Peterson and Martin Seligman, *Character Strengths and Virtues* (New York: Oxford University Press, 2004).
50. Bok, *Our Underachieving Colleges*, 150.
51. Howard Kirschenbaum, "From Values Clarification to Character Education: A Personal Journey," *Journal of Humanistic Counseling, Education and Development* 39,.1 (2000): 17.
52. Ernest T. Pascarella and Patrick T. Terenzini, *How College Affects Students: A Third Decade of Research,* Vol. 2 (San Francisco, CA: Jossey-Bass, 2005), 350–51.
53. Ibid., 351.
54. Reuben, *The Making of the Modern University*, 269.
55. Ibid.
56. Alasdair MacIntyre, *After Virtue: A Study in Moral Theory* (Notre Dame, IN: University of Notre Dame Press, 1984).
57. Alasdair MacIntyre, *Three Rival Versions of Moral Enquiry: Encyclopedia, Genealogy and Tradition* (Notre Dame, IN: University of Notre Dame Press, 1990), 225–226.
58. Ibid., 231.
59. Ibid., 234.
60. MacIntyre, *After Virtue*, 263.
61. Ibid., 205.
62. Ibid.
63. Ibid., 222.
64. Ibid., 263.
65. Bart Pattyn, "Is It Wrong to Teach What Is Right and Wrong? The Debate at K.U.Leuven" (Brussels, Ethical Forum, 29 November 2007), http://www.fondationuniversitaire.be/common_docs/EF6/Pattyn2.pdf (accessed 15 September 2008).
66. Ibid., 5.
67. Ibid., 4.
68. Ibid.

Five   Who Are We? The Identities Universities Use To Provide Moral Orientation

1. Charles Taylor, *Sources of the Self: The Making of the Modern Identity* (Cambridge, MA: Harvard University Press, 1989), 28.

2. See Lee S. Duemer, Sheila Delony, Kathleen Donalson, and Amani Zaier, "Behavioral Expectations of 110 Nationally Ranked Liberal Arts Colleges," *Journal of College & Character* 10, 2 (November 2008): 1–14.

3. Anne Colby, Thomas Ehrlich, Elizabeth Beaumont, Jason Stephens, *Educating Citizens: Preparing America's Undergraduates for Lives of Moral and Civic Responsibility* (San Francisco, CA: Jossey-Bass, 2003), 52.

4. We will draw primarily upon the qualitative analysis results reported in Colby et al., *Educating Citizens.* In addition, our own research addressed has involved the qualitative analysis of schools that represent the types chosen listed in *The Templeton Guide.* These institutions, in order of discussion include: Yale University (Research University—Very High Research Activity, New Haven, Connecticut); Colorado State University (Research University—Very High Research Activity/Fort Collins, Colorado); the United States Air Force Academy (Baccalaureate College-Diverse Fields/Colorado Springs, Colorado); Mary Baldwin College (Master's Colleges and Universities—Smaller Programs/Staunton, Virginia); Hampden-Sydney College (Baccalaureate College—Arts and Sciences/Hampden-Sydney, Virginia), and Hillsdale College (Baccalaureate College—Arts and Sciences Hillsdale, Michigan).

5. Derek Bok, *Our Underachieving Colleges: A Candid Look at How Much Students Learn and Why They Should Be Learning More* (Princeton: Princeton University Press, 2006); Nannerl Keohane, *Higher Ground: Ethics and Leadership in the Modern University* (Durham, NC: Duke University Press, 2006); Adrianna Kezar, Tony Chambers, and John Burkhardt, eds., *Higher Education for the Public Good* (San Francisco, CA: Jossey-Bass, 2005); Harold Shapiro, *A Larger Sense of Purpose* (Princeton: Princeton University Press, 2005).

6. By liberal democracy we mean "a political system marked not only by free and fair elections, but also by the rule of law, a separation of powers, and the protection of basic liberties of speech, assembly, religion, and property" Fareed Zakaria, "The Rise of Illiberal Democracy," *Foreign Affairs* 76 (1997): 22.

7. Carol Schneider, "Liberal Education and the Civic Engagement Gap," in *Higher Education for the Public Good*, eds. Adrianna Kezar, Tony Chambers, and John Burkhardt (San Francisco, CA: Jossey-Bass, 2005), 127–145.

8. Shapiro, *A Larger Sense of Purpose*, 90.

9. Ibid., 97.

10. Ibid., 103.

11. Ibid., 104.

12. Colby et al., *Educating Citizens.*

13. Ibid., 13.

14. Ibid., 66.

15. United States Air Force, "Fact Sheet," http://www.usafa.af.mil/superintendent/pa/factsheets/quick.htm (accessed February 21, 2009).

16. Jeffrey Stout, *Democracy and Tradition* (Princeton: Princeton University Press, 2004), 3.
17. Colby et al., *Educating Citizens*, 66.
18. Ibid., 91.
19. Ibid., 66–67.
20. Ibid., 67.
21. Ibid.
22. Ibid.
23. Personal interview with administrator from the USAF Academy Center for Character Development by Perry L. Glanzer, August 5, 2008, U.S. Air Force Academy.
24. United States Air Force Academy, "Character," http://academyadmissions. com/character/ (accessed February 21, 2009).
25. Personal interview with administrator from the USAF Academy Center for Character Development by Perry L. Glanzer, August 5, 2008, U.S. Air Force Academy.
26. United States Air Force Academy, "Honor," http://academyadmissions. com/character/honor.php (accessed February 21, 2009).
27. Ibid.
28. Ibid.
29. See United States Air Force Academy, "Center for Character Development," http://www.usafa.af.mil/Commandant/cwc/?catname=cwc (accessed March 11, 2009).
30. John Lyons, "Upon What Authority Might We Teach Morality?" *Philosophy and Literature* 22, 1 (1998): 156.
31. Ibid., 158.
32. Colby et al., *Educating Citizens*, 227–28.
33. Ibid., 60.
34. Ibid., 60–61.
35. Turtle Mountain Community College, "The Spirit Within Us," http:// www.turtle-mountain.cc.nd.us/ (accessed October 3, 2008).
36. Colby et al., *Educating Citizens*, 63.
37. Ibid., 86.
38. Ibid.
39. D.C. Gilman, "Inaugural Address of Daniel Coit Gilman as First President of The Johns Hopkins University" (2007), http://www/jhu. edu/125th/links/gilman.html (accessed March 11, 2009).
40. See, e.g., the original rationales of women associated with starting female educational institutions in *Readings in American Educational Thought: From Puritanism to Progressivism*, eds. Andrew J. Milson, Chara Haussler Bohan, Perry L. Glanzer, and J. Wesley Null (Greenwich, CT: Information Age, 2004), 115–49.
41. Carol Gilligan, *In a Different Voice: Psychological Theory and Women's Development* (Cambridge, MA: Harvard University Press, 1982); Nel Noddings, *Caring: A Feminine Approach to Caring and Moral Education* (Berkeley: University California Press, 1984).

42. Bruce Wilshire, *The Moral Collapse of the University: Professionalism, Purity and Alienation* (Albany: State University of New York Press, 1990), 256.
43. One exception would be Harvey C. Mansfield, *Manliness* (New Haven, CT: Yale University Press, 2006).
44. Hampden-Sydney College, "General Education Goals," http://www.hsc.edu/academics/ (accessed February 24, 2009).
45. Ibid.
46. Hampden-Sydney College, "Academic Catalogue," http://www.hsc.edu/academics/catalogue/2008–09pdf/24–50academics.pdf (accessed February 26, 2009).
47. Ibid.
48. Hampden-Sydney College, "Student Life Catalogue," http://www.hsc.edu/studentlife/thekey/pdf2008–09/08StuGovtOfficers.pdf (accessed February 26, 2009).
49. Hampden-Sydney College, "The Honor Code," http://www.hsc.edu/honorcode/ (accessed February 26, 2009).
50. Personal interview with student life administrator by Perry L. Glanzer, October 28, 2008, Hampden-Sydney College.
51. Hampden-Sydney College, "The Honor Code," http://www.hsc.edu/honorcode/ (accessed February 26, 2009).
52. Mary Baldwin College, "Mission," http://www.mbc.edu/about/mission.asp (accessed February 24, 2009).
53. Ibid.
54. Mary Baldwin College, "History," http://www.mbc.edu/vwil/history.asp (accessed February 24, 2009).
55. Personal Interview with Mary Baldwin administrator by Perry L. Glanzer, October 27, 2008.
56. Mary Baldwin College, "History," http://www.mbc.edu/vwil/history.asp (accessed February 24, 2009).
57. Personal Interview with Mary Baldwin administrator by Perry L. Glanzer, October 27, 2008.
58. Ibid.
59. Mary Baldwin College, "Student Handbook," http://www.mbc.edu/student/studenthandbook/honorsystem.asp (accessed February 24, 2009).
60. Mary Baldwin College, "4 Year Plan," http://www.mbc.edu/docs/admin_docs/reg_4yearplan2006plus.pdf (accessed February 24, 2009).
61. See Alasdair MacIntyre, *After Virtue*, 203.
62. Colby et al., *Educating Citizens*.
63. Kezar et al., *Higher Education for the Public Good*; Shapiro, *A Larger Sense of Purpose*.
64. Shapiro, *A Larger Sense of Purpose*, 97.
65. John H. Robinson, "Why Schooling Is So Controversial in America Today," *Notre Dame Journal of Law, Ethics and Public Policy*, 3 (1988), 532.
66. Colby et al., *Educating Citizens*, 13.
67. Fish, *Save the World on Your Own Time*, 71.

68. Alasdair MacIntyre, *Dependent Rational Animals: Why Human Beings Need the Virtues* (Peru, IL: Carus, 2001), 132.
69. For background on some of these cases see "Supreme Court Punts," *Inside Higher Ed*, http://www.insidehighered.com/news/2009/07/01/truth (accessed July 2, 2009).
70. Center for Law and Religious Freedom, "Center Blog," http://religious-freedom.blogspot.com/2007/12/another-cls-chapter-derecognized-this.html (accessed March 11, 2009).

Six Searching for a More Human Moral Education: Three Approaches

1. H. John Sommerville, *The Decline of the Secular University* (New York: Oxford University Press, 2008), 24.
2. Christopher Peterson and Martin Seligman, *Character Strengths and Virtues: A Handbook and Classification* (Oxford and New York: Oxford University Press, 2004).
3. Ibid., 5.
4. Perry Glanzer and Andrew Milson, "Legislating the Good: A Survey and Evaluation of Contemporary Character Education Evaluation," *Educational Policy*, 20, 3 (2006): 525–50.
5. Colorado State University, "Facts and Figures," http://www.colostate.edu/features/facts-figures.aspx (accessed February 21, 2009).
6. See Character Fort Collins, http://www.characterfortcollins.org/aboutus.html (accessed June 25, 2009).
7. Character First, "What Is Character First?" http://www.characterfirst.com/aboutus/ (accessed February 28, 2009).
8. Interview with CSU student life administrator by Perry L. Glanzer, August 4, 2008, Colorado State University.
9. Ibid.
10. Ibid.
11. Colorado State University, "All Character Traits," http://campusofcharacter.colostate.edu/values/all.asp (accessed February 28, 2009).
12. Interview with CSU student life administrator by Perry L. Glanzer, August 4, 2008, Colorado State University.
13. Ibid.
14. Templeton Foundation, *Colleges That Encourage Character Development: A Resource for Parents, Students and Educators* (Philadelphia: Templeton Foundation Press, 1999), 58, 85, 300.
15. Interview with CSU student life administrator by Perry L. Glanzer, August 4, 2008, Colorado State University.
16. Anthony T. Kronman, *Education's End: Why Our Colleges and Universities Have Given Up on the Meaning of Life* (New Haven, CT: Yale University Press, 2007), 229.

17. Ibid., 259.
18. Ibid.
19. Yale University, "About Yale," http://www.yale.edu/about/history.html (accessed February 12, 2009).
20. George Marsden, *The Soul of the American University: From Protestant Establishment to Established Nonbelief* (New York: Oxford University Press, 1994).
21. Yale University, "History of Yale Divinity School," http://www.yale.edu/divinity/abt/Abt.HistMish.shtml (accessed February 12, 2008).
22. Yale University, "The Undergraduate Curriculum," http://www.yale.edu/yalecollege/publications/ycps/chapter_i/curriculum.html (accessed February 12, 2009).
23. Ibid.
24. Yale University, "A Brief History of Yale," http://www.library.yale.edu/mssa/YHO/brief_history.html (accessed February 12, 2009).
25. Julie Reuben, *The Making of the Modern University: Intellectual Transformation and the Marginalization of Morality* (Chicago: University of Chicago Press, 1996), 261–62.
26. Personal Interview with Yale University administrator by Todd C. Ream, October 24, 2008.
27. Ibid.
28. *Yale News*, "Orthodox Jews Relieved by 'Yale Five' Loss," http://www.yaledailynews.com/articles/printarticle/25 (accessed March 3, 2009).
29. Ibid.
30. Ibid.
31. Perry L. Glanzer, Michael Beaty, and Larry Lyon, "Moral and Civic Education at Religious Research Universities: Exploring Faculty Support and Resistance," *Religious Education* 100, 4 (Fall 2005): 386–403.
32. See, e.g., Marsden, *The Soul of the American University*; Sommerville, *The Decline of the Secular University*.
33. Sommerville, *The Decline of the Secular University*, 24.
34. C. John Sommerville, *Religion in the National Agenda: What We Mean by Religious, Spiritual, Secular* (Waco, TX: Baylor University Press, 2009).
35. James Engell and Anthony Dangerfield, *Saving Higher Education in the Age of Money* (Charlottesville: University of Virginia Press, 2005), 166.
36. James Hunter, *The Death of Character: Moral Education in an Age Without Good or Evil* (New York: Basic Books, 2000).
37. Kronman, *Education's End*, 251.
38. Ibid., 254.
39. Gould Wickey and Ruth A. Eckhart, *A National Survey of Courses in Bible and Religion in American Universities and Colleges* (Indiana Council on Religion in Higher Education, 1936).
40. Douglas Sloan, "The Teaching of Ethics in the American Undergraduate Curriculum, 1876–1976," in *Ethics Teaching in Higher Education*, eds.

Daniel Callahan and Sissela Bok (New York: Plenum Press, 1980). Sloan notes "it would be difficult to draw a hard and fast line between the ethical and nonethical dimensions of what was taught" in a course such as "the life and teachings of Jesus" (p. 52). Still, as Sloan (1980) observed, further study is needed to ascertain the role of ethics in the curriculum of these colleges (p. 53).

41. Ibid.
42. Hastings Center Report, *The Teaching of Ethics in Higher Education* (New York: Institute of Society, Ethics and Life Sciences, 1980), 19. It is not clear, however, the evidence used for this assertion.
43. Arthur Holmes, *Shaping Character: Moral Education in the Christian College* (Grand Rapids, MI: Eerdmans, 1991).
44. Jennifer A. Lindholm, Katalin Szelényi, Sylvia Hurtado, and William S. Korn, *The American College Teacher: National Norms for the 2004–2005 HERI Faculty Survey* (Los Angeles: Higher Education Research Institute, UCLA, 2005); Linda J. Sax, Alexander W. Astin, William S. Korn, and Shannon K. Gilmartin, *The American College Teacher: National Norms for the 1998–1999 HERI Faculty Survey* (Los Angeles: Higher Education Research Institute, UCLA, 1999).
45. Glanzer, Beaty, and Lyon, "Moral and Civic."
46. Allen Fisher, "Religious and Moral Education at Three Kinds of Liberal Arts Colleges: A Comparison of Curricula in Presbyterian, Evangelical, and Religiously Unaffiliated Liberal Arts Colleges," *Religious Education 90, 1* (Winter 1995): 30–49.
47. George Kuh, "Do Environments Matter? A Comparative Analysis of the Impress of Different Types of Colleges and Universities on Character," *Journal of College and Character* 2 (2002). http://www.collegevalues.org/articles.cfm.
48. Donna Freitas, *Sex & the Soul: Juggling Sexuality, Spirituality, Romance, and Religion on America's College Campuses* (New York: Oxford University Press, 2008), 67.
49. Steven P. McNeel, "College Teaching and Student Moral Development" in *Moral Development in the Professions: Psychology and Applied Ethics,* Eds., James R. Rest and Darcia Narvaez (Hillsdale, NJ: Lawrence Erlbaum Associates), 26–47; Ernest T. Pascarella and Patrick T. Terenzini, *How College Affects Students: A Third Decade of Research*, vol. 2 (San Francisco, CA: Jossey-Bass, 2005), 351–52.
50. James R. Rest, *Moral Development: Advances in Research and Theory* (New York: Praeger, 1987); D.G. Shaver, "Moral Development of Students Attending a Christian, Liberal Arts College and a Bible College," *Journal of College Student Personnel 26*, 400–404.
51. Steven P. McNeel, "College Teaching and Student Moral Development."
52. Pascarella and Terenzini, *How College Affects Students*, 352.
53. Hardwick-Day. *Brand Archeology: Excavating for Position, Persona and Attitude.* (Minneapolis, MN: Hardwick Day, 2003).

54. Templeton Foundation, *Colleges That Encourage Character Development,* v.
55. Douglas Jacobsen and Rhonda H. Jacobsen, "The Ideals and Diversity of Church-Related Higher Education" in *The American University in a Postsecular Age,* Eds., D. Jacobsen and R.H. Jacobsen (New York: Oxford, 2008), 63–80.

Seven Moral Education in the Christian Tradition: Contemporary Exemplars

1. John Howard Yoder, *The Priestly Kingdom* (South Bend, IN: Notre Dame Press, 1984), 44.
2. When we first started our research, the largest group included the CCCU institutions (103) followed by the LFN institutions (70). We excluded the three Canadian CCCU institutions. In addition, fourteen schools were part of both coalitions.
3. Jennifer A. Lindholm, Katalin Szelényi, Sylvia Hurtado, and William S. Korn, *The American College Teacher: National Norms for the 2004–2005 HERI Faculty Survey* (Los Angeles: Higher Education Research Institute, UCLA, 2005); Linda J. Sax, Alexander W. Astin, William S. Korn, and Shannon K. Gilmartin, *The American College Teacher: National Norms for the 1998–1999 HERI Faculty Survey* (Los Angeles: Higher Education Research Institute, UCLA, 1999); George Kuh, "Do Environments Matter? A Comparative Analysis of the Impress of Different Types of Colleges and Universities on Character," *Journal of College and Character* 2 (2002), http://www.collegevalues.org/articles. cfm.
4. John Templeton Foundation, Ed. *Colleges that Encourage Character Development.* (Radnor, PA: John Templeton Foundation, 1999).
5. Robert Benne, *Quality with Soul: How Six Premier Colleges and Universities Keep Their Faith with Their Religious Tradition* (Grand Rapids, MI: Eerdmans, 2002).
6. Our methods and analysis were taken largely from the methods of qualitative research found in Juliet Corbin and Anselm Strauss. *Basics of Qualitative Research: Techniques and Theory for Grounded Theory Development,* 3rd ed. (Thousand Oaks, CA: Sage, 2008).
7. Morningside College, http://www.morningside.edu/.
8. Seattle Pacific University, 2007–2008 Undergraduate Catalogue, http://www.spu.edu/acad/ugcatalog/20078/generalinfo/aboutSPU.asp (accessed May 10, 2008).
9. George Fox University, "Mission Statement," http://www.georgefox. edu/about/beliefs/mission.html (accessed March 10, 2009).
10. University of Dallas, "Mission Statement," http://www.udallas.edu/ about/mission.cfm (accessed May 10, 2008).

11. Calvin College, "Mission," http://www.calvin.edu/about/mission.htm, (accessed May 10, 2008).
12. Eastern Mennonite University, "EMU Mission Statement," http://www.emu.edu/president/mission, (accessed May 10, 2008).
13. Anne Colby, Thomas Ehrlich, Jason Beaumont, and Jason Stephens, *Educating Citizens: Preparing America's Undergraduates for Lives of Moral Responsibility* (San Francisco, CA: Jossey-Bass, 2003), 52–71.
14. James T. Burtchaell, *The Dying of the Light: The Disengagement of Colleges and Universities from Their Christian Churches* (Grand Rapids, MI: Eerdmans, 1998).
15. John W. Wright, "How Many Masters? From the Church-Related to an Ecclesially Based University," *Conflicting Allegiances: The Church Based University in a Liberal Democratic Society*, eds. Michael L. Budde and John Wright (Grand Rapids, MI: Brazos Press, 2004), 23.
16. David Kirp, *Shakespeare, Einstein, and the Bottom Line: The Marketing of Higher Education* (Cambridge, MA: Harvard University Press, 2003), 11.
17. Seattle Pacific University, Admissions View Book, 2003, 6.
18. Calvin College, Admissions View Book, 2003.
19. Personal interview with Xavier faculty member by Perry L. Glanzer, October 12, 2004, Xavier University.
20. Michael Davis, *Ethics and the University* (New York: Routledge, 1999).
21. Perry L. Glanzer, Todd C. Ream, Pedro Villarreal III, and Edith Davis, "The Teaching of Ethics in Christian Higher Education: An Examination of General Education Requirements," *Journal of General Education 53* (2004): 184–200.
22. Perry L. Glanzer and Todd Ream, "Has Teacher Education Missed Out on the 'Ethics Boom?' A Comparative Study of Ethics Requirements and Courses in Professional Majors of Christian Colleges and Universities," *Christian Higher Education* 6 (July 2007): 271–88.
23. Colby et al., *Educating Citizens*, 52.
24. Holmes, *Shaping Character*, 13–17.
25. St. Olaf College, Admissions View Book, 7.
26. Interview with student life administrator by Perry L. Glanzer, 7 May 2004, St. Olaf College.
27. Benne, *Quality with Soul*, 87–91, 126–34; Burtchaell, *The Dying of the Light*.
28. St. Olaf College, "St. Olaf Mission Statement," http://www.stolaf.edu/about/mission.html (accessed March 7, 2009).
29. St. Olaf College, Admissions View Book, 2003, 7.
30. Ibid.
31. Ibid.
32. St. Olaf College, "R.I.C.H. Statement," http://www.stolaf.edu/about/guidingdocuments/rich.html (accessed March 7, 2009).

33. University of St. Thomas, "Mission, Vision and Convictions Statement," http://www.stthomas.edu/aboutust/mission/default.html (accessed March 7, 2009).
34. Terrence J. Murphy, *A Catholic University: Vision and Opportunities* (Collegeville, MN: Liturgical Press, 2001).
35. University of St. Thomas, Academic Catalog, 2002–2004, 42.
36. Interview with student life administrator by Perry L. Glanzer and Todd C. Ream, 8 May 2004, University of St. Thomas.
37. Holmes, *Shaping Character*, 14.
38. Interview with university administrator #1 by Perry L. Glanzer, November 6, 2003, University of Dallas.
39. Interview with university administrator #2 by Perry L. Glanzer, November 6, 2003, University of Dallas.
40. University of Dallas, "UD's distinctive approach," http://www.udallas.edu/undergrad/distinctivecont.cfm (accessed June 29, 2009).
41. Seattle Pacific University, "2008–2009 Seattle Pacific University Facts," http://www.spu.edu/info/facts/index.asp (accessed March 7, 2009).
42. Ibid.
43. Personal interview with Seattle Pacific University administrator #1 by Pedro Villareal, November 17, 2003, Seattle Pacific University.
44. Ibid.
45. Seattle Pacific University, "Student Handbook," http://www.spu.edu/depts/studentlife/studenthdbk.html (accessed March 9, 2009).
46. Xavier University, "Mission Statement," www.xavier.edu/mission/ (accessed March 7, 2009).
47. Personal interview with Xavier student development administrator #1 by Perry L. Glanzer, October 12, 2004, Xavier University.
48. Ibid.
49. Xavier University, "Mission Statement," www.xavier.edu/mission/ (accessed March 7, 2009).
50. Xavier University, Admissions View Book, 37.
51. George Fox University, "About Our Christian University," http://www.georgefox.edu/about/index.html (accessed March 12, 2009).
52. Personal interview with George Fox administrator #1 by Todd C. Ream, November 12, 2003, George Fox University.
53. Personal interview with George Fox administrator #2 by Todd C. Ream, November 12, 2003, George Fox University.
54. Personal interview with Bethel University administrator #1 by Todd C. Ream, May 7, 2004, Bethel University.
55. Mark A. Noll, *The Scandal of the Evangelical Mind* (Grand Rapids, MI: Eerdmans, 1994), 8.
56. Bethel University, "Mission and Vision," http://www.bethel.edu/about-bu/mission-vision.html (assessed March 12, 2009).
57. Personal interview with Bethel University administrator #1 by Todd C. Ream, May 7, 2004, Bethel University.

58. Personal interview with Bethel University administrator #2 by Todd C. Ream, May 7, 2004, Bethel University.
59. Bethel University, "Becoming Whole and Holy Persons," http://seminary.bethel.edu/catalog/programs/covenant (accessed March 12, 2009).
60. Ibid.
61. Ibid.
62. Personal interview with Xavier student development administrator by Perry L. Glanzer, October 12, 2004, Xavier University.
63. Personal interview with Seattle Pacific University administrator by Pedro Villareal, November 17, 2003, Seattle Pacific University.
64. Personal interview with Calvin College administrator by Perry L. Glanzer and Todd C. Ream, October 13, 2004, Calvin College.
65. Personal interview with Calvin College faculty member #1 by Perry L. Glanzer and Todd C. Ream, 13 October 2004, Calvin College.
66. Cornelius Plantinga, *Engaging God's World: A Christian Vision of Faith, Learning, and Living* (Grand Rapids, MI: William B. Eerdmans, 2002), xi.
67. Ibid, xii.
68. Calvin College, *Expanded Statement of Mission* (Grand Rapids, MI: Calvin College, 2004), 11.
69. Calvin College, *All Things* (Grand Rapids, MI: Calvin College, 2002), 3.
70. Calvin College, *Catalog*, 33.
71. Ibid.
72. Ibid., 88.
73. Ibid., 13.
74. Calvin College, *Student Handbook* (Grand Rapids, MI: Calvin College, 2007), i.
75. Ibid., 21.
76. Personal interview with Calvin College administrator #2 by Perry L. Glanzer and Todd C. Ream, October 13, 2004, Calvin College.
77. Ibid.
78. Personal interview with Calvin College administrator #3 by Perry L. Glanzer and Todd C. Ream, October 13, 2004, Calvin College.
79. Ibid.
80. Donald B. Kraybill, *The Upside-Down Kingdom* (Scottdale, PA: Herald Press, 2003), 19.
81. Personal interview with EMU administrator by Perry L. Glanzer and Todd C. Ream, March 11, 2004, Eastern Mennonite University.
82. Eastern Mennonite University, *Undergraduate Catalog, 2002–2003* (Harrisonburg, VA: Eastern Mennonite University, 2002), 23.
83. Ibid.
84. Ibid., 2.
85. Eastern Mennonite University, *Undergraduate Catalog, 2002–2003* (Harrisonburg, VA: Eastern Mennonite University, 2002), 23.
86. Ibid., 30.

87. Ibid., 49.
88. Eastern Mennonite University, 2008–2009 *Student Handbook* (Harrisonburg, VA: Eastern Mennonite University, 2008), 7.
89. Ibid., 44.
90. Personal interview with EMU administrator by Perry L. Glanzer and Todd C. Ream, March 11, 2004, Eastern Mennonite University.
91. Ibid.

Eight   Moral Identity, Moral Autonomy, and Critical Thinking

1. Donna Freitas, *Sex & the Soul: Juggling Sexuality, Spirituality, Romance, and Religion on America's College Campuses* (New York: Oxford, 2008), 70.
2. Perry L. Glanzer and Konstantin Petrenko, "Religion and Education in Post-Communist Russia: Making Sense of Russia's New Church-State Paradigm," *Journal of Church and State* (Winter 2007): 53–73.
3. For an additional argument supporting this point in general see Christopher J. Eberle, *Religious Convictions in Liberal Politics* (New York: Cambridge University Press, 2002).
4. Paul Berman, ed., *Debating P.C.: The Controversy over Political Correctness on College Campuses* (New York: Laurel, 1992).
5. E.g., see Derek Bok, *Our Underachieving Colleges: A Candid Look at How Much Students Learn and Why They Should Be Learning More* (Princeton: Princeton University Press, 2006),, 58–72; Anne Colby, Thomas Ehrlich, Jason Beaumont, and Jason Stephens, *Educating Citizens: Preparing America's Undergraduates for Lives of Moral Responsibility* (San Francisco, CA: Jossey-Bass, 2003), 16–17.
6. For a thorough discussion of this disagreement see Elmer John Thiessen, *In Defense of Religious Colleges and Schools* (Montreal: McGill-Queen's University Press, 2001), 133–42 and Elmer John Thiessen, *Liberal Education, Indoctrination & Christian Nurture* (Montreal: McGill-Queen's University Press, 1993).
7. Thiessen, *In Defense of Religious Colleges and Schools*, 135.
8. Donna Freitas found students at Catholic university campuses unfamiliar with their own tradition's teaching on sexual ethics. Freitas, *Sex & the Soul*.
9. Robert F. Pace, *Halls of Honor: College Men in the Old South* (Baton Rouge: Louisiana State University Press, 2004), 4–5.
10. University of Virginia, "History of the Honor Committee," http://www.virginia.edu/honor/intro/honorhistory.html (accessed March 5, 2009).

11. Helen Lefkowitz Horowitz, *Campus Life: Undergraduate Cultures from the End of the Eighteenth Century to the Present* (New York: Alfred A. Knopf, 1987), 36.
12. Donald L. McCabe, Linda Klebe Treviño, Kenneth D. Butterfield, "Cheating in Academic Institutions: A Decade of Research," *Ethics & Behavior* 11 (3), 219–232. They note from a qualitative study, "Contextual influence on cheating that were emphasized by students included the degree to which the code is deeply embedded n a culture of integrity; the degree to which a school has a supportive, trusting atmosphere; competitive pressures; the severity of punishments; the existence of clear rules regarding unacceptable behavior; faculty monitoring; peer pressure to cheat or not to cheat; the likelihood of being caught or reported; and class size" (p. 226).
13. Pace, *Halls of Honor*, 8.
14. Ibid., 9.
15. Lee S. Duemer, Sheila Delony, Kathleen Donalson, and Amani Zaier, "Behavioral Expectations of 110 Nationally Ranked Liberal Arts Colleges," *Journal of College & Character* 10, 2 (November 2008): 8.
16. See Donald McCabe, "Academic Dishonesty & Educational Opportunity," *Liberal Education*, 91.3 (2005): 26–31; Donald McCabe and Linda Klebe Treviño, "Honesty and Our Honor Codes," *Academe* 88, 1 (2002): 37–42; Donald McCabe, Linda Klebe Treviño, and Kenneth D. Butterfield, "Honor Codes and Other Contextual Influences on Academic Integrity: A Replication and Extension to Modified Honor Code Settings," *Research in Higher Education* 39.3 (2002): 236–274; Donald McCabe, Linda Klebe Treviño and Kenneth D. Butterfield, "Cheating in Academic Institutions: A Decade of Research," *Ethics and Behavior* 11.3 (2001): 219–232; Donald McCabe and G. Pavela, "Some Good News about Academic Integrity," *Change* 33.5 (2000): 32–39; Donald McCabe and Linda Klebe Treviño, "Academic Dishonesty: Honor Codes and Other Contextual Influences," *The Journal of Higher Education* 64.5 (1993): 533–538.
17. McCabe, Treviño, and Butterfield, "Cheating in Academic Institutions."
18. Ibid., 225.
19. E.g., one study found that one of the schools with the highest levels of cheating was an honor code school. See ibid., 224.
20. Sarah Roberts-Cady, "The Role of Critical Thinking in Academic Dishonesty Policies," *International Journal for Educational Integrity* 4.2 (December 2008): 60–66.
21. Duemer et al., "Behavioral Expectations of 110 Nationally Ranked Liberal Arts Colleges," 8.
22. McCabe and Treviño, "Honesty and Honor Codes."
23. Rhodes College, "The Honor System," www.rhodes.edu/images/content/CampusLife/Honor_Constitution.pdf (accessed February 2, 2009).

24. Duemer et al., "Behavioral Expectations of 110 Nationally Ranked Liberal Arts Colleges," 8.
25. Wheaton College, "The Honor Code," wheatoncollege.edu/Catalog/Contents/WheatonCommunity/HonorCode.html (accessed February 2, 2009).
26. Duemer et al., "Behavioral Expectations of 110 Nationally Ranked Liberal Arts Colleges," 8.
27. D. Gehring, E. Nuss, and G. Pavela, *Issues and Perspective on Academic Integrity*, NASPA Monograph Series (Columbus, OH: National Association of Student Personnel Administrators).
28. Pace, *Halls of Honor*, 27.
29. See the chapter on "Integrity" in Christopher Peterson and Martin Seligman, *Character Strengths and Virtues* (New York: Oxford University Press, 2004).
30. Hillsdale College, "History and Mission," http://www.hillsdale.edu/about/history.asp (accessed February 26, 2009).
31. Ibid.
32. Ibid.
33. Personal Interview #2 with Hillsdale administrator by Todd C. Ream, October 17, 2009, Hillsdale College.
34. Personal Interview #1 with Hillsdale administrator by Todd C. Ream, October 17, 2009, Hillsdale College.
35. Hillsdale College, "Honor Code," http://www.hillsdale.edu/about/honorcode.asp(accessed February 26, 2009).
36. Holmes, *Shaping Character*, 20.
37. See Freitas, *Sex & the Soul*.
38. Ibid., 33.
39. Ibid., 35.
40. Amy Gutmann, *Democratic Education* (Princeton: Princeton University Press, 1987), 44.
41. Harvard University, Faculty of Arts and Sciences, *Report of the Task Force of General Education* (Cambridge, MA: Harvard University, 2007), 2.
42. Ibid., 1–2.
43. David Brooks, "What Life Asks of Us," *The New York Times*, 27 January 2009.
44. Thiessen, *In Defense of Religious Schools and Colleges,* 139.
45. Ibid., 140–41.
46. MacIntyre, *Three Rival Versions of Moral Enquiry.*
47. Interview with student life administrator #1 by Perry L. Glanzer, May 7, 2004, St. Olaf College.
48. Ibid.
49. Interview with student life administrator #2 by Perry L. Glanzer, May 7, 2004, St. Olaf College.
50. Ibid.

51. Personal interview with Calvin College administrator #1 by Perry L. Glanzer and Todd C. Ream, October 13, 2004, Calvin College.
52. Personal interview with George Fox administrator #2 by Todd C. Ream, November 12, 2003, George Fox University.

Nine Christian Humanism and Christ-Centered Education: The Redemptive Development of Humans and Human Creations

1. John Dewey, *The School and Society and the Child and the Curriculum* (Chicago: University of Chicago Press, 1990), 34.
2. Duane Litfin, *Conceiving the Christian College* (Grand Rapids, MI: Eerdmans, 2004), 65.
3. See, e.g., Nicholas Wolterstorff, *Educating for Shalom: Essays on Christian Higher Education*, eds. Clarence Joldersma and Gloria Stronks (Grand Rapids, MI: Eerdmans, 2004).
4. David Dockery, "Preface" to *The Integration of Faith and Learning: A Basic Bibliography* at http://www.uu.edu/centers/christld/bibliog/ (accessed May 8, 2007).
5. For a recent example, see Douglas Jacobsen and Rhonda Hustedt Jacobsen, *Scholarship & Christian Faith: Enlarging the Conversation* (New York: Oxford University Press, 2004).
6. William Hasker, "Faith-Learning Integration: An Overview," *Christian Scholars Review* 21 (1992): 234.
7. *Christian Scholar's Review*, http://www.csreview.org/ (accessed January 22, 2008).
8. Baylor Institute for Faith and Learning, http://www.baylor.edu/ifl/ (assessed January 22, 2009).
9. Pepperdine Center for Faith and Learning, http://www.pepperdine.edu/centerforfaithandlearning/ (assessed January 22 2009).
10. Whitworth College, "Weyerhaeuser Center for Christian Faith & Learning," http://www.whitworth.edu/FaithCenter/Index.aspx (assessed, January 22, 2009).
11. We find in intriguing that when listing the challenges facing Christian higher education, Litfin does not mention the integration of faith and learning with the learner.
12. Al Wolters, *Creation Regained: Biblical Basics for a Reformational Worldview* 2nd ed. (Grand Rapids, MI: Eerdmans, 2005), 43–44.
13. Ibid., 70–71.
14. Ibid., 121.
15. See, e.g., William Lane Craig and Paul M. Gould, eds., *The Two Tasks of the Christian Scholar* (Wheaton, IL: Crossway, 2007).

16. We should note that we believe our vision will be consistent with what many Christian thinkers, such as George Marsden and Nicholas Wolterstorff, suggest that we do: interpret and live all of life within the Biblical drama of creation, fall, redemption, and restoration. George Marsden, *The Outrageous Idea of Christian Scholarship* (New York: Oxford, 1996); Nicholas Wolterstorff, *Educating for Shalom: Essays on Christian Higher Education*, eds. Clarence Joldersma and Gloria Stronks (Grand Rapids, MI: Eerdmans, 2004). In particular, our vision remains distinct from what Wolterstorff labels, "the Christian humanist model" where the goal is "to induct the student into the great cultural heritage of humanity" (pp. 87, 88). We believe redemptive development would require a more critical interaction and appropriation of that heritage.

17. E.g., see Harry Lee Poe, *Christianity in the Academy* (Grand Rapids, MI: Baker Academic, 2004); Paul J. Dovre, ed., *The Future of Religious Colleges* (Grand Rapids, MI: Eerdmans, 2002); Robert Benne, *Quality with Soul: How Six Premier Colleges and Universities Keep Their Faith with Their Religious Tradition* (Grand Rapids, MI: Eerdmans, 2002); Alice Gallin, *Negotiating Identity: Catholic Higher Education since 1960* (Notre Dame, IN: University of Notre Dame Press, 2000); John Wilcox and Irene King, *Enhancing Religious Identity: Best Practices from Catholic Campuses* (Washington, DC: Georgetown University Press, 2000); James T. Burtchaell, *The Dying of the Light: The Disengagement of Colleges and Universities from Their Christian Churches* (Grand Rapids, MI: Eerdmans, 1998); Richard T. Hughes and William B. Adrian, *Models for Christian Higher Education: Strategies for Success in the Twenty-First Century* (Grand Rapids, MI: Eerdmans, 1997); George Marsden, *The Soul of American University: From Protestant Establishment to Established No Belief* (New York: Oxford University Press, 1994); and Douglas Sloan, *Faith and Knowledge: Mainline Protestantism and American Higher Education* (Louisville, KY: Westminster/John Knox, 1994).

18. Arthur Holmes, *Shaping Character: Moral Education in the Christian College* (Grand Rapids, MI: Eerdmans, 1991).

19. See, e.g., Richard Hays, *The Moral Vision of the New Testament: A Contemporary Introduction to New Testament Ethics* (San Francisco, CA: Harper, 1996).

20. Willem Wardekker and Siebren Miedema, "Denominational School Identity and the Formation of Personal Identity," *Religious Education* 96.1 (2001): 37.

21. See Arthur Chickering and Linda Reisser, *Education and Identity* (San Francisco, CA: Jossey-Bass, 1996).

22. Erik Erikson, "Identity and the Life Cycle," *Psychological Issues Monograph 1* (1959): 1–171.

23. Chickering and Reisser, *Education and Identity*, 49.

24. See Wardekker and Miedema "Denominational School Identity and the Formation of Personal Identity"; Taylor; Alasdair MacIntyre, *After*

Virtue (Notre Dame, IN: Notre Dame Press, 1984); and Alasdair MacIntyre, *Three Rival Versions of Moral Enquiry: Encyclopedia, Genealogy, and Tradition* (Lanham, MD: Rowan & Littlefield, 1990).

25. See, e.g., the seventeen narratives in *Journal of Counseling & Development* 77 (1999 Winter): 4–53.

26. Wardekker and Miedema, "Denominational School Identity and the Formation of Personal Identity," 37.

27. D. A. Snow and R. Machalek, "The Sociology of Conversion," *Annual Review of Sociology* 10 (1984): 167–90.

28. Augustine, "On the Morals of the Catholic Church" in *Christian Ethics: Sources of the Living Tradition*, eds. Waldo Beach and H. Richard Niebuhr, 2nd ed. (New York: Alfred A. Knopf, 1973).

29. Robert Maynard Hutchins, *The Higher Learning in America* (New Haven, CT: Yale University Press, 1936), 70–71.

30. Richard Foster, "Spiritual Formation Agenda," *Christianity Today* (January 2009): 31.

31. Anthony T. Kronman, *Education's End: Why Our Colleges and Universities Have Given Up on the Meaning of Life* (New Haven, CT: Yale University Press, 2007), 77.

32. Kenneson, "Worship, Imagination and Formation," *The Blackwell Companion to Christian Ethics*, eds. Stanley Hauerwas and Samuel Wells (Malden, MA: Blackwell, 2004), 54.

33. Augustine, *Confessions*, 44.

34. Kenneson, "Worship, Imagination and Formation," 65.

35. See the various essays in Hauerwas and Wells. *The Blackwell Companion to Christian Ethics.*

36. Jim Foder, "Reading the Scriptures: Rehearsing Identity, Practicing Character," in *The Blackwell Companion to Christian Ethics*, 141.

37. See Hauerwas and Wells, *The Blackwell Companion to Christian Ethics.*

38. David Smith and Barbara Carvill, *The Gift of the Stranger: Faith, Hospitality and Foreign Language Learning* (Grand Rapids, MI: Eerdmans, 2000), 90.

39. Frederick Rudolph, *Curriculum, A History of the American Undergraduate Course of Study since 1636* (San Francisco, CA: Jossey-Bass, 1977), 1.

40. William R. Reid, "Curriculum as an Expression of National Identity," *Journal of Curriculum and Supervision* 15 (2000): 113–22.

41. Stanley Hauerwas, *Christian Existence Today: Essays on Church, World, and Living in Between* (Durham, NC: Labyrinth, 1988), 249.

42. Holmes, *Shaping Character*, 70–71.

43. Hauerwas, *Christian Existence Today*, 239.

44. C. John Sommerville, *The Decline of the Secular University* (New York: Oxford, 2006), 67.

45. *Oxford English Dictionary* [online] http://dictionary.oed.com/entrance.dtl

46. We also believe there are redemptive ways to tell this story that take into account the contributions of the various communities and histories within the Christian story and their gifts and limitations. See, e.g., Richard T. Hughes, *How Christian Faith: Can Sustain the Life of the Mind* (Grand Rapids, MI: Eerdmans, 2001).

47. See Wilcox and King, *Enhancing Religious Identity*.

48. For more details about our methods and the results see Perry L. Glanzer and Todd Ream, "Whose Story? Which Identity? Fostering Christian Identity at Christian Colleges and Universities," *Christian Scholars Review* 35 (2005): 13–27.

49. John Howard Yoder, *The Christian Witness to the State*, 2nd ed. (Scottdale, PA: Herald Press, 2001), 13.

50. We should note that we do not believe that a required church history course such as this one is the central key to forming Christian identity. Adding a course is rarely a solution to a problem that requires the whole community to reevaluate its identity and fundamental priorities. E.g., we also suggest a much greater focus on the role of memory and the Christian story in communal worship, campus art and architecture, and more.

51. Wardekker and Miedema, "Denominational School Identity and the Formation of Personal Identity," 40.

Ten   A More Human Christian Education: Cultivating and Ordering the Great Identities

1. Nicholas Wolterstorff, *Educating for Shalom: Essays on Christian Higher Education*, eds. Clarence Joldersma and Gloria Stronks (Grand Rapids, MI: Eerdmans, 2004), 26.

2. Anthony T. Kronman, *Education's End: Why Our Colleges and Universities Have Given Up on the Meaning of Life* (New Haven, CT: Yale University Press, 2007), 77.

3. Anne Colby, Elizabeth Beaumont, Thomas Ehrlich, Josh Corngold, *Educating for Democracy: Preparing Undergraduates for Responsible Political Engagement* (San Francisco, CA: Jossey-Bass, 2008), 4.

4. Alasdair MacIntyre, *Three Rival Versions of Moral Enquiry: Encyclopedia, Genealogy and Tradition* (Notre Dame, IN: University of Notre Dame Press, 1990), 171. MacIntyre particularly mentions the Ninth Edition of the Encyclopedia Britannica.

5. Harvard University, Faculty of Arts and Sciences, *Report of the Task Force of General Education* (Cambridge, MA: Harvard University, 2007).

6. Derek Bok, *Our Underachieving Colleges: A Candid Look at How Much Students Learn and Why They Should Be Learning More* (Princeton: Princeton University Press, 2006).

7. Wolterstorff, *Educating for Shalom*, 34.
8. Ibid., 34.
9. William G. Perry, Jr., *Forms of Intellectual and Ethical Development in the College Years: A Scheme* (San Francisco, CA: Jossey-Bass, 1999/1968).
10. Perry L. Glanzer, Michael Beaty and Larry Lyon, "Moral and Civic Education at Religious Research Universities: Exploring Faculty Support and Resistance," *Religious Education 100*, 4 (Fall 2005): 386–403.
11. H. Richard Niebuhr, *Christ and Culture* (New York: Harper, 1956).
12. C. John Sommerville, *The Decline of the Secular University* (New York: Oxford, 2008), 8.
13. Donna Freitas, *Sex & the Soul* (New York: Oxford University Press, 2008).
14. Fish, *Save the World on Your Own Time* (New York: Oxford University Press, 2008), 67.
15. John W. Wright, "How Many Masters? From the Church-Related to an Ecclesially Based University," *Conflicting Allegiances: The Church-Based University in a Liberal Democratic Society*, eds. Michael L Budde and John Wright (Grand Rapids, MI: Brazos Press, 2004), 22.
16. Jeff Astley, Leslie Francis, John Sullivan, and Andrew Walker, eds., *The Idea of a Christian University: Essays on Theology and Higher Education* (Bucks, UK: Paternoster Press, 2004), 180.
17. Colby et al., *Educating for Democracy*.
18. In this respect, conversations about liberal democracy undertaken with a Christian orientation may be more critical than education within the liberal democratic tradition where voting is often treated as a sacrament. See Ted Lewis, ed., *Electing Not to Vote: Christian Reflections on Reasons for Not Voting* (Eugene, OR: Cascade Books, 2008).
19. Paul J. Wadell and Darin H. Davis, "Tracking the Toxins of *Acedia*: Reenvisioning Moral Education," in *The School Heart: Moral Formation in Higher Education*, eds. Douglas V. Henry and Michael D. Beaty (Waco, TX: Baylor University Press, 2008), 181.
20. Neil Postman, *The End of Education* (New York: Vintage Books, 1995), 4.
21. Douglas Jacobsen and Rhonda Hustedt Jacobsen, *Scholarship & Christian Faith: Enlarging the Conversation* (New York: Oxford, 2004), 27.
22. V. James Mannoia, *Christian Liberal Arts* (Lanham, MD: Rowman & Littlefield, 2000), 155.
23. George Kuh, John Schuh, Elizabeth J. Whitt, and Associates, *Involving Colleges: Successful Approaches to Fostering Student Learning and Development outside the Classroom* (San Francisco, CA: Jossey-Bass, 1991).
24. Stanley Hauerwas, *A Community of Character* (South Bend, IN: Notre Dame Press, 1983), 130.
25. Personal interview with Seattle Pacific University administrator by Pedro Villareal, November 17, 2003. Seattle Pacific University.

26. John Berkman, "Being Reconciled: Penitence, Punishment, and Worship" in *The Blackwell Companion to Christian Ethics. The Blackwell Companion to Christian Ethics*, eds. Stanley Hauerwas and Samuel Wells (Malden, MA: Blackwell, 2004).

Conclusion Transforming Human Animals into Saints

1. Tom Wolfe, *I Am Charlotte Simmons* (New York: Farrar, Straus, Giroux, 2004).
2. Ibid., 3.
3. Ibid., 4.
4. Ibid.
5. Mary Anne Glendon, "Off at College," *First Things, 150* (2005): 41.
6. Donna Freitas, *Sex & the Soul* (New York: Oxford University Press, 2008), 68.
7. Stanley Hauerwas, *A Community of Character* (South Bend, IN: Notre Dame Press, 1983), 131.

Select Bibliography

Abbott Andrew. "The Aims of Education Address." *University of Chicago Record* 37 (2002): 4–8.

Aquinas, Thomas. *Summa Theologica: A Concise Translation.* Edited by Timothy McDermott. Westminster, UK: Christian Classics, 1989.

Astley, Jeff, Leslie Francis, John Sullivan, and Andrew Walker, eds. *The Idea of a Christian University: Essays on Theology and Higher Education.* Bucks, UK: Paternoster Press, 2004.

Augustine. *The Confessions of Saint Augustine.* Translated by John K. Ryan. New York: Doubleday, 1960.

———. "On the Morals of the Catholic Church." In *Christian Ethics: Sources of the Living Tradition*, edited by Waldo Beach and H. Richard Niebuhr, 110–17. 2nd ed. New York: Alfred A. Knopf, 1973.

Barber, David. *A Hard Rain Fell: SDS and Why It Failed.* Jackson: University Press of Mississippi, 2008.

Barzun, Jacques. *The American University: How It Runs, Where It Is Going.* Chicago, IL: University of Chicago Press, 1968/1993.

Beauchamp, Thomas L., and James F. Childress. *Principles of Biomedical Ethics.* New York: Oxford University Press, 1979.

Belenky, Mary, Blythe McVicker Clinchy, Nancy Rule Goldberger, and Jill Mattuck Tarule. *Women's Ways of Knowing: The Development of Self, Voice, and Mind.* New York: Basic Books, 1997.

Bellamy, Edward. *Looking Backward.* Boston, MA: Houghton Mifflin, 1926.

Benne, Robert. *Quality with Soul: How Six Premier Colleges and Universities Keep Their Faith with Their Religious Tradition.* Grand Rapids, MI: Eerdmans, 2002.

Bergman, Roger. "Why Be Moral? A Conceptual Model from Developmental Psychology." *Human Development* 45.2 (2002): 104–124.

Berkman, John. "Being Reconciled: Penitence, Punishment, and Worship." In *The Blackwell Companion to Christian Ethics. The Blackwell Companion to Christian Ethics*, edited by Stanley Hauerwas and Samuel Wells, 95–109. Malden, MA: Blackwell, 2004.

Berman, Paul, ed. *Debating P.C.: The Controversy over Political Correctness on College Campuses.* New York: Laurel, 1992.

Bok, Derek. *Beyond the Ivory Tower: Social Responsibilities of the Modern University.* Cambridge, MA: Harvard University Press, 1982.

———. *Our Underachieving Colleges: A Candid Look at How Much Students Learn and Why They Should Be Learning More.* Princeton, NJ: Princeton University Press, 2006.

Booth, Wayne C. "Introducing Professor Mearsheimer to His Own University." *Philosophy and Literature* 22.1 (1998): 174–178.

Brooks, David. "The Organizational Kid." *Atlantic Monthly* (April 2001): 40–54.

———. "What Life Asks of Us." *The New York Times*, 27 January 2009, A31.

Browning, Don S. *Christian Ethics and the Moral Psychologies.* Grand Rapids, MI: Eerdsmans, 2006.

Burtchaell, James T. *The Dying of the Light: The Disengagement of Colleges and Universities from their Christian Churches.* Grand Rapids, MI: Eerdmans, 1998.

Chickering, Arthur, and Linda Reisser, *Education and Identity.* San Francisco, CA: Jossey-Bass, 1996.

Clouser, Roy. *The Myth of Religious Neutrality: An Essay on the Hidden Role of Religious Belief in Theories.* Notre Dame, IN: University of Notre Dame Press, 2005.

Colby, Anne, and William Damon. *Some Do Care: Lives of Contemporary Moral Commitment.* New York: Free Press, 1992.

Colby, Anne, Thomas Ehrlich, Elizabeth Beaumont, and Jason Stephens. *Educating Citizens: Preparing America's Undergraduates for Lives of Moral Responsibility.* San Francisco, CA: Jossey-Bass, 2003.

Colby, Anne, Elizabeth Beaumont, Thomas Ehrlich, Josh Corngold. *Educating for Democracy: Preparing Undergraduates for Responsible Political Engagement.* San Francisco, CA: Jossey-Bass, 2008.

Coles, Robert. *The Moral Life of Children.* Boston, MA: Atlantic Monthly Press, 1986.

Cook, Kaye V., Daniel C. Larson, and Monique D. Boivin. "Moral Voices of Women and Men in the Christian Liberal Arts College: Links between Views of Self and Views of God." *Journal of Moral Education* 32, 1 (2003): 77–89.

Corbin, Juliet, and Anselm Strauss. *Basics of Qualitative Research: Techniques and Theory for Grounded Theory Development.* 3rd ed. Thousand Oaks, CA: Sage, 2008.

Craig, William Lane, and Paul M. Gould, eds., *The Two Tasks of the Christian Scholar.* Wheaton, IL: Crossway, 2007.

Davis, Michael. *Ethics and the University.* New York: Routledge, 1999.

Dewey, John. *The School and Society and the Child and the Curriculum.* Chicago: University of Chicago Press, 1990.

Dewey, John, and James Tufts. *Ethics.* New York: Holt, Rinehart, and Winston, 1908.

Dovre, Paul J., ed. *The Future of Religious Colleges.* Grand Rapids, MI: Eerdmans, 2002.

Duemer, Lee S., Sheila Delony, Kathleen Donalson, and Amani Zaier. "Behavioral Expectations of 110 Nationally Ranked Liberal Arts Colleges." *Journal of College & Character* 10.2 (November 2008): 1–14.

Eberle, Christopher J. *Religious Convictions in Liberal Politics*. New York: Cambridge University Press, 2002.

Edwards, Mark. *Religion on Our Campuses: A Professor's Guide to Communities Conflicts and Promising Conversations*. New York: Palgrave Macmillan, 2006.

Engell, James, and Anthony Dangerfield. *Saving Higher Education in the Age of Money*. Charlottesville: University of Virginia Press, 2005.

Erasmus, Desiderius. "De Pueris Statim Ac Liberaliter Instituendis Liberllus" [That Children Should Straightaway from Their Earliest Years Be Trained in Virtue and Sound Learning]. In *Desiderius Erasmus Concerning the Aim and Method of Education* by W. H. Woodward. New York: Teachers College Press, 1964/1529.

Erikson, Erik. "Identity and the Life Cycle." *Psychological Issues Monograph* 1 (1959): 1–171.

Fiering, Norman. *Moral Philosophy at Seventeenth Century Harvard: A Discipline in Transition*. Chapel Hill: University of North Carolina, 1981.

Fish, Stanley. "Aim Low: Confusing Democratic Values with Academic Ones Can Easily Damage the Quality of Education." *The Chronicle of Higher Education* 49 (May 16, 2003): C5.

———. "The Case for Academic Autonomy." *The Chronicle of Higher Education* 50 (July 23, 2004): C1–C4.

———. "Save the World on Your Own Time." *The Chronicle of Higher Education* 23 (January 2003) http://chronicle.com/jobs/news/2003/01/2003012301c/careers.html (accessed September 15, 2008).

———. *Save the World on Your Own Time*. New York: Oxford University Press, 2008.

Fisher, Allen. "Religious and Moral Education at Three Kinds of Liberal Arts Colleges: A Comparison of Curricula in Presbyterian, Evangelical, and Religiously Unaffiliated Liberal Arts Colleges." *Religious Education* 90.1 (Winter 1995): 30–49.

Foder, Jim. "Reading the Scriptures: Rehearsing Identity, Practicing Character." In *The Blackwell Companion to Christian Ethics*, edited by Stanley Hauerwas and Samuel Wells, 141–55. Malden, MA: Blackwell, 2004.

Foster, Richard. "Spiritual Formation Agenda." *Christianity Today* (January 2009): 28–33.

Freitas, Donna. *Sex & the Soul: Juggling Sexuality, Spirituality, Romance, and Religion on America's College Campuses*. New York: Oxford, 2008.

Gallin, Alice. *Negotiating Identity: Catholic Higher Education since 1960*. Notre Dame, IN: University of Notre Dame Press, 2000.

Gehring, D. and E. Nuss, and G. Pavela. *Issues and Perspective on Academic Integrity*. NASPA Monograph Series Columbus, OH: National Association of Student Personnel Administrators.

Geiger, Roger. *To Advance Knowledge: The Growth of the American Research Universities, 1900–1940*. New York: Oxford University Press, 1986.

Gilligan, Carol. *In a Different Voice: Psychological Theory and Women's Development*. Cambridge, MA: Harvard University Press, 1982.

Gilman, Daniel C. "Inaugural Address of Daniel Coit Gilman as First President of The Johns Hopkins University." (2007), http://www/jhu.edu/125th/links/gilman.html (accessed March 11, 2006).

Glanzer, Perry. *The Quest for Russia's Soul: Evangelicals and Moral Education in Post-Communist Russia*. Waco, TX: Baylor University Press, 2002.

Glanzer, Perry L., and Andrew J. Milson. "Legislating the Good: A Survey and Evaluation of Contemporary Character Education Legislation." *Educational Policy* 20, 3 (2006): 525–50.

Glanzer, Perry L., and Konstantin Petrenko. "Religion and Education in Post-Communist Russia: Making Sense of Russia's New Church-State Paradigm." *Journal of Church and State* (Winter 2007): 53–73.

Glanzer, Perry L., and Todd Ream. "Has Teacher Education Missed Out on the 'Ethics Boom?' A Comparative Study of Ethics Requirements and Courses in Professional Majors of Christian Colleges and Universities." *Christian Higher Education* 6 (July 2007): 271–88.

———. "Whose Story? Which Identity? Fostering Christian Identity at Christian Colleges and Universities." *Christian Scholars Review* 35 (2005): 13–27.

Glanzer, Perry L., Michael Beaty, and Larry Lyon. "Moral and Civic Education at Religious Research Universities: Exploring Faculty Support and Resistance." *Religious Education* 100, 4 (Fall 2005): 386–403.

Glanzer, Perry L., Todd C. Ream, Pedro Villarreal III, and Edith Davis. "The Teaching of Ethics in Christian Higher Education: An Examination of General Education Requirements." *Journal of General Education* 53 (2004): 184–200.

Glendon, Mary Anne. "Off at College." *First Things* 150 (2005): 41.

Goodman, John F., and Howard Lesnick. *The Moral Stake in Education*. New York: Longman, 2001.

Gutmann, Amy. *Democratic Education*. Princeton, NJ: Princeton University Press, 1987.

Hardwick-Day. *Brand Archeology: Excavating for Position, Persona and Attitude*. Minneapolis, MN: Hardwick Day, 2003.

Harvard University, Faculty of Arts and Sciences. *Report of the Task Force of General Education*. Cambridge, MA: Harvard University, 2007.

Hastings Center Report. *The Teaching of Ethics in Higher Education*. New York: Institute of Society, Ethics and Life Sciences, 1980.

Hastings Center Staff. "The Teaching of Ethics in American Higher Education." in *Ethics Teaching in Higher Education*, edited by Daniel Callahan and Sissela Bok, 153–70. New York: Hastings Center, 1980.

Hauerwas, Stanley. *Christian Existence Today: Essays on Church, World, and Living in Between*. Durham, NC: Labyrinth, 1988.

———. *A Community of Character: Toward a Constructive Christian Social Ethic*. South Bend, IN: Notre Dame, 1981.

Hauerwas, Stanley, and Samuel Wells, eds., *The Blackwell Companion to Christian Ethics* Malden, MA: Blackwell, 2004.

Hays, Richard. *The Moral Vision of the New Testament: A Contemporary Introduction to New Testament Ethics*. San Francisco, CA: Harper, 1996.

Hofstadter, Richard, and Wilson Smith, eds. *American Higher Education: A Documentary History*, Chicago, IL: University of Chicago Press, 1961.

Holmes, Arthur. *Shaping Character: Moral Education in the Christian College*. Grand Rapids, MI: Eerdmans, 1991.

Horowitz, Helen Lefkowitz. *Campus Life: Undergraduate Cultures from the End of the Eighteenth Century to the Present*. New York: Alfred A. Knopf, 1987.

Hughes, Richard T. *How Christian Faith: Can Sustain the Life of the Mind*. Grand Rapids, MI: Eerdmans, 2001.

Hughes, Richard T., and William B. Adrian. *Models for Christian Higher Education: Strategies for Success in the Twenty-First Century*. Grand Rapids, MI: Eerdmans, 1997.

Hunter, James Davison. *The Death of Character: Moral Education in an Age without Good or Evil*. New York: Basic Books, 2000.

Hutchins, Robert Maynard. *The Higher Learning in America*. New Haven, CT: Yale University Press, 1936.

Jacobsen, Douglas, and Rhonda Hustedt Jacobsen. *Scholarship & Christian Faith: Enlarging the Conversation*. New York: Oxford, 2004.

John Templeton Foundation, ed. *Colleges that Encourage Character Development*. Radnor, PA: John Templeton Foundation, 1999.

Kandel, Isaac L., *The Dilemma of Democracy*. Cambridge, MA: Harvard University Press, 1934.

Kenneson, Philip. "Worship, Imagination and Formation." In *The Blackwell Companion to Christian Ethics*, edited by Stanley Hauerwas and Samuel Wells, 53–67. Malden, MA: Blackwell, 2004.

Keohane, Nannerl. *Higher Ground: Ethics and Leadership in the Modern University*. Durham, NC: Duke University Press, 2006.

Kerr, Clark. *The Uses of the University*. Chicago, IL: University of Chicago Press, 1995.

Kezar, Adrianna, Tony Chambers, and John Burkhardt, eds. *Higher Education for the Public Good*. San Francisco, CA: Jossey-Bass, 2005.

Kirp, David. *Shakespeare, Einstein, and the Bottom Line: The Marketing of Higher Education*. Cambridge, MA: Harvard University Press, 2003.

Kirschenbaum, Howard. "From Values Clarification to Character Education: A Personal Journey." *Journal of Humanistic Counseling, Education and Development* 39.1 (2000): 4–20.

Kohlberg, Lawrence. *The Philosophy of Moral Development: Moral Stages and the Idea of Justice, Essays on Moral Development, Vol. 1.* San Francisco, CA: Harper and Row Publishers, 1981.

Kohlberg, Lawrence, and Mayer, R. "Development as the Aim of Education." *Harvard Educational Review* 42 (1972): 449–96.

Kraybill, Donald B. *The Upside-Down Kingdom.* Scottdale, PA: Herald Press, 2003.

Kronman, Anthony T. *Education's End: Why Our Colleges and Universities Have Given Up on the Meaning of Life.* New Haven, CT: Yale University Press, 2007.

Kruesler, Abraham. *Contemporary Education and Moral Upbringing in the Soviet Union.* Ann Arbor, MI: University Mircofilms International, 1976.

Kuh, George. "Do Environments Matter? A Comparative Analysis of the Impress of Different Types of Colleges and Universities on Character." *Journal of College and Character* 2 (2002): http://www.collegevalues.org/articles.cfm. (accessed June 29, 2009).

Kuh, George, John H. Schuh, Elizabeth J. Whitt and Associates. *Involving Colleges: Successful Approaches to Fostering Student Learning and Development Outside the Classroom.* San Francisco, CA: Jossey-Bass, 1991.

Lewis, Harry. *Excellence without a Soul: How a Great University Forgot Education.* New York: Public Affairs, 2006.

Lewis, Ted, ed. *Electing Not to Vote: Christian Reflections on Reasons for Not Voting.* Eugene, OR: Cascade Books, 2008.

Lindholm, Jennifer A., Katalin Szelényi, Sylvia Hurtado, and William S. Korn. *The American College Teacher: National Norms for the 2004– 2005 HERI Faculty Survey.* Los Angeles, CA: Higher Education Research Institute, UCLA, 2005.

Litfin, Duane. *Conceiving the Christian College.* Grand Rapids, MI: Eerdmans, 2004.

Luther, Martin. *Three Treatsies.* Translated by Charles M. Jacobs. Philadelphia: Fortress Press, 1970.

Lyons, John. "Upon What Authority Might We Teach Morality?" *Philosophy and Literature* 22.1 (1998): 155–160.

Lyotard, Jean-Francois. *The Postmodern Condition: A Report on Knowledge.* Minneapolis: University of Minnesota Press, 1984.

MacIntyre, Alasdair. *After Virtue: A Study in Moral Theory.* Notre Dame, IN: University of Notre Dame Press, 1984.

———. *Dependent Rational Animals: Why Human Beings Need the Virtues.* Chicago, IL: Open Court, 1999.

———. *Dependent Rational Animals: Why Human Beings Need the Virtues.* Peru, IL: Carus, 2001.

———. *Three Rival Versions of Moral Enquiry: Encyclopedia, Genealogy and Tradition.* Notre Dame, IN: University of Notre Dame Press, 1990.

Mannoia, V. James. *Christian Liberal Arts.* Lanham, MD: Rowman & Littlefield, 2000.

Mansfield, Harvey C. *Manliness,* New Haven, CT: Yale University Press, 2006.

Marsden, George. *The Outrageous Idea of Christian Scholarship.* New York: Oxford, 1997.

———. *The Soul of American University: From Protestant Establishment to Established No Belief.* New York: Oxford University Press, 1994.

Mather, Cotton. *Diary of Cotton Mather.* New York: Ungar, 1957.

McCabe, Donald. "Academic Dishonesty & Educational Opportunity." *Liberal Education* 91.3 (2005): 26–31.

McCabe, Donald, and G. Pavela. "Some Good News about Academic Integrity." *Change* 33.5 (2000): 32–39.

McCabe, Donald, and Linda Klebe Treviño. "Academic Dishonesty: Honor Codes and Other Contextual Influences." *The Journal of Higher Education* 64.5 (1993): 533–538.

———. "Honesty and Our Honor Codes." *Academe* 88.1 (2002): 37–42.

McCabe, Donald, Linda Klebe Treviño, and Kenneth D. Butterfield. "Cheating in Academic Institutions: A Decade of Research." *Ethics and Behavior* 11.3 (2001): 219–232.

———. "Honor Codes and Other Contextual Influences on Academic Integrity: A Replication and Extension to Modified Honor Code Settings." *Research in Higher Education* 39.3 (2002): 236–74.

McNeel, Steven P. "College Teaching and Student Moral Development." In *Moral Development in the Professions: Psychology and Applied Ethics,* edited by James R. Rest and Darcia Narvaez, 26–47. Hillsdale, NJ: Lawrence Erlbaum Associates.

Mearsheimer, John. "The Aims of Education Address." *The University of Chicago Record* 32 (1997): 5–8.

———. "Mearsheimer's Response: Teaching Morality at the Margins." *Philosophy and Literature* 22.1 (1998): 193–98.

Meyer, D.H. *The Instructed Conscience: The Shaping of the American National Ethic.* Philadelphia: University of Pennsylvania Press, 1972.

Milson, Andrew J., Chara Haussler Bohan, Perry L. Glanzer, and J. Wesley Null, eds. *Readings in American Educational Thought: From Puritanism to Progressivism.* Greenwhich, CT: Information Age, 2004.

Morison, Samuel. *The Founding of Harvard College.* Cambridge, MA: Harvard University Press, 1935.

Morrison, Jeffrey. *John Witherspoon and the Founding of the American Republic.* Notre Dame, IN: University of Notre Dame Press, 2005.

Myers, David, and Malcolm Jeeves. *Psychology: Through the Eyes of Faith.* New York: Harper San Francisco, 2003.

Nemtsova, A. "In Russia, Corruption Plagues the Higher-Education System." *The Chronicle of Higher Education* 54 (February 22, 2008): 1.

Niebuhr, H. Richard. *Christ and Culture.* New York: Harper, 1956.

Noddings, Nel. *Caring: A Feminine Approach to Caring and Moral Education.* Berkeley: University California Press, 1984.

Noll, Mark A. *The Scandal of the Evangelical Mind.* Grand Rapids, MI: Eerdmans, 1994.

Novak, Michael. "God in the Colleges: The Dehumanization of the University." In *The New Student Left,* edited by Mitchell Cohen and Dennis Hale, 253–64. Boston: Beacon Press, 1967.

Pace, Robert F. *Halls of Honor: College Men in the Old South.* Baton Rouge: Louisiana State University Press, 2004.

Pascarella, Ernest T., and Patrick T. Terenzini. *How College Affects Students: A Third Decade of Research.* vol. 2. San Francisco, CA: Jossey-Bass, 2005.

Pattyn, Bart. "Is It Wrong to Teach What Is Right and Wrong? The Debate at K.U.Leuven." Brussels, Ethical Forum (November 2007), http://www.fondationuniversitaire.be/common_docs/EF6/Pattyn2.pdf (accessed September 15, 2008).

Perry, William G. Jr. *Forms of Intellectual and Ethical Development in the College Years: A Scheme.* San Francisco, CA: Jossey-Bass, 1999/1968.

Peterson, Christopher, and Martin Seligman. *Character Strengths and Virtues: A Handbook and Classification.* Oxford and New York: Oxford University Press, 2004.

Plantinga, C. *Engaging God's World: A Christian Vision of Faith, Learning, and Living.* Grand Rapids, MI: William B. Eerdmans, 2002.

Poe, Harry Lee. *Christianity in the Academy.* Grand Rapids, MI: Baker Academic, 2004.

Postman, Neil. *The End of Education: Redefining the Value School.* New York: Vintage Books, 1995.

Ravitich, Diane. *The Troubled Crusade.* New York: Basic Books, 1983.

Rawls, John. *Political Liberalism.* New York: Columbia University Press, 1996.

Reid, William R. "Curriculum as an Expression of National Identity." *Journal of Curriculum and Supervision* 15 (2000): 113–22.

Rest, James R. *Moral Development: Advances in Research and Theory.* New York: Praeger, 1987.

Rest, James, Darcia Narvaez, Muriel J. Bebeau, and Stephen J. Thoma. *Post-Conventional Moral Thinking: A Neo-Kohlbergian Approach.* Mahwah, NJ: L. Erlbaum Associates, 1999.

Reuben, Julie. *The Making of the Modern University: Intellectual Transformation and the Marginalization of Morality.* Chicago, IL: University of Chicago Press, 1996.

Roberts-Cady, Sarah. "The Role of Critical Thinking in Academic Dishonesty Policies." *International Journal for Educational Integrity* 4.2 (December 2008): 60–66.

Robinson, John H. "Why Schooling Is So Controversial in America Today." *Notre Dame Journal of Law, Ethics and Public Policy* 3 (1988): 519–33.

Rudolf, Frederick. *Curriculum: A History of the American Undergraduate Course of Study Since 1636.* San Francisco, CA: Jossey-Bass, 1977.

Sax, Linda J., Alexander W. Astin, William S. Korn, and Shannon K. Gilmartin. *The American College Teacher: National Norms for the 1998–1999 HERI Faculty Survey.* Los Angeles, CA: Higher Education Research Institute, UCLA, 1999.

Schneider, Carol. "Liberal Education and the Civic Engagement Gap" In *Higher Education for the Public Good,* edited by Adrianna Kezar, Tony Chambers, and John Burkhardt. San Francisco, CA: Jossey-Bass, 2005, 127–145.

Schwehn, Mark. *Exiles from Eden: Religion and the Academic Vocation in America.* New York: Oxford University Press, 1993.

Schwinges, Rainer. "Student Education, Student Life" In *A History of the University in Europe, Vol. I,* edited by H.D. Ridder-Symeons, 195–243. New York: Cambridge University Press, 1992.

Shapiro, Harold. A *Larger Sense of Purpose.* Princeton, NJ: Princeton University Press, 2005.

Shaver, D.G. "Moral Development of Students Attending a Christian, Liberal Arts College and a Bible College." *Journal of College Student Personnel* 26 (1987): 400–404.

Shweder, R.A. "Liberalism as Destiny." *Contemporary Psychology* 20 (1982): 421–24.

Sloan, Douglas. *Faith and Knowledge: Mainline Protestantism and American Higher Education.* Louisville, KY: Westminster/John Knox, 1994.

———. "The Teaching of Ethics in the American Undergraduate Curriculum, 1876–1976" In *Ethics Teaching in Higher Education,* edited by Daniel Callahan and Sissela Bok, 1–57. New York: Plenum Press, 1980.

Smith, Christian. *Moral, Believing Animals: Human Personhood and Culture.* New York: Oxford University Press, 2003.

———. *What Is a Person? Rethinking Humanity, Social Life, and the Moral Good from the Person Up* (Chicago: University of Chicago Press, forthcoming).

Smith, David, and Barbara Carvill. *The Gift of the Stranger: Faith, Hospitality and Foreign Language Learning.* Grand Rapids, MI: Eerdmans, 2000.

Smith, James K. A. *Desiring the Kingdom: Worship, Worldview, and Cultural Formation.* Grand Rapids, MI: Baker Academic, 2009.

Smith, William. *Professors and Public Ethics: Studies of Northern Moral Philosophers Before the Civil War.* Ithaca, NY: Cornell University Press, 1956.

Snow, D. A. and R. Machalek. "The Sociology of Conversion." *Annual Review of Sociology* 10 (1984): 167–90.

Sommerville, C. John. *Religion in the National Agenda: What We Mean by Religious, Spiritual, Secular.* Waco, TX: Baylor University Press, 2009.

Sommerville, H. John. *The Decline of the Secular University.* New York: Oxford, 2008.

Stepp, Laura Sessions. *Unhooked: How Young Women Pursue Sex, Delay Love and Lose at Both.* New York: Riverhead Books, 2006.

Stout, Jeffrey. *Democracy and Tradition.* Princeton, NJ: Princeton University Press, 2004.

Taylor, Charles. *Sources of the Self: The Making of the Modern Identity.* Cambridge, MA: Harvard University Press, 1989.

Templeton Foundation. *Colleges That Encourage Character Development: A Resource for Parents, Students and Educators.* Philadelphia, MA: Templeton Foundation Press, 1999.

The Committee on the Student in Higher Education. *The Student in Higher Education.* New Haven, CT: Haven Foundation, 1968.

Thiessen, Elmer John. *In Defense of Religious Colleges and Schools.* Montreal, Canada: McGill-Queen's University Press, 2001.

———. *Liberal Education, Indoctrination & Christian Nurture.* Montreal, Canada: McGill-Queen's University Press, 1993.

Tweksbury, D. *The Founding of American Colleges and Universities Before the Civil War.* New York: Teachers College, Columbia University, 1932.

Twenge, Jean M. *Generation Me: Why Today's Young Americans Are More Confident, More Assertive, Entitled—and More Miserable Than Ever Before.* New York: Free Press, 2006.

Wadell, Paul J., and Darin H. Davis. "Tracking the Toxins of *Acedia*: Reenvisioning Moral Education." In *The School Heart: Moral Formation in Higher Education*, edited by Douglas V. Henry and Michael D. Beaty, 133–54. Waco, TX: Baylor University Press, 2008.

Wardekker, Willem, and Siebren Miedema. "Denominational School Identity and the Formation of Personal Identity." *Religious Education* 96.1 (2001): 36–48.

Wayland, Francis. *The Elements of Moral Science.* Cambridge, MA: Belknap Press of Harvard University Press, 1963.

———. *Thoughts on the Present Collegiate System in the United States.* Boston: Gould, Kendall & Lincoln, 1842.

Wilcox, John, and Irene King. *Enhancing Religious Identity: Best Practices from Catholic Campuses.* Washington, DC: Georgetown University Press, 2000.

Wilshire, Bruce. *The Moral Collapse of the University: Professionalism, Purity and Alienation.* Albany: State University of New York Press, 1990.

Wolfe, Alan. "The Potential for Pluralism." In *Religion, Scholarship and Higher Education,* edited by Andrea Sterk, 23–39. Notre Dame, IN: University of Notre Dame Press, 2002).

Wolfe, Tom. *I Am Charlotte Simmons.* New York: Farrar, Straus, Giroux, 2004.

Wolters, Al. *Creation Regained: Biblical Basics for a Reformational Worldview.* 2nd ed. Grand Rapids, MI: Eerdmans, 2005.

Wolterstorff, Nicholas. *Educating for Shalom: Essays on Christian Higher Education.* Edited by Clarence Joldersma and Gloria Stronks. Grand Rapids, MI: Eerdmans, 2004.

———. *Reason within the Bounds of Religion*, rev ed. Grand Rapids, MI: Eerdsmans, 1999.

Wright, John W. "How Many Masters? From the Church-Related to an Ecclesially Based University." In *Conflicting Allegiances: The Church Based University in a Liberal Democratic Society*, edited by Michael L. Budde and John Wright, 13–28. Grand Rapids, MI: Brazos Press, 2004.

Yoder, John Howard. *The Christian Witness to the State.* 2nd ed. Scottdale, PA: Herald Press, 2001.

———. *The Priestly Kingdom.* South Bend, IN: Notre Dame Press, 1984.

Index